Violent Silence

Paul Mayersberg was born in Cambridge in 1941 and was educated at Dulwich College. During the 1960s he worked as a critic and journalist on film topics.

During the 1970s and '80s he worked as a screenwriter and his credits include *The Man Who Fell To Earth* and *Merry Christmas Mr Lawrence*. His films as writer/director are *Captive* (1986), *Nightfall* (1988) and *The Last Samurai* (1990).

Violent Silence is his second novel. His first novel, *Homme Fatale* was published in 1991.

VIOLENT SILENCE

Paul Mayersberg

ARROW

First published 1992

1 3 5 7 9 10 8 6 4 2

© Paul Mayersberg 1992

First published in the United Kingdom by Sinclair-Stevenson in 1992

Arrow edition 1993
Random House, 20 Vauxhall Bridge Road, London SW1V 2SA

Random House Australia (Pty) Limited
20 Alfred Street, Milsons Point, Sydney,
New South Wales 2061, Australia

Random House New Zealand Limited
18 Poland Road, Glenfield
Auckland 10, New Zealand

Random House South Africa (Pty) Limited
PO Box 337, Bergvlei, South Africa

Random House UK Limited Reg. No. 954009

A CIP catalogue record for this book
is available from the British Library

ISBN 0 09 930691 3

Printed and bound in Great Britain by
Cox & Wyman Ltd, Reading, Berkshire

**This book is for
Paul Buck**

Part One

1

He had been there on Tuesday morning sitting alone at the same table in the dining room. After the game Pandora had a late breakfast with her tennis partner, Beverly, who was the mother of a school friend of her daughter. She liked the room in the Bel Air Hotel. It was old-fashioned, luxurious, a large dining room in pale green and pink. Apple and salmon were two of her favorite colors.

Today was Friday and she was back with Beverly. The man looked at her frequently. When she looked back at him she had to smile. It was acceptable as a conventional smile of recognition. The fact was she liked the look of him. He seemed to epitomize the cool Californian man. He had a tanned, bland intelligence. Pandora came from New Hampshire. She had married a young architect, Alec Hammond, thirteen years ago. They had moved out to Los Angeles. Their daughter Paulette had been born here twelve years ago, and they had stayed.

More than her marriage, the birth of Paulette had changed Pandora, turned her into the stable woman she now was. Her father, Alfred Harten, was a nineteenth century man. He inherited wealth which allowed him to pursue his private interest in classical Greek and Roman culture. After the death of her mother when she was six, Harten retreated into a world of his own. Little Pandora grew up privileged, in a large old farmhouse, alone except for a succession of English nannies and her pony, Smoky. At school she had been a rebel. In college she had had a few brushes with the law over drugs. Wayward, was her father's word for her.

3

Glancing again at the man across the dining room Pandora remembered her early troubles with men, escapades that had upset her father. She had been promiscuous. She had taken risks, but for some reason had never gotten pregnant. For a time she thought she never would. She was relieved. But it worried her that she might die childless.

Pandora met Alec Hammond when her father hired a firm of architects to convert two barns into a guesthouse on the Harten estate. She had liked him immediately. He was a serious young man, different from the men in her crowd. He was not sarcastic. He was mature. He had goals in life. He had had to struggle. He didn't have a chip on his shoulder. But above all he had an innocent air. He was clean and fresh. She liked that. Alec Hammond lifted what she saw as the curse of sterility from her life. He made her pregnant. He gave her Paulette. For that she loved him. He made her happy. She became content.

The man was still in the dining room at eleven thirty when Beverly had to go. The place was empty apart from him. The waiters had already set the tables for lunch. Crystal wine goblets on the apple green cloths. Like the rooms in the hotel the tables were waiting for new occupants. She signed her Diner's slip and waited.

He was looking at her again when a tall, dark-haired woman came running into the dining room. She was looking for him. She came up to his table, opened her purse, pulled out a gun and aimed it at the man's head.

'I'm going to blow you away,' she said. Her voice was husky and shaky.

'No, you're not,' the man said evenly.

Pandora was scared. She wondered whether to call for help or intervene.

The dark-haired woman's finger tightened on the trigger.

'Put it away,' he said.

The waiter came back with the credit card and receipt inside a green leather folder. He saw the gun.

'Hey!' The waiter called out.

4

The woman jerked around. The man coolly snatched the gun from her hand. She burst into tears.

'Sorry about this,' the man said to the waiter. 'It's not loaded.'

The dark-haired woman ran out of the dining room.

'Shall I get the manager?' asked the waiter.

'No, no. Just forget it. Thank you.' He handed the waiter a fifty dollar bill.

'That's not necessary.'

'Please take it. Then you can give that lady over there her receipt.'

'Thank you sir.'

The waiter came up to Pandora. He shrugged. She thanked him and gave him a five dollar bill. The man came over to her as the waiter left.

'Sorry about that. Were you scared?'

'Yes, I was a bit.'

'The gun wasn't loaded.'

'Oh.'

'You're shaking.'

'No, not really.'

He put his hand on her quivering arm. It didn't stop, her quivering.

'Let's move out of here. Enough excitement for the moment, don't you think?'

'I guess so.' Pandora was still shaking.

They left the main building of the hotel. They walked together along the curving path towards the bungalow area. It was a walk through a miniature jungle, a beautifully kept jungle of sweating greenery and single flowers, aflame like daytime candles.

Pandora had no idea why she was walking with this man. Perhaps he was going to tell her what the incident had been about. Perhaps he wanted to ask her to keep quiet about it, like the waiter. Perhaps he was going to offer her a drink to steady her nerves. Well, she could use a drink.

'My shack's over there,' he said pleasantly.

They walked over the little bridge towards a group of terracotta colored bungalows, each with its own palm tree and

5

garden. Hardly shacks. The most expensive hotel accomodation in Los Angeles.

Suddenly Pandora stopped with a cry. The man turned and saw that her high heel had stuck between two wooden slats in the bridge. She laughed. She wiggled her shoe.

'Take your foot out.'

He bent down and with both hands removed her foot from the shoe. He noticed the pale freckles on her skin that went naturally with her sandy blonde hair. She hopped.

He twisted the shoe heel around to try and release it. It was difficult. She watched as he gave the shoe a jerk. The heel snapped.

'I'm sorry.' He looked up at her apologetically.

'That's all right,' she said.

It wasn't all right really. It was a nuisance.

He tried to tug the heel out. It was wedged.

'They don't make shoes like they used to,' he said.

'They're Ferragamo,' she said.

'Come on,' he addressed the wedged heel.

'Look, leave it. It's OK.' She took off the other shoe. He stood up. She smiled and walked on. He held her broken shoe, but didn't offer to give it to her.

Pandora knew he was watching her as she walked barefoot through the garden towards the bungalow he had pointed to. She wondered what had happened to the crazy, dark-haired woman. She thought she might even be in the bungalow waiting. Wait a minute, what am I doing, she thought.

'Here we are.'

He unlocked the door for her. This is crazy, Pandora thought. She went in ahead of him. She was suddenly very conscious of her body. She walked barefoot on the salmon carpet. A real log fire burned in the drawing room grate. It wasn't cold enough for a fire.

He kicked the door closed. He advanced on her as if he intended to kill her. She didn't back off. She held her shoe in one hand, her purse in the other. He hadn't even thought of locking the door. She was pleased about that.

6

Suddenly, she stopped quivering altogether. It was all right. She wasn't afraid. He stopped a foot away from her. They looked at each other. She simply wasn't afraid.

Pandora dropped her purse and handed him her shoe. He put it with the other one and tossed them onto the couch. One of them bounced off.

He took the gun out of his jacket pocket and gave it to her. It was a Smith & Wesson. It seemed a dangerous thing to do, to give her the gun. Then she remembered it wasn't loaded. She had fired a .38 like this at her gun club. She didn't like it as a weapon. It was too heavy.

The man took off his jacket and began to get undressed in front of her. This was ridiculous. She couldn't get over not being scared. The guy could be any nut, any pervert, anyone.

She watched him removing his clothes, pulling off his loafers, bending for his socks. He paused slightly before taking down his undershorts. Pandora was determined not to look at his genitals. She looked into his blue eyes. For a man as dark-haired as he the sky-blue eyes were a surprise.

He stood in front of her naked as if he wanted her to be sure she knew what she was getting. She saw the scar. It was six inches long, stretching from below his muscular chest to his navel. He reached forward, gripped the top of her yellow dress and tore it away from her as if it had been made of paper.

Pandora swayed with the sudden force of it. She was momentarily shocked. No man had ever done that to her before. He rubbed the dress over his body like a towel. When he took it away it revealed his erection. He opened her bra at the front. A small, pink satin bow covered the two hooks. He watched her breasts come free. She felt his surprise. They were fuller than he expected. This was the pleasure of beautifully cut underwear.

Pandora pulled the bra off herself and reached both hands down to the panties. For a woman of her age her stomach was quite firm, almost flat. She bent and pushed the panties down past her knees to her ankles. With a little kick she stepped out of them. As she straightened up, he picked her up by the waist.

They both heard the cracking sounds in her back as the small bones moved in their joints.

He was incredibly strong. She was not a small woman but he held her as if she were the weight of a child. She put her arm around his neck and drew breath as he eased into her. The only thing that felt heavy to her was her head. Her neck didn't seem able to control it as he moved her up and down slowly. She could feel the weight of her hair as her head moved from side to side before it fell with a slap onto his shoulder.

Pandora lost control and didn't regain it for several minutes. It was shock treatment. His electricity raged through her body. As they slid in and out of each other she had the feeling of transference. Something she couldn't do anything about. The sensation was wonderful but it wasn't confined to her body. It seemed to invade her spirit. When she swallowed him it was like taking a potion.

As he bent her forward over the soft fleshy upholstery of a chair she was somehow condemned. Not for a crime but for a pleasure. She expected pain as he entered her. There was only excitement. And it came in waves, a surging possession.

Later, he licked her clean like a dog. She tensed again as his tongue stroked her eye-lids. Her pale, wide nipples filled with blood and went dark as if a cloud had passed across the sun. He had taken her apart and now he was putting her back together. She was soon the way she was before. As good as new. No one would know what had happened to her.

Except perhaps the dark-haired woman. Nobody had tried to come into the bungalow, but the thought crossed Pandora's mind that the woman had been there all the time, hiding in a closet, watching and listening.

Nothing in the drawing room suggested the presence of a woman. There were no clues at all even as to who the man was. The only surprising thing she noticed was the small pile of books on the coffee table. *The Classical World*, *The Satyricon* by Petronius, Caesar's *Gallic Wars*.

He kissed her softly, almost lovingly as if he was thankful.

She put her hand between his legs under his swollen balls. He moved away.

He left her on the salmon pink carpet and went into the bathroom. Pandora rolled over on her back. Her pale skin was damp and pink like the carpet. She felt wonderful and completely without guilt. She had amazed herself. She had not made love to a total stranger since her marriage. She hadn't wanted to after Paulette was born. Which made this incident, and that's what it was, an incident, all the more remarkable.

She sat up. She picked up the gun from the coffee table. She idly checked the cartridge. She stiffened. The gun was fully loaded. The safety was engaged but the gun was loaded. So he had lied. Why? To make her feel more at ease probably. She wondered who the woman really was.

He came back into the room. He was now wearing fresh white undershorts. He had combed his hair. He had freshened up. She could smell the soap. He smiled at her. Pandora pointed the gun at him.

'Why didn't you say it was loaded?'

'I didn't want to alarm you. Or the waiter.'

She longed to ask him what he did, why he was staying at the hotel. But she couldn't. That was part of their unspoken pact. No names, no questions, no information. It was just an incident, a wildly pleasurable encounter. There was no past behind it, no future ahead of it.

Pandora stood up. She saw her broken shoe and her torn dress.

'I must be going,' she said, putting the gun down.

'Come with me.' He took her hand and led her into the bedroom which they had never reached. On the way he stroked her sticky ass. His hand, which had been a weapon a while ago, was now disarmed, friendly, the safety on.

He took her to the clothes closet and opened it. Inside there were three dresses hanging.

'Choose one,' he said.

He pulled them out and put them on the bed. She laughed. It was like a boutique. The dresses were simple, expensive.

'Try the red one.'

'I never wear red.'

He picked up the red chenille dress.

'It won't suit me.'

She put it on over her head. For a few seconds as she moved her body into it, she could see nothing but red. The fit was perfect. She looked at herself in the mirror. He stood behind her, watching.

Pandora was surprised. She looked very good. Different, but interesting. He was right.

'I'll send it back to you.'

'No. Keep it.'

She knew what he meant. They wouldn't have any further contact. She would keep it as a souvenir. He left her without a word. She went into the bathroom and washed her hands. She found a comb and ran it through her drying hair. She looked at herself in the bathroom mirror. Red suited her. Why had she never known that before?

When Pandora came back into the drawing room, he was picking up her things.

'I don't have any shoes to offer you.'

'I'll manage.'

He handed her her bra and panties. She didn't try to put them on. She opened her purse and popped them in.

Without a word he threw the torn yellow dress onto the log fire. For a moment, she was shocked to see her dress burning. But he was right again. Destroy the evidence.

'I must go.'

'Of course.'

He came forward and kissed her breasts through the red dress.

'Goodbye,' he said.

Pandora held out her hand. He smiled and shook it firmly. It was all over.

She left the bungalow. Three hours had passed. It had seemed much longer. She walked barefoot back across the bridge. She looked down for the heel that had stuck. But it was gone. One of the hotel gardeners must have found it and removed it.

She didn't go back through the hotel, not in her bare feet. She didn't want to encounter the waiter again, not in her red dress. She went around.

She crossed the shaded parking lot and over to her white BMW. The concrete was hot under her soles. She unlocked the car door and climbed in. Now her thighs started to ache a bit. She settled herself in the seat. Her bottom hurt, but not badly.

She drove slowly out the hotel area. As she stopped at the gate she noticed a Ford Mustang parked a few yards away. There was someone in it, sitting alone behind the tinted window, at the wheel. She wondered if it was the dark-haired woman from the dining room. So what. It was over now. But the woman would have clocked her license plate. PANDORA.

2

I drove away from the Bel Air Hotel shaking. How could I explain what happened? How could I account, to myself I mean, for what I had just done? It was awful. No, not awful, incredible. It was so unlikely, so unlike me. I do not jump into bed with men I meet casually. Ever. Apart from my husband I don't sleep with anyone. I don't cheat. I don't have to. I don't fool around. I don't want to. That stuff's just not me. Occasionally, I've been curious about other men. Who hasn't? It was natural enough. But the thing was so sudden, so violent, it shook me. Even now I could still feel my joints clicking.

I consider that I have an excellent sexual life with Alec, especially when I hear some of my girlfriends complaining. I need sex. I enjoy sex. It's the best entertainment there is. Alec makes me feel good. He always has, from the start. We have fun together in bed and, when Paulette's asleep, around the house and in the pool. I didn't need this. So why did I do it? I wasn't drunk. I wasn't forced. It wasn't rape.

When I first realized the man was looking at me I thought there must be something wrong with me. My clothes, or hair, or way of eating perhaps. But he was looking directly at my face. There was nothing wrong with it. He just liked it. Well, OK, I found the man attractive.

As a matter of fact, I liked him instinctively. I suppose I was flattered as well as astonished by his proposition. After all, I am thirty-six-years-of-age. But that doesn't explain it. Why didn't I just say thanks but no thanks? Maybe the appearance of the woman had somehow triggered my response, my yes. Was she his lover or ex-lover, wife or ex-wife? When she threatened him with the gun I was scared. For him. But I was also excited. She seemed so passionate, so jealous, unafraid to lose control like that in a public place.

Had it really been her in the parking lot? What was she doing now, this woman? Had she gone back to kill him? Perhaps he was dead now as I drove, the smell of Pandora still on his skin, the last woman he'd had. I could smell him on me as I turned on to Sunset Boulevard.

I thought about Alec, wondering. Could he provoke me like that? Could there be a situation where I would threaten Alec like that? With death? I was not by nature a jealous person. I hadn't had reason to be. In fact, Alec was out of town. Flagstaff, Arizona.

He was in pre-production, designing sets for a movie that was going to start shooting in a month. A sudden thought. Did Alec being away have anything to do with this morning? No. No, Alec was often out of town for weeks and this had never happened before. No, that was just a coincidence. But then, would I have done it if Alec had been home right now? No. No, I guess not. No, definitely not.

I drove to Gelson's in Century City on the way home. I didn't have to think about picking Paulette up from school today. She had a music lesson with a friend whose maid would drop her back at around five thirty. So I was on my own for a while. Just as well. I could use the breathing space. To celebrate, I bought some frozen yoghurt. Raspberry with hazelnut topping. No one would ever know. We all have our secrets.

At the supermarket check-out I glanced at the carousel of best-selling paperbacks. Jackie Collins, Judith Krantz, Sally Beauman; I never seem to finish those books. To me they always end up the same. I like Gore Vidal. Although I have to confess I still haven't gotten through *Hollywood*. On impulse I picked up *Dark Angel* and put it with the frozen yoghurt and the smoked whitefish and the onion bagels.

'You smell great,' the check-out girl said. 'What are you wearing?'

'Thank you. I'm glad you like it.' What should I say? That it's the smell of this guy I've just been screwing in bungalow seventeen at the Bel Air Hotel?

Alec and I lived five minutes from Century City, just south of Beverly Hills in Rancho Park. We were one street away from Ray Bradbury, our Guatamalan gardener told me. I used to read science fiction in school, I liked those cut-off, imagined worlds that were always on the brink of destruction. But it turned out that S.F. was a *bête noire* of Alec's. So I stopped reading the stuff. Alec liked old-fashioned realism. Theodore Dreiser was his cup of tea.

That man in the bungalow had an unusual taste in books. *The Classical World* and the others. Not the kind of thing you expected to find in Los Angeles hotel rooms. The subject reminded me of growing up. My father was a classical scholar. He still is, although he's not been well recently and I ought at least to call him. He named me Pandora. Reluctantly, I think, because I'm sure he wanted a boy. He still calls me Pan. In Greek *pan* means everything, and I guess that's what he wanted from me. He didn't get it though, poor man.

Alec, on the other hand, has always called me Dora. Dora sounds like a doll's name, but because of Alec I've gotten used to it. Occasionally, he calls me that as he comes. Then I love it. When we first met I'm sure he chose Dora just to be different from my father, to show he wanted a different me, a person my father couldn't see. In a sense Alec took me away from my father. After my marriage we were never really close. I guess Alec changed me when he changed my name. I was Pan Harten one day, Dora Hammond the next. Just like that. Overnight. It was a metamorphosis. It was scary at the time, but necessary. I was more than ready to leave home, eager to change, and I never used Harten after my marriage on my check books.

I've always called myself, signed myself, Pandora, the full version. I came to realize that I'm definitely made up of two parts, two women. Pan and Dora. Before Alec, and after. What happened in that bungalow at the Bel Air Hotel belongs to the world of Pan. Between the ages of thirteen and twenty three, when we got married, I was Pan. I haven't had anything to do with her until today. Dora is husband and daughter and home. She has never missed being Pan. Until today. There was a twinge today. In the past Pan was generally disapproved of, whereas in the present Dora is widely admired. This man had for a short while hurled me back to that former, wayward existence. Wayward was my father's word.

On the way home I switched on the car radio. It was pre-set to the classical station, Alec's favorite. He loved listening to music while he drove, while he worked, even while we made love. But Alec's classical was different from my father's classical. Alec's classical was in fact romantic: Brahms, Beethoven, Mendelssohn. My father's classical was strictly Bach. I certainly can't be accused of marrying my father. For another thing, Alec Hammond liked children. And women. You can smell it on a man, a liking or a distaste for us. It's a perfume. The Bel Air bungalow was drenched in it. On the other hand I have no idea whether or not the man liked me personally.

I was nearly home when it came, like a wind from nowhere. A sudden silence. The music from the car radio stopped. I froze. I could hear nothing. It wasn't just the music that had cut out. I couldn't hear the traffic sounds on Pico. I was in silence. I'd gone deaf.

'Oh God,' I said out loud. But I couldn't hear my own voice. 'Don't panic, just hang on. It'll go away.'

I tried to relax, one hand on the steering wheel, the other holding the stick shift.

But it scared me. The deafness had happened earlier, in the bungalow, with the man.

When he came into me for the first time the sound around me cut out. In my excitement it had seemed somehow natural. I had already pretty much lost control of my mind. The pleasure I felt was intensified. I went to pieces. I flowed in and out of myself. It was a shock effect that ricocheted on and on. I found that I wasn't reaching for a climax. It was different. There was no straining in me, no yearning. I was in an unending chain reaction that would never stop. The silence was excruciating, more powerful than orgasm.

When the sound did come back it was with an amplified roar. I was in a storm at sea, deafened, tossed. His breathing was the gale. His hands were the lashing waves, twenty feet high. His penis was the unseen rock on which I was aground. I had no will. I was riven. I floundered in ecstasy as I sank into the black foaming water. I must have shouted. I sank in the crashing horror, happy.

Now in my car the sound came back on, with a loud clap, music and traffic together. I was relieved. I realized that without hearing anything I had accelerated to compensate. I slowed and changed down, my damp hand palm down on the shift. But it wasn't the shift. It was flesh, tense, slightly soft. It was a man's penis. I was holding the head of a cock. I snatched my hand away, looked down, expecting to see . . . But it was just the black head of the stick shift. This wasn't happening. I didn't need this. It mustn't happen.

I had one thought in my head. Was this kind of hallucination going to happen again? I looked at the shift. How long was it going to be before I could look at it again without remembering that sensation. Wait a minute. Don't exaggerate this thing. You didn't actually see anything. You felt what you imagined was his cock. You didn't actually hallucinate. Maybe that was natural, after what happened. The memory of arousal was a pulse in my whole body, a beat. Look out!

I braked at a set of lights I hadn't noticed. 'Be careful. Oh please, let me forget it, the whole fucking thing. Don't let me get wet. This is ridiculous. I don't need it. Go away!'

I was talking to myself. 'Think of something. Anything. Concentrate. Watch the road.' I watched the tail of the car ahead. I just stared at the Arizona license plate. Arizona. Alec. Would Alec believe this? Would he believe that his Dora had done this, felt like this, so without control? Maybe he'd understand. Alec was a gentle soul. Maybe he wouldn't understand how I felt today. Maybe he would be disgusted, feel betrayed. Because that man today could have done anything to me. Anything he wanted. At the time. In those two hours, after the silence.

I ate my yoghurt lying in the tub. The afternoon sun blazed through the open bathroom window. A strong beam of light hit the surface of the water. It lit my thighs and sex like a flashlight. I was embarrassed. I don't know why. I was alone. Yes, I do too. It was guilt. It was as if the sunlight was a burning glass, or an eye that had seen what I had done. I soaped myself to make the water cloudy. The sun couldn't penetrate the sudsy surface. I thought again about what had happened. What did it really mean? The intense pleasure of touching, holding, sucking a man I didn't even know, as if he was the love of my life, what did that signify? A flaw in my character.

I decided to shave my armpits. God knows why. I hadn't bothered to do that since Alec left for Arizona, proving I'm not real Beverly Hills material. The hair under my arms, being blonde, was quite pretty. I knew I shouldn't have used his razor. When the phone rang I was startled and jerked my left hand. I nicked my right armpit. Shit.

Clasping a Kleenex under my arm, I picked up the phone by the bed with the other hand. Water dripped from me onto the bedcover.

'Hello . . .'

There was a pause. I waited.

'Hello . . .'

Nothing. I was uneasy, almost scared. It was one of those calls. I knew it.

'You're blonde . . . aren't you . . . ?'

'Hang up, asshole.'

'Touch yourself. I want you to touch yourself.' A disguised voice, a Southern drawl.

Why didn't I hang up myself? Then and there. He blew into the phone. The rush of sound hurt my ear.

Shit. Hang up Pandora. Hang up.

'Are you touching yourself? I know you want to.'

I was about to slam the phone down, but there was something

17

in the adopted voice that was familiar. Who was it? Who the fuck? Then I knew. It was the man from the hotel. My skin prickled. Was that why I hadn't hung up?

'Listen. What happened, happened. It's over, pal.'

Now he paused. 'What happened Dora?'

I jumped. It was Alec's voice.

'Alec.' The relief.

He laughed. 'What happened?'

He had done this to me once before, made a dirty phonecall. I had liked it then.

'Nothing, darling. I've had a couple of calls. Some sicko.'

'Oh really? When? You didn't tell me.'

'I didn't want to worry you.'

'I am worried. Have you called the police?'

'What can they do?'

'That's not the point. Call them.'

'OK. I will.'

'I'm sorry I scared you. But you must call the police.'

'How's it going?'

'Pretty good. The usual chaos. How's our daughter?'

'She's fine. She's at a music lesson.'

I prayed he wouldn't go back to what I had blurted out. Shit. How could I have been so stupid? 'What happened, happened. It's over, pal.' That was pretty unambiguous.

Luckily, Alec was preoccupied with his own problems on the movie. He talked for a while. I hardly heard him. How could I have been so dumb?

'You will call the police, won't you?'

'Of course I will.' I could feel he wanted to go. Thank God.

'I'll try and get back Friday night.'

'Just make sure you're back by Saturday.'

'Have you arranged a party?'

'Just be back.'

'I love you, Dora.'

'Me too. With all my heart.'

'Whatever happens, I'll love you.'

'Come home soon,' I said.

I lay back on the bed. I looked at myself. That female angle, looking down through my breasts to my pubic hair. I slapped myself smartly between my legs.

That's it. Never again. Rub yourself all you want. Get a vibrator. Go blind. But for Christ's sake never do a thing like that again. Promise?

'I promise,' Pan said to Dora.

The bleeding in my armpit had stopped. It hadn't been much to begin with. Then I wondered, had I done it on purpose? To wound myself. To punish Pandora for what she'd done.

I'm a sound sleeper, but I didn't sleep at all well for the next two nights. I read chapter after chapter of *Dark Angel*. I didn't really like it. It was too close to home. A woman rummaging around in her past. I put it with *Hollywood*.

Paulette had the teenage habit of trying on my clothes. I found her in front of the mirror wearing the red dress. I should have thrown it away. I didn't because I liked it. Maybe I will now.

'It doesn't suit you,' I told her.

'One day it will,' she said.

'I bought it.'

'It's great. Sexy.'

That night I think I needed Paulette more than she needed me. We were real pals, my daughter and I. She was better for me than any son could have been. And far better than any man. Except for Alec, of course. They just didn't come any better. I was so fucking lucky.

Three days later I was back in the leafy parking lot of the Bel Air Hotel. I had arranged to meet Beverly in the usual place for breakfast. When I made the arrangement I was scared. But what of? He wouldn't be there. And if he was that wouldn't happen again. Ever.

Of course, he wasn't there. He'd been staying in the hotel and now he'd moved on. But all the time I talked with Beverly I kept looking over to his table. I was kind of proud of my bravery in coming back to the hotel. I hardly listened to what she was telling me. I could smell him. Stop it. Stop it, Pandora. Beverly had discovered that her Hollywood husband, Jimbo, was having an affair with her cousin in Santa Barbara. She wanted sympathy and advice.

'These things happen,' I said.

'Not to me they don't,' said Beverly. 'What would you do?'

'I'd let it ride.'

'If Hammond was having an affair, would you let that ride?'

'I'd prefer not to know.'

'Me too. But I do know. So now what do I do?'

I was tempted to say, go and have an affair of your own. Get your revenge. But that was dumb. And I knew it. I don't know why I even thought it. What was I thinking, revenge?

'Wait it out for a while. These things usually take care of themselves.'

'I wonder how you'd feel if it was Hammond.'

'I guess you never know till it happens.'

It was curious the way Alec's friends and associates all called him Hammond. I called him Alec, and always had. For the first time it struck me that he was like me in that way. We both had two names. Why hadn't that occurred to me before? Was he two people in one? No, Alec was constant, consistent to a fault. Except sometimes when he drank.

Over the next few days I began to forget the face of the man in the bungalow. The man whose name I didn't know. Now I remembered only his body. And then even that became vague in outline. His scar remained. I couldn't forget that. But my clearest memory was how I had felt, the electric release, the enigmatic silence, the panic of sensual freedom. Panic, yes. I couldn't think of that word without remembering my father telling me its origin. It had been one of his bedtime stories. Or bedtime educations. Pan was the son of Hermes and the Greek god of shepherds. He loved music and invented the flute. He lived in the forest and he used to creep up on travelers. He would appear suddenly and scare them out of their wits. They would be paralysed with fear, struck dumb with terror. That, Daddy told me, was where we got the word panic, from Pan.

Panic was a silent state. Silence and fear. His Pan certainly knew about those two things.

With difficulty I returned to the comfort of being Dora. Alec would be home soon. Everything would be back to normal. Thinking back on his phonecall I was puzzled by something he'd said. It had stuck in my memory. After Alec's heavy breathing bit, after I had got out of my jam of thinking he was the man from the Bel Air, it came right at the end of our conversation. Alec had said: 'Whatever happens, I'll love you.' And I said: 'Come home soon.' But what did he mean, 'whatever happens'? What could happen? Or was he referring to what had happened? No, he couldn't possibly know about that, that was impossible. So then what did he mean, 'whatever happens I'll love you.'? In my guilty state it never entered my head that Alec might be talking about himself, referring to something he'd done.

Part Two

1

No one on the set had formally introduced them. As the production designer on the movie, Hammond was frequently away from the set for hours at a time selecting, buying, adapting materials for construction. Only intermittently did he see other members of the crew. He had noticed Betty May, saw she was very young and assumed she was a runner or third assistant director. She was pale-skinned, dark-haired, wore dark glasses, jeans and a shirt. Nothing special.

At lunch one day she sat down next to him at one of the trestle tables set out under a canvas tent in the desert south of Flagstaff. She looked kind of nervous, he thought. She looked even younger in close-up. She was uncertain. She seemed new to film work. He introduced himself and asked her what she did.

'I'll be doing some doubling and maybe some stunts.'

'Stunts? That's very brave of you.'

'Well, I don't think it'll be anything too difficult.'

'You won't be jumping off burning buildings or anything like that.'

'Lord no. I hope not.' Her face creased into a fearful, school-girl smile.

Hammond told her his job. She seemed very interested, but knew practically nothing about making movies. She assumed he painted the scenery.

Hammond thought no more about her until late that night when he got back from the Lake location. He had been supervising the construction of a jetty. It was after ten when he sat down tired in the Old Silver coffee shop. He saw her sitting by herself at a nearby table. An Edward Hopper image, she was an ad for loneliness. Most of the crew had already eaten. The place was overlit and almost empty. She smiled shyly at him. He waved her to come over.

Betty May brought her Coke and sat down. She was wearing carefully torn jeans, exposing her knees and a thin white cotton shirt which exposed nothing.

'What have you been doing today?' he asked her.

'Not much really.'

'You'll be busier when we start shooting.'

Betty May watched Hammond eat his chilli omelette. He felt watched.

'Made any friends yet?'

'Everybody seems so busy.'

Hammond thought she looked sad, as if she had a recent troubled past. After eating he looked at his watch. It was nearly eleven. The girl had shown no sign of wanting to leave. As an Old Silver regular, Hammond signed the check and got up. She stood up with him. They left the coffee shop and walked down the road to the rectangle of motel cabins. The wind was rolling a Coke can back and forth.

'This one's mine,' Hammond said, as they reached cabin eleven.

'I'm in seventeen,' she said.

'Goodnight, Betty May. Sleep well.'

Hammond leaned forward to kiss her on the cheek. She put her arm round his back and drew him against her. He could feel her body pressing firmly against his shirt. She kissed him quite suddenly on the lips. Hammond was instantly aroused, instantly worried.

'Look, this isn't such a great idea,' he said. He glanced around. Sooner or later on a movie set everybody knew everything about everybody else.

'Can I come in? Just for a minute?'

He looked at her. She had tears in her eyes. How could he resist? Hammond unlocked the cardboard door to his cabin and they went in. Betty May sat on the bed. He switched on a lamp which gave the dreary room a yellow glow. He closed the drapes.

'What's the matter? Why are you crying?'

He questioned her as he retrieved the vodka bottle from the fridge. She didn't reply.

'Do you want a drink?'

She shook her head. He poured some vodka into a glass for himself, decided against weakening it with ice, and sat beside her on the bed.

'Where do you come from?' he asked.

'From L.A. The Valley.'

'How did you get into this sort of work?'

'It just happened. I was offered a job.'

'That happened to me too,' Hammond said. 'I used to be an architect. One day someone offered me a job to design and build a set for a movie.'

'I guess I just wanted to get away from home,' she said.

'What's really the matter, Betty May?'

'You are.'

Hammond felt the suddenness of her desire. Dora used to be like that when he first met her. Unexpected flashes of desire. He loved that in her. He remembered Dora in her house, in what had been her nursery when she was a little girl. They made love for the first time awkwardly in her painted cot. Remembering her rabbit and the lion-shaped pillows it had seemed to Hammond that he was literally cradle-snatching. At the time Dora was much older than this girl, but she had seemed like a teenager.

Betty May stood up. Her clean short-nailed fingers began to undo the buttons of her white shirt. She started at the waist, pulling the shirt out from her jeans.

'I want you to see me.'

She left her shirt on, open. Then she unzipped her jeans. Hammond wanted to tell her to stop. If he saw this girl naked he would have to make love to her, he knew that.

She pulled her jeans down over her thighs. Her panties edged down at the same time. Hammond saw her blonde pubic hair.

He felt a strange, sensual jolt. He hadn't realized her hair was dyed. Below the waist she also reminded him of Dora. He sat on the bed, his cold vodka in his wet hand, watching her strip. Betty May made no attempt to be seductive. This was a strip without the tease.

She kicked her jeans away with her flip-flops and stood before him, her hands simply at her sides. She was completely still, a statue of flesh.

'When we first sat together at lunch I wanted you to see me like this.' Her immobility was unbearable.

'You're very beautiful.' Hammond felt himself getting hard. He was embarrassed, feeling suddenly middle-aged in front of this girl who was only a few years older than his daughter. He reached forward and took her hand. She stepped towards him and stopped. Her pubic hair was level with his face. She looked down on his head. He leaned forward and kissed her skin above her panties. She pulled them down an inch to encourage him. Her warmth and a smell of marjoram enveloped him. He moved his tongue in her soft hair. He felt her stomach twitch.

'I want to see you too. Is that all right?' A simple request in a controlled tone.

Hammond stood up. She moved back. He looked for some-where to put his drink. She took it from him and held it while he removed his jacket. She rolled the chill glass between her breasts as he pulled off his shirt.

Hammond leaned forward and kissed her lips. Her mouth opened only very slightly. She was waiting. He licked her lips. She touched his tongue with hers. He reached down to unfasten his western belt buckle.

'Let me,' she said, and handed the glass back to him. She pulled his belt away. The leather clicked through the loops of Hammond's gray cotton pants. She hung the belt around her neck.

After she had unzipped him Betty May gently turned him around. She pulled his pants down, bending her knees. Ham-mond heard the snapping sounds of her joints. This girl may be young, he thought, but she must be experienced. There was an assurance in her manner. She must have slept with many men, he thought.

She pushed him gently backwards and onto the musty motel bed. She slipped his shoes off and removed his socks, massaging his feet.

Desire overcame Hammond. He fought to keep the physical control he was used to with Dora. But this was nothing like sex with his wife. There was no reassurance, no certain knowledge of the outcome, no next-day calm at the back of his mind. Betty May had an uncomfortable originality about her.

Beneath the peach-like fuzz of the blonde hair of her thighs, he discovered a surprising muscularity. There was a tense firmness in her breasts. Apart from the inside of her mouth there seemed to be no really soft areas of her body, unlike Dora.

Stop making comparisons. This wasn't Dora. She was a young girl. Think of this as an experiment, he told himself. He inhaled the slightly oily smell of her, a natural body lotion, woodsy, herbal.

She opened her legs for him, wider and wider. It wasn't an invitation for his cock but for his eyes. She wanted to be looked at, examined carefully, thought about. It was medical, gynaecological. Parting her flesh folds was shocking to him. He felt like a doctor who wasn't sure what he was looking for. She was a child with the body of a woman, capable of giving birth. Like the rest of her torso her vulva was oddly unripe. He put his mouth to her firm sex. His feelings were sensual, his thoughts clinical. He couldn't get the fact of her youth out of his mind. She was newly-built.

He remembered his student days as an architect. He recalled an interpretation of the ever-narrowing folds at the arching entrance to a Gothic cathedral. The way in to the house of God was the way into the body of a woman. With his head between her legs there came a sensation of drowning. No, not drowning. She wasn't that wet. It was a feeling of not being able to breathe properly. It was enticing, willingly giving up your right to breathe. She was made of sun-warmed soapstone.

29

When he got up and moved into her, her legs slowly closed. Very slowly, as he moved in and out, she became stronger. She gripped him as if she were holding his penis tightly between her hands. It was overwhelming. She was trying to rid him of his consciousness. Let your mind go, she was saying. I'm going to take your intellect away.

He was scared. He didn't want to let go. But what was he holding on to? What was he scared of? What territory did he think she wanted to occupy? He had the disturbing sensation that Betty May was drawing him towards death, into some state without consciousness. He clung desperately to his self-awareness. But in the end he had to let go. The tighter she became the more his mind crumbled. Her arms were strong around his hips. He was in an *Aikido* hold. In a long, pounding orgasm, he gave in, collapsed. He shook for a while in her arms. He was lost and didn't think about her at all.

Hammond felt as if he had experienced sex for the first time. He'd been taught in the arms of an older woman. A ridiculous feeling. The girl wasn't twenty. She took his left hand and put the fingers where his cock had been. He rubbed her quite violently. She yelled as she came. The sound scared him. She bit his shoulder. Hammond felt the extraordinary willfulness of her sexuality. She was having her way with him.

At around three thirty in the morning Betty May left the cabin without saying goodbye. Hammond was silent too. The chill night air of the desert blew into the stuffy room before she closed the door. He smelled the scent of night-flowering jasmine. It was cruelly similar to the perfume of Pandora's soap.

It seemed to Hammond like one of those movie affairs that burst into flame, often intensely, but which extinguish themselves naturally by the end of the production. They were common enough, safety valves for overheated emotional states, adolescent romances for people of any age. They had clear rules. They were enacted in their own film space and within a defined period of time. Partners back home knew that they must happen and tried not to care or think about it. They knew detective work was a mistake. It would blow everything out of all proportion. Pandora never asked him about that.

Hammond had had two such affairs in the past, both enjoyable and harmless. But there was something about Betty May that touched him more deeply than any girl before. He couldn't figure quite what it was. Her innocence certainly. Her youth naturally. The fact that she wanted him, picked him out, was an irresistible source of attraction. She had aroused a paternal instinct in him. He tried not to think of Paulette when he was with her.

Sexually, Betty May was more complex than he had guessed. After two or three nights together she began to demand aggression from him. He wasn't used to that. He loved sex with Dora, it was equal in aggression and submission. Usually, they took it in turns to bring each other to orgasm. They seldom seriously tried to come simultaneously. It didn't seem necessary. There was a slow, seductive patience in their love-making. Pandora loved having it done to her. It was her trust in him that made her so desirable. And essential.

Betty May would get him excited and then demand that he hit her, slap her across her back and thighs. Hammond had never done this to a woman. He didn't understand it. It was against his nature, contrary to his instincts. Pleasant, likeable people didn't behave like this. He had read about sadistic sex, but it had never turned him on. He had no urge for it. Suddenly, it was expected of him.

His first thought was to tell Betty May that it just wasn't his way. But looking down at her strong naked body, raised, waiting for him to act, he was nervous of what she would think if he refused. He would look like a wimp, somehow not man enough for this young girl. He was on the edge of panic. Come on, Hammond, she wants it. It won't hurt you. Show a little courage. After all, what happened between a man and a girl, who didn't know each other, in an anonymous motel room in the middle of nowhere, in the middle of the night was unlikely to trouble anyone else. No one would know.

He tickled her. He didn't know where to begin. He slapped

her, tentatively at first. She immediately wanted more and harder. The sound of the slaps unnerved him at first. He was abusing a young girl. How could he ever explain it? He saw, after several blows across the backs of her thighs, that Betty May's muscles tensed with pleasure and excitement. She lay face down on the bed. He couldn't see her face. The sounds she made were muffled by the pillow she clung to. He judged the movements, the undulations, the spasms of her body. He found that he could gauge her responses as accurately as if he were watching her face. When he understood that she loved it, he began to like it too.

It excited him. The sensuality released another man inside him. He became aware of a troubling violence in his character. With Betty May he came near to losing control. On one occasion he ejaculated without being inside her, without any contact with his penis. He shot onto her thighs from above. That had never happened in his life before. It shook him. Betty May shook him. He was stirred by the look of triumph on her face when she made him come. It was a look of love. It touched him. The mix of sexual abandon and hugging affection confused him. He came close to tears. And Hammond never cried.

2

SCENE 103. EXTERIOR. DESERT. SHACK. MORNING

HELGA *comes out of the door of the shack into the yard. No sooner has she pulled the door closed behind her than she turns at the sound of a car. She is immediately scared.*

A MAN *jumps out of the still moving car. He carries a sub-machine gun.* HELGA *cries out as the* MAN *opens fire. Bullets splatter her body. Spurting blood, she is blown backwards through the door and into the shack.*

That was how Helga's death read in the screenplay. The young actress playing her would just do the close-ups. Betty May was her stunt double. She would do the physical action. Mel Harris, the director, shot the actress before lunch. At two thirty he started work on the action.

The seven explosive charges inside Betty May's Levi shirt and jacket were detonated simultaneously. Blood spurted from the holes. The seven vinyl blood bags continued to discharge the dark shiny liquid as Betty May was thrown backwards through the door of the shack. Invisible wires attached were yanked violently from inside the shack. The effect was startlingly realistic. Mel Harris yelled 'Cut'. The watching crew clapped and cheered. The stunt had worked first time.

In designing the shack, Hammond had built the door out of light balsa wood, the kind model plane-makers use. So when Betty May was thrown back against it, her body smashing the wood, she wouldn't be hurt. The set was Hammond's department, but the scene was the work of the special effects team,

33

and of Charles Wildman, the stunt co-ordinator, who was Betty May's boss.

Hammond knew something had gone wrong. They cheered outside but he was inside the shack. He saw what the others did not. He watched Betty May yanked back through the splintering door, trailing the fine electric charge wires from under her specially-cut jeans. She screamed. She had no control of the action. She hit an upright pole that was part of the interior construction of the shack. Hammond winced at the thud. He heard the air whistle out of her lungs. Betty May collapsed at Wildman's feet, a fallen puppet, entangled in his wires.

Hammond ran over to her. She was lying quite still, unconscious. He crouched over her body facing Wildman. When he reached out to lift her head Wildman shouted at him.

'Don't touch her!'

Hammond froze. The medic rushed in from outside. Mel Harris was in a panic.

'Get her to hospital,' the medic said, listening to Betty May's heart, his head pressed between the breasts that only the night before had been in Hammond's hands.

'Get a chopper. Fast.' The medic told Mel.

There was the sound of a woman crying. Hammond looked round to see his assistant, Rosie Holden, in tears. He couldn't cry. It had been an accident, a sickening accident. But he had seen something before that horrible moment that stuck in his mind. It wouldn't go away.

There had been a look in Wildman's eyes as he operated the machine which controlled the wires of Betty May's harness. An indelible look. A look of intense, repressed violence, a look of power, grim and shocking. Hammond would never forget it. Wildman knew he had seen it.

Neither man went with Betty May to the hospital. At the end of shooting that day Mel announced to the crew that Betty May was dead. She had died of internal bleeding. She never regained consciousness.

Nobody on the movie wanted to blame Wildman. There were worried exchanges among members of the crew that night in the

Old Silver coffee shop. Hammond was acutely aware that blame could also be levelled at him. People asked each other questions. Why was the upright pole allowed to remain on the set where it could be a hazard? That was hindsight. No one thought Betty May would come back that far inside the shack. Had it been strictly necessary for Wildman to use that amount of force? Yes, he argued, otherwise the effect wouldn't have worked properly. It would have looked feeble, as if she had deliberately thrown herself back. So then why had Wildman used such an inexperienced stunt woman? That was the producer's responsibility, Wildman pointed out. Early on, before they started, the production office had refused to sanction more expenditure in the stunt department. It was not the fault of any one person. That was the consensus.

Hammond was in a state of shock. He couldn't sleep that night. Betty May was still in his bed. He could smell her. He walked around the motel forecourt in the moonlight. He stopped outside her own cabin. He opened the door. He went into the darkness. The room was tidy. He pulled back the bedclothes, looking for God-knows what. Nothing. Sheets gray and dry. It was as if Betty May had never been there, never existed. The title of the movie was apt. *Ghost Town*. Now she was a ghost.

In the remaining weeks of the shoot Hammond did not talk to Wildman. An unspoken tension grew between them. It was an internal version of the generally uneasy atmosphere on and off the set. There was a silent pact among the cast and crew not to talk about Betty May Lefevre. Her father in Los Angeles was suing the production company for negligence. Two men from an insurance company came out to Flagstaff to interview separately the principal crew members about the circumstances of the accident in order to prepare a report. Hammond and Wildman were both questioned. The short interviews after work were conducted in private and there was no comparing notes. Hammond did not reveal his feelings about Wildman, but the memory of the man's face stayed with him. His growing hatred began to occupy even his dreams. Every two or three days he called Pandora and sometimes spoke to Paulette who said always how much she missed him.

He detected a nervousness in Pandora's voice on the phone. He knew she was worried about her father back East. The old man hadn't been well. But beyond that he worried whether she had somehow heard about his relationship with Betty May. When he thought of it he felt sick. He was guilty, not so much about his affair with her as a fact he wanted to conceal, but about his special feeling for the girl herself. She had meant something to him, something he found it difficult to define, perhaps because everything was so colored by her death. Or was it murder? Wildman had killed her. Hammond had no doubts about that. And he was an unwitting accomplice. Every night he needed a few shots of vodka to sleep.

In fact, Wildman was not around too much. There were only two or three scenes which required a stunt co-ordinator. He was often away for several days at a time. Wildman's absence from the scene was a more powerful provocation than his presence. His not being there gave Hammond the feeling that the man had gotten away with it. Wildman was running around somewhere, free as a bird.

He returned for the last two days of the shoot. At the final wrap party held in a steak joint Hammond knew he could not let Wildman go away, disappear for ever without being called to account. Fuelled by vodka at two thirty in the morning Hammond asked him to leave the restaurant. They left the party, the dancing, the drunken laughter, and stepped into the chill desert air.

'I know one thing,' Hammond said. 'She died because of you. You're not going to get away with it.'

'Accidents happen,' Wildman said.

'You put her at risk. Unnecessary risk.'

'Everybody knows stunting's a dangerous business. Betty May knew what she was getting into.'

'You knew. She didn't.'

36

'She signed the release form. Mel accepted it.'

'Mel only knew what you told him. You told him the stunt was safe.'

'Not safe. Minimal risk.'

'Bull.' Hammond felt a surge of hatred. Wildman's tone was cold. He seemed almost casual.

'She's dead. It was an accident. That's all there is to it.'

Wildman had had enough of the conversation. He started to go back inside. Hammond grabbed his arm. Wildman turned. There was cold fury in his face. Hammond thought he was going to hit him.

'That's not all there is to it. You're not going to walk away from this.'

'Get this Hammond. It was your set that killed her. You're forgetting that. If that pole hadn't been there she'd be alive now.'

Yes, the fucking pole was his fault. He knew that. It was a factor, but that was not why she died.

'You're a sadistic fuck. Her father's suing the company. If it goes to court –'

'– it won't go to court. The company will settle. Her father will get the money. And that'll be the end of it.'

'Not for me.'

'Not for you? What do you mean, not for you?'

'You killed Betty May. You gave her a job she couldn't handle. She died. That's called murder. You're not going to get away with it.'

'You wouldn't give a fuck about it if you hadn't been screwing her. That's the bottom line.'

How did he know that? No one knew. Had she told him? Hammond's stomach churned. If it got to court everything would come out. Maybe other people knew. If they didn't Wildman would surely tell them. Hammond could see Dora's face when she heard about it. And Paulette too. That really was the bottom line. He said nothing. Wildman smiled and went back into the restaurant to enjoy the party.

Hammond stayed outside, mocked by the screeching

laughter. He was confused. He was nauseous. He was drunk. He'd been a fool. He needed a good night's sleep but he knew he wouldn't get it. Not for a long time.

3

In the quiet days and bad nights that followed Hammond's return to Los Angeles, he hardly registered his wife's moods. He didn't see that she was as preoccupied as he. There were times when she didn't seem to hear what he said. He ignored them, grateful to be left isolated in his own confusions.

Pandora went to Doctor Fleming, the family physician, to tell him about her bouts of deafness. He sent her to a clinic for tests. No one could find anything wrong physically. The specialist suggested that it might have a psychological cause.

'What do you mean?' Pandora was panicky.

'I think you should see a neurologist first.'

He made an appointment for her. She broke it at the last minute. She didn't tell Hammond about any of it. It'll go away on its own, she told herself.

'Darling, I haven't seen that dress before. I thought you didn't like red.'

Pandora took it off.

'I like it.'

'I said I liked it.'

'It doesn't suit me. It was a mistake.'

Her tone was cold. Hammond left it at that.

Other times she clung to him as if she was afraid of losing him. Hammond passed off these switches in behavior as female temperament. He was preoccupied with one thing only. Betty May's death. The finality of that memory made him practically impotent. Twice a week he made love to Dora, as usual, but with some difficulty. He didn't think he betrayed it. There were times when she seemed almost to be making love to herself. She hoped he wasn't aware of it.

One night they went out to a seafood dinner with friends. Pandora uncharacteristically drank a whole bottle of French Chablis. Hammond counted six glasses. He noticed them because he himself wasn't drinking that night. He was going to drive them home. And he'd had a skinful at lunch thinking about Betty May.

While he was brushing his teeth in the bathroom, Pandora slotted a cassette into the bedroom radio-cassette player, and waited for him, fully dressed. As Hammond came out of the bathroom she began her striptease. He knew what to do. He turned out the bathroom light and got into bed. The music Pandora loved best for her stripping was a love theme from a French movie. It was smoochy, not bump and grind.

This was the first time since he returned from Arizona that she had drunk enough to perform. When Pandora was tipsy she was happy. And when she was happy she liked to take her clothes off just for him. Her striptease was a small ritual between them. It was her answer to Hammond's occasional dirty phone-call. They both enjoyed it. Pandora used to joke that if all else failed financially she could support them as a stripper in an L.A. club.

Slowly she began to undo the buttons of her dress, one at a time from the neck to the knees. She kept this salmon pink dress especially for her performance. Having undone the last button Pandora turned away from him and eased the dress off her shoulder and down her back. Under the dress she wore a pale green silk petticoat. He smiled at her as she put one foot on the dressing table stool and reached under the petticoat to unsnap her stocking which was clipped to a garter belt.

As he watched her, images of Betty May came into Hammond's mind. He didn't want the memory but he couldn't stop it. He tried with all his strength to concentrate on Dora and forget Betty May. That was all over. Over. Yet now he could feel her thighs clamping his cheeks. He wanted Pandora to stop.

She stood up after the second stocking was off and slowly shrugged her way out of the petticoat which slid to the floor with an electric crackle. Carefully, Pandora eased her foot into the material and kicked it upwards. The silken bundle landed on the bed in front of Hammond. He reached forward and put it to his face. For God's sake, Dora, finish this.

She was enjoying herself. She enjoyed herself right up to the point where she unhooked her bra. The fall of her breasts suddenly reminded her of the anonymous man in the Bel Air Hotel. Why? Why now? She tried to dispel the thought, the memory of her undressing in front of him. She could see his scar, his erection. Go away. Go away. She gritted her teeth as she reached down for her panties. She pulled the elastic out and let it slap back against her skin.

The sound was like a whiplash to Hammond. Why had she done that? Other memories surfaced. His hand slapping Betty May's thighs. Her fingers digging into his buttocks. His fingers squeezing her nipples. The shock of seeing that pain was pleasure to her.

Pandora held her breasts, one in each hand, offering them to her audience. Then she shook them gently. It was so different from what she was remembering. Her legs spread over the couch as the man eased into her from behind. The soft pleasure of her little performance for Alec had given way to a sensation of danger. 'Get out of my body.'

It was too late. She felt the liquid between her legs. For Hammond too the memories were vivid. He saw Betty May's buttocks not Dora's. He felt the peach fuzz of youth. 'God, I just want to forget.'

Pandora was trembling now. She prayed that he wouldn't notice. She had to bring this dumb game to an end. When she squeezed her thighs together in the last sequence of her naked dance, she could feel it coming. She closed her eyes to try and halt it. The images were flashbulbs going off in her head. The way he had used her like a doll, doing anything he wanted, and that frightening feeling of insemination.

Thank God, the fucking music's coming to an end, Hammond

41

thought. She always ended her strip the same way, covering her sex with one hand and crossing her right arm over her breasts. In the language of the stripper it represented a return to modesty. Pandora's hand on her blonde pubic hair was wet.

She climbed on the bed and moved towards him like a snake swimming. That was what she always did after the strip. But this time she moved as fast as she could. 'Quickly. I can't stand it.' And when he hauled her into his arms, she came. Hammond held her quivering body. They fell asleep in each other's arms without making love, her hand on his softening penis.

He awoke out of a miserable dream. He had been with Betty May. It was hideous thinking of her dead when in his mind she was alive. Lying in bed with Dora he was betraying her with a dead girl. It was somehow more of a betrayal now than it had seemed at the time.

Hammond couldn't stay in bed with these memories. He got up. She felt him move.

'Are you all right?' she whispered.

'Just restless.'

Sleepily, Pandora put out her arm and touched his face to reassure him. There was a rumble of distant thunder.

Hammond went downstairs and sat on the patio by the pool. There was a flash of lightning. He remembered Wildman's face.

'Get out of my mind. Both of you.' He hissed at the black sky. How long would it be before they went, vanished, the pair of them, the girl and Wildman?

When it started to rain, splashing onto the shiny surface of the pool, drumming on the umbrellas, soaking his pajamas, he went back inside the house, never more lost.

The next morning he woke up with a start. He knew what had to be done. He had dreamt it. It was simple. In order to exorcise the ghost of Betty May Lefevre he would have to kill Charles Wildman.

4

In Hammond's dream Wildman had tried over and over to kill him. Attack followed lethal attack. No sooner had he gotten away from the knife fight in a supermarket than he found himself on a deserted beach. Wildman had tried to club him to death with a rock. What finally woke him was a struggle in a pool. Wildman was drowning him, pulling him under. When he finally lost consciousness, his lungs full of water, he came to with a start. He was in bed beside Pandora. The sound of his cry had made her jump. She herself had only just awakened from a nightmare of her own.

'Alec, what is it?' His anguished face frightened her. Pandora had never seen that twisted look of terror before. For a few moments Hammond had the face of another man, someone she didn't recognize.

'A nightmare.' He could feel the water. He coughed, retched. His legs kicked downwards. His eyes were stinging with the chlorine from the pool.

'Tell me. What was it? What did you dream?' Had it been a nightmare like hers?

He couldn't answer her. She held his shaking body. She watched his face muscles relax.

'God. It must have been awful.' Was it possible they had dreamed the same dream?

Hammond could still hear the flat, underwater echoing. He still felt the life bubbling from his mouth and nose.

'I was drowning.'

'You're all wet.' She stroked his damp chest. Drowning had not been in her dream.

Hammond's body was covered with sweat. His hair was soaking as if he had just crawled out of the pool, out of his nightmare. Pandora handed him a glass of water.

'No more water,' he said. It wasn't funny.

Pandora wanted to say that she too had had a nightmare, to comfort him. But she didn't. She couldn't. Pandora's dream had started off like a love affair, promising everything.

She had been so looking forward to seeing him again, the man. She had gone to the police and they had traced him through his scar. He was staying in a motel somewhere near the beach. Like a teenager on a date Pandora was elated as she drove over. She sang in the car. She was still humming when she walked into the room, high on expectation. He was there. He was lying naked on the bed. He was pushing into a woman. Pandora screamed and screamed. Her cries were deafening. She knew what was coming. A silence. She started to haul the woman away from him. She saw his penis sliding out of the woman's body like a sword. His rigid and shining flesh dripped with blood.

The woman fell from the bed onto the floor. The pearls from her necklace ran across the worn rug like mercury.

Pandora leapt onto the man. The head of his cock pressed into her navel. She saw that she was naked herself. She wasn't surprised. She gripped his shoulders. He struggled. The scar shone with sweat. She slapped his face, in silence, threatened to kill him. He kicked to get away. She bent his penis sideways. She knelt at his slender waist. She overpowered him, pressing the bone of her elbow into his throat hard against his Adam's apple.

Pandora had no pity for him. He was an object. She wanted to smash him. He could have been crying. She heard nothing. He seemed to be giving in. She felt nothing. In anger she grabbed him between his legs. There was a handful of pubic hair between her clenched fingers. He had no penis.

Suddenly, she caught sight of herself from across the room.

44

There was no mirror. She was both the observer and the observed, double. She watched a blonde woman raping a man. The woman was in a frenzy, a crazed butcher hacking up an animal while it was still alive. Seeing herself in action, Pandora lurched towards orgasm.

Everything went electric white, lightning reflected in a mirror. The explosion in her head brought the sound crashing back. Pandora's body shook in an internal earthquake.

Panting, Pandora looked at the sleeping form of her husband in the bed beside her. By the time she had recovered and was beginning to forget parts of the dream, Hammond started to wake. He was twisted around himself like a serpent. She tried to analyse her dream. But as she struggled to make sense of it all she started to forget the parts.

Hammond was less fortunate. For days afterwards the feeling that Wildman was going to kill him stayed in the front of his mind. Wildman was there while he was marketing for Pandora at Gelson's. Hammond was on line for the check-out. He didn't wait to count his change. He got out. Then he saw Wildman outside the school when he went to pick up Paulette. He tried never to be alone. He kept to crowded places. He stopped going to the movies. One afternoon he looked out of his studio window and there was Wildman lounging by the pool insolently waiting for him. Hammond became a prisoner of fantasy and fear.

Wildman replaced Betty May as the dominant figure in his consciousness. There seemed to be no solution to his state of panic, no release. Exactly what to do came to him as he was talking to his ex-assistant in the art department. Rosie was working over at Paramount. As he talked to her he became aware that there was someone on the line, listening. It couldn't have been Pandora because she was out of the house. Paulette was at school. The maid had left for the day.

'Rosie, just stop talking for a second, would you?'

'Why, what did I say?'

'Nothing, nothing. I just want to listen.' He could hear a soft breathing on the phone. 'Get off the line, whoever you are,' Hammond shouted.

'I didn't hear anything,' Rosie said.

'I did. I still can. Get off the line, you hear me? Get off my fucking phone. Listen Rosie, I'll call you back in a little while,' said Hammond. 'Sorry about this.'

He put the phone down. He stared at it for a long while. He half-expected it to ring. It did ring. He hesitated. The machine picked up. When Pandora was at home during the day Hammond let her answer it. At night Paulette took care of the calls.

Somehow Pandora caught the phone disease too, the unease. She became nervous of answering, except when she was alone. Even then she didn't know how she would handle a call from him. In bed at night she was terrified of dreaming her nightmare again. Around town during the day she was terrified of seeing him again. There were moments when she begged him to appear anywhere, anytime, just so she could face it down. Lay the ghost.

Hammond was aware that his dream and the subsequent sightings of Wildman were fantasy trips. He wasn't that crazy. But there was a truth in his imagination. Wildman wasn't just getting to him. He was inside his mind. Like a virus the man was undermining his whole nervous system. Hammond was sick and Wildman was the disease. It had to be cured. Hammond could not go on living with it. But the thing would take courage. Courage.

He found a number for Wildman in the cast and crew list for *Ghost Town*. Betty May Lefevre was on the list too as a stunt person but there was no phone number or address for her. She had never existed.

He called the number and got a machine. He didn't leave a message. He called on and off for the next two days until finally he heard Wildman's voice in person.

It had taken courage, but courage without planning. Hammond hadn't figured out exactly what he intended to say. He knew only that he wanted to kill the man.

Wildman recognized his voice. 'Hammond. How strange. I was thinking about you.'

'Do you know why I've called?' Hammond was suddenly calm.

'You want to meet.'

'I want to settle it.'

'Fine. Let's do it.' Wildman was unequivocal.

'When?'

'It's your call, Hammond.'

'Where?'

'That's up to you.'

'I'll get back to you.'

'It's your call. I'm ready. Don't leave it too long.'

Wildman hung up. Hammond was pleased how simple the call had been after all. Simple. Who was he kidding? Simple? Crazy more like.

This was the end of the twentieth century in California, U.S.A., and here were two adult men challenging each other to a duel. It was crazy. Who would believe it? What would Dora say if he went home and casually announced to her at dinner that he was fixing to fight a duel within a few days and that he might not return alive. What would she say? And how would he go about explaining it to Paulette? Daddy's going out to kill someone, darling. Or maybe Daddy himself will get killed. Don't be upset. These things happen. You'll understand it when you're a bit older.

For two days Hammond prowled around his studio, looking at books and picture references, searching for a clue to the choice of weapons. How could he fight a duel with Wildman that would put them on equal terms? Guns? Hammond didn't own a gun and had never fired a weapon in his life. Dora kept two guns. She was a good shot. He never really understood her interest. She was such a peace-loving creature.

He went through the alternatives. He considered swords, knives, crossbows, even the Roman gladiators' trident and net. He had to smile thinking of Wildman and himself performing a scene out of *Quo Vadis?* But this was deadly serious.

The solution finally came to him. He found a book he had read years ago called *Car* in which a man ate a Cadillac piece by

47

piece in front of an audience. Cars. They would fight in cars. It was simple. The more he thought about it the more right the simplicity seemed. Hammond's intense hatred for Wildman sustained him through many hesitations and second thoughts about this decision.

Hammond bought the ten year old Oldsmobile from a dealer in Tarzana. The machine cost $1,800. He paid the guy cash.

'I give three months warranty on parts,' said the salesman.

'That's plenty.' The car would be a write-off within two weeks.

Hammond drove the car to the studio lot and parked it in Rosie's space. He couldn't very well take it home. Rosie was away scouting locations in Hawaii and wouldn't be back for a few days.

Now he had the weapon. Next, he needed the place. Where would the duel be conducted? Hammond looked through his own reference library of landscape photographs. Over the years he had built up a substantial collection of pictures of potentially interesting movie locations. That was part of his job. Hammond was in the habit of taking a camera everywhere he went. When he visited or discovered a place he photographed it for possible future use. So when a director wanted a particular location for a scene in a script Hammond had examples ready. He had a reputation for that. He was considered a better designer for exterior work than for building sets in the studio. He instinctively preferred real places to made-up, invented sets. Maybe that was why he would never have made it as an architect. Hammond was brilliant at converting places to suit the scene required, re-dressing them, enhancing them. He had a wonderful memory for places. He never worked on fantasy movies or science fiction. That work was for other designers with a different kind of imagination, perhaps with more imagination.

He studied photographs he had taken over the last ten years, remote areas that were none the less accessible to Los Angeles. Hammond could see that the fantasy element he avoided in his work had incongruously entered his life. He came across a set of Polaroids of a terrain that could work. Several square miles of flats in the desert beyond San Bernardino County. Hammond had seen them scouting locations for a motorcycle picture made.

On Sunday morning he drove the Oldsmobile to get used to its feel. He went out to the flats. He was alone at dawn on the highway inside his weapon. There was no traffic to speak of and driving fast he arrived in under an hour.

The flats, a vast lake rimmed by mountains, were just as Hammond remembered. Strangely, after five or six years even the wreck of a motorcycle seemed to be in the same place. It was a perfect setting. He was pleased.

On the way back he called Wildman. Get it settled. There was no answer. Not even the machine. He dialed again. Still no answer. He was irritated. He wanted to get on with it. Now. He was scared his resolve might weaken.

He drove on another twenty miles towards L.A. and made the call again, this time from a roadside diner. Wildman answered. Hammond had come to hate the man's low voice and unconcealed arrogance. He informed him of the place, gave a map reference, then casually said they would fight in cars. That was his decision. Wildman agreed, casually. Hammond wondered if the man was impressed by his solution to the problem of a choice of weapons.

'When do you want to do this?' Wildman wanted to know.

'That's your call. Soon.'

'Next Wednesday?'

'Good enough. People don't go out to the flats much during the week.'

'Shall we say midday? I have an appointment later.'

'You'd better cancel it. You won't be there.'

'I'm never late.'

'One thing,' Hammond said. 'If it happens to rain we'll have to re-schedule. You can't drive on the flats when it's wet. There's solid rock under the sand and the rain-water just lies there. There's no purchase for the tires.'

'I'll watch the weather reports.'

'Midday Wednesday, then.'

'Why are you doing this? I'm as existential as the next man, but . . . what are you trying to prove?'

'That you can't get away with it.'

'That's pretty high-minded. People get away with things every day. Haven't you noticed? Read the papers. Only a small percentage of crimes are ever solved.'

'By the cops, yes. But the cops have nothing to do with this. This is outside the law. We both know that. You were right, of course. The company settled out of court. What was it? Fifty grand for her father. That's the law for you. I'm talking about justice.'

'What happens if I win?' Wildman asked. 'You die and I live. Does that mean that justice will be done?'

'You won't win.'

'Did that girl really mean so much to you? She was a tramp.'

'Wednesday. Noon.'

'So be it.'

5

Hammond's teeth were clenched together. His jaw was locked. He was mindless.

His Oldsmobile swerved and rammed into the door on the driver's side of the Bentley Continental. The metallic jolt was far greater than he expected. He shot forward. His spine held. His tight safety belt tore violently into his ribs. His bones were near to breaking. His escaping breath whistled through his teeth. He knew his body was safe. He swung the wheel of the Olds and accelerated away. He felt the gas pedal in his head. The tires spun on the sandy surface of the flats. He could feel the spin in his sweating hands. He was the car.

In his Bentley Wildman was relieved that Hammond hadn't attacked him full on. The coachwork of the Bentley was stronger than the ten year old Oldsmobile, but the sheer weight of the Olds' engine could have crippled him right away. He knew Hammond hadn't thought this thing through. And that gave him an edge.

Wildman regained control of his car, as it glided from the impact. Now he started after Hammond, praying to catch him before the man had time to turn and attack again.

Hammond second guessed Wildman. He was all instinct. He slowed the Olds to let the Bentley gain ground. The long hood of the British car raced towards his rear. It was fast and slow. Hammond swerved to his left as Wildman bore down on him. He could see Wildman's face in his mind. He wanted to smash it. He flung the wheel to the right. The skid put the Olds out of control for a few seconds, a few long seconds. Hammond was prepared for that. Sweat ran down his back like mercury. He braked carefully. He was in control.

Wildman watched the Oldsmobile skating helplessly across the flats. He loved the way it went. It wasn't dangerous. It was funny. There was plenty of light between them.

The flats at the foot of the San Bernadino mountains stretched for twenty miles. It was the surface of another planet. There were no nearby towns or identifying landmarks. The flats shimmered like a vast lake. The two cars were metal creatures locked in battle. Or mating in some obscure ritual.

For a moment Wildman was uncertain whether to pursue the Oldsmobile or slow down and wait. Hammond was not a very skilful driver. And his car wasn't built for combat. He was an amateur. Wildman was a brilliant driver and his Bentley was highly maneuverable for its weight and length. He had fixed it up. He was a professional.

Hammond knew that Wildman would be confused by his skid. Good. He knew the guy was a better driver. It didn't matter. He knew he had one winning tactic at his disposal. The head-on crash. That was the strike that would knock Wildman in his fancy car right out of the box. Out of the game. But that head-on collision could also cost Hammond his life. Safety belt or no, the impact could be disastrous for him. Could be, but wouldn't be. He had to destroy Wildman. It was simple. That determination gave him invincibility.

Wildman was doing a cool fifty when he saw Hammond coming out of the skid. He relaxed his shoulders. He slowed to forty. Thirty. The Oldsmobile turned to face him. A stupid junk car. It started towards him, gathering speed. This was what Wildman had most feared. Maybe Hammond had done his homework after all. For Wildman the only way out of a head-on crash was a last minute dodge. He knew the sandy surface of the flats wasn't ideal for that. But there was no question of Wildman backing off. He would finish Hammond today. Here and now, under the midday sun. This thing had gone on long enough.

Hammond thundered towards Wildman. He heard himself

yelling for blood, for revenge. He was vaguely aware it wasn't him at the wheel of the Oldsmobile. It was another guy, a secret man who lived inside Hammond's head. The other was coming out now, into his own. Hammond knew Wildman must be afraid. He turned on the car radio, the classical music station. A Monteverdi chorus accompanied him as he drove towards death. But it wasn't going to be his.

Wildman was ready. He didn't want to go too fast. He mustn't lose the steering. He watched the oncoming Oldsmobile. He waited, waited, then wrenched the wheel. His timing was good. But he was unlucky. He hit a patch of loose sand on the flats. The wheels didn't respond fully to the instruction of the steering.

Hammond was still accelerating when he saw that Wildman wasn't going to make it. He screamed for blood. The Oldsmobile tore into the Bentley, just as it was turning away from the onslaught. He saw Wildman had misjudged his speed. The mistake would cost him the battle. Hammond yelled. A cry of war.

The Oldsmobile hit the left headlamp and rammed on into the hood. Hammond fancied that Wildman cried out. The Bentley's front left wheel rose several inches into the air. The continuing, unstoppable force of the oncoming Olds slowly toppled Wildman's car. The Bentley tumbled like a toy, over and over.

Hammond laughed. He eased up on the gas and turned the wheel. He watched the rolling Bentley with pleasure. The car exploded even before it had come to a stop. Then he felt something going wrong with the Oldsmobile. The engine spluttered and soon gave out. The choral music had already stopped.

Hammond pressed the starter over and over but it was out. He braked. His softly rolling car came to a full stop. Hammond looked back at the sheet of flame and oily black smoke. He breathed deeply again and again. He had imagined that Wildman would die crushed in the twisted metal. Now he could see Wildman was being incinerated.

Hammond got out of his car. He walked slowly towards the burning Bentley. He tried to see inside the car which was full of smoke. He waited impatiently for the moment of triumph. A sight of Wildman dead. Then he saw the man's face. It was still and black. He loved the sight of the sooty mask of death. He didn't want to leave.

Now for the first time in minutes he felt nervous. He realized he had cut himself on something. His left hand was bleeding. As he walked back to the Oldsmobile he saw he was limping. As he became increasingly aware of pain, the secret man, the other, went back to where he lived deep in Hammond's psyche.

His left leg was in agony. He tried to open the hood of the Olds. It was impossible. Far away a small plane flashed silver in the sunlight. He must go, get away from here. Get out.

There was still no one in sight. People never strayed this far, five miles or more, from the highway. There was nothing to stray for, nothing to see, nothing to do, no shelter. Hammond was alone.

The flames were dying around the funeral pyre of the Bentley as Hammond abandoned his car and limped as quickly as he could towards the highway. He couldn't see it. It was quite a walk. He didn't care. Wildman was dead. Hammond was a happy man.

6

Hammond had known he would have to rely on hitching a ride back to L.A. This had always been a danger. Whoever picked him up now would certainly remember him, especially with his freshly cut hand and his limp, hard to disguise. His physical pain was increasing by the throbbing minute but the memory of Wildman, his blackened face and twisted body trapped in his blazing antique car, was a soothing anaesthetic.

He stopped hobbling and waited beside the open highway. The long straight road through the desert was an arrow pointing homeward. A big frozen food truck rumbled past him, wailing like a ship at sea. The vehicle made no attempt to stop. Hammond was enveloped in a cloud of dust. As he raised his aching hand to rub his eyes he realized that the truck hadn't stopped because he hadn't raised his hand to ask. If he was to hitch the hundred and twenty miles back he would have to act like a hitchhiker.

The third car that came along stopped. The driver was a woman. Somehow he hadn't expected that. She was jet black-haired, intelligent looking and wore jet black sunglasses.

'I'm going to Glendale,' she said without expression. 'That any good to you?'

'Thank you. Yes. I can arrange a ride from there.'

Hammond got in. It was disconcerting not seeing the woman's eyes. He couldn't guess what she was thinking or even how old she was. Thirty-two or thirty-three. The woman drove fast and well. Her legs looked slim in dark tights. He began to feel safer because she didn't speak or appear even to look at him. She wasn't curious. That in itself was curious.

She had the radio on. His preferred classical station. Hammond liked that. It was soothing, ballet music or an orchestral suite of some kind. Hammond listened to this same station when he was working at home. He was going home. Working alone in his studio room, the concertos and symphonies were like friends from the past, invisible but reassuring. He never got really specific ideas from the music itself. After all, there wasn't a whole big connection between designing the set for a cheap hotel room in Flagstaff, Arizona, and the second movement of Mahler's 'Resurrection' symphony. But what the music gave him was an atmosphere of concentration in which he could let his mind work freely and productively. It was a kind of silence. Peace of mind had been very important in the last few weeks, ever since he had come to realize that he had to rid himself, and everyone else, of Charles Wildman.

'It's Roussel.'

'I'm sorry?' Hammond hadn't expected her to speak.

'This music. It's by Albert Roussel.' She pronounced the name in what seemed to Hammond an authentic French accent. 'It's actually a ballet called *The Spider's Banquet*.'

'I don't know it.'

'Very few people do. It came out in 1913 in Paris, but it was overshadowed by *The Rite of Spring* . . .'

'That I know, of course.'

'Now this is pretty much forgotten.'

She had a way of talking as if she were addressing people in general.

'Are you a musician?'

'Dancer. Used to be.' She spoke without looking at him, no regret in her tone.

A buzzer sounded. Hammond started. He hadn't clocked that the car had a telephone. The woman picked up the receiver from beside the dash. She said nothing, just listened. Hammond was sure he could hear the distant dialog of a man's voice.

He was suddenly, irrationally scared. They were looking for

him, the cops. They'd discovered the burned-out car, they'd identified Wildman. Someone had reported seeing him leaving the scene. Someone else had just witnessed him getting into this car, maybe someone in a car going in the opposite direction. The cops had put it all together. And now, an hour later, they'd found him and called this woman's phone. It was a preposterous scenario, he knew that. But he couldn't stop imagining it all the same. He was that nervous. It was something he'd have to get rid of.

'I should be there in about ninety minutes . . .' The woman spoke into the phone.

For the first time she turned to look at him from behind the glasses. Was she trying to say, mind your own business, this is private.

Hammond could see himself in her black lenses. She wasn't a cop. He looked away, out of the window, trying to act deaf. He blinked. The desert landscape went in and out of focus. Stop thinking like this, he shouted to himself, inside his head. Stop imagining things.

'Everything's fine,' the woman said. 'I agree . . . look, we can discuss it later . . .' She listened to what the man said, then replaced the phone in its clasp.

Of course she wasn't a cop. She was just a woman probably having an affair with someone. She didn't look married. He wondered if he looked married. Unaccountably he had the crazy idea of telling this woman everything that had happened. Of course, he didn't. He had considered telling Dora about it all, a while back. But it was too late now. It was over.

The open desert was behind them now. The woman was driving into a built-up area. She slowed and stopped at the first set of lights. *The Spider's Banquet* was still playing on the radio. Strange title, Hammond thought. It fit though. Wildman was a spider, catching people like flies in his web. A dead spider now. A ruined web.

The woman had shown no curiosity at all about Hammond. She had never even looked as if she wanted to ask a question, like what happened to you? Where's your car? Or, do you live in Los Angeles? Nothing.

Now that they were stopping and starting in traffic Hammond found himself glancing at the woman more frequently. She was very good-looking in an unapproachable kind of way. Not at all his type. The women Hammond was usually attracted to were talkative, open types like Dora. And like Betty May.

This woman seemed to belong to another breed. He couldn't imagine trying to seduce her. Where would he start? She didn't look as if she'd respond to flattery. He wouldn't dare put his hand out to touch her, even in a friendly way. What would she feel like? Her skin was very pale, whitened by her black clothes. It would probably bruise easily. He shifted in his seat. He ached. There was no fat on this woman at all. No folds to grip. She seemed hard, unyielding. She would photograph beautifully in black and white. Yes. He could imagine her in a broad-brimmed hat, naked. But he couldn't see himself making love to her.

A picture suddenly flashed into Hammond's mind. He could see this woman with Wildman. They were together in bed. In that motel maybe. She was on top of Wildman, swaying back and forth, up and down. And there was music playing. It was *The Rite of Spring*, the movement Stravinsky called *The Game of Rape*, violent, ritualistic, pounding, screaming, intense, wrestling life with death. Wildman was her man. He could make her come because she would want him. She would embrace the cruelty. This woman would go to the edge.

She turned off the radio. Silence. He looked around. Glendale.

'Here we are,' she said. 'I can drop you here.'

'Thank you.'

Of course, she didn't ask him where he was going nor how he might get there. Hammond summoned his courage and held out his hand. Quietly, she took it. They shook hands. Her grip was crisp, but not dismissive. His bruised hand hurt. He winced, trying to make it look like a smile, and opened the door to get out.

'One thing,' she said.

Hammond hadn't expected her to speak again. Her voice was suddenly soft, serious.

'You can do one thing for me. If anyone asks, I didn't pick you up. You were never in my car.'

'I understand,' Hammond said.

'I know you do.'

He looked at her. What did she know? He prayed for her to take her glasses off. She didn't. He closed the door. She drove off quickly into a gap in the gathering traffic.

Everyone has something to hide, Hammond thought. It was reassuring. It meant he wasn't alone.

7

Again Hammond needed a ride home. He went into the bar area of The Laughing Shrimp, a seafood place across the street from where the woman had dropped him.

He called a taxi. He sat up at the bar and referred to a vodka martini. He started by spilling it. Control was what he needed now. A cocktail of icy alcohol and conscious forgetting.

He was going home to Dora, for the second time. It would be the beginning of a second aftermath. The first had been the day following the movie wrap party. He had driven himself all the way back from Flagstaff, a thousand miles of desert dreaming and memory sickness. Since that time his life, it seemed to him, had been made up of car drives, long and short like drinks, ending today in a willful crash. Now the driving was over. He should relax. Now he was being driven. The coming taxi would complete the cycle.

Sitting up at the bar of The Laughing Shrimp in Glendale, Hammond studied the mirrored lines of shining bottles. He looked at his own face. Dazed by a river of recollection he pressed the vodka against the mark on his forehead. Would that become a duelling scar, a permanent emblem of his bravery?

'Hammond.'

A man's voice blasted through the bar hubbub, over the roaring TV commercial, right into Hammond's silent thoughts.

'Wildman.' Hammond stiffened with instant fear.

'Anyone here call a cab? Name of Hammond.'

Hammond swung around. A young man was standing a few feet away squinting through bar smoke. Hammond breathed out with relief. He waved, greeting his driver as a rescuing friend.

'Here. Be right with you.'

He drained his second vodka martini. He left a two dollar tip on the bar and eased off the stool. His frame ached. His head throbbed. But the alcohol had slowed the shaking in his hands.

He grabbed a couple of mints from the bowl beside the cash desk on his way out. A pathetic habit, that, to disguise the smell of his breath. Dora didn't like him drinking during the day. It was true he had gone through a period after they were first married when he drank far too much. He admitted it. Dora had been genuinely worried about him. And she wasn't just being the nagging new wife. It worried him too. Hammond had been on the brink of becoming an angry afternoon drunk. He had agreed that it wasn't good for anyone, least of all Paulette. Nowadays he drank much, much less.

The taxi driver, who lived in Glendale, wasn't that familiar with the West Side of Los Angeles. Hammond told him the best route to Rancho Park. As he sat back he became aware that the car was an Oldsmobile, but a much later model than the one he had just escaped from, but none the less an Olds. Hey, you can't jump on every coincidence, every association. That's the business of dreams.

Just think of your home, Hammond told himself. That's your anchor. You're sitting in a safe car going home to your wife and daughter and normality. The madness is over. Think about Dora, for Christ's sake.

'Hey, be careful,' Hammond admonished his driver as the guy accelerated to overtake a truck on the freeway. 'You're going way too fast.'

'OK.'

'Why risk getting a ticket?'

Hammond saw the dining table had been meticulously set.

'What's the occasion?' Pandora had used their best dinner service, her father's Royal Copenhagen. Alfred Harten never

61

bought new things to give people. The linen napkins were Delft blue, the tablecloth her favorite salmon pink.

'I just felt like it,' Pandora said.

Unknowingly she was celebrating the death of Wildman. Hammond put his arms around her from behind. He squeezed her breasts. She sighed. He pressed his fingers into her dress. He felt the stitching of her bra.

'You'll have to wait,' she whispered.

Pandora took his right hand in hers and brought it to her lips. She kissed the open palm.

'What's this? Did you cut yourself?' She looked at a wound he had received in the car when Wildman smashed into him.

Hammond had his story ready.

'In a washroom at the studio. Some idiot left some broken glass in the basin. I didn't see it.'

'I'll put something on it.'

He didn't protest as Pandora led him to the downstairs bathroom. She carefully fitted a plaster across his hand.

She noticed the mark on his forehead and smiled. 'How did the meeting go? Did you get into a fight?'

'No. But it's still not a go-project.'

'Maybe it'll do you good to have a week or two off. You haven't stopped for months.' Pandora was worried about the cuts.

'I'm not happy if I stop,' Hammond said.

She turned away. She could see the vivid scar on the man's body, feel its toughened skin on her lips.

Hammond went up to shower and examined his body. There were several bruises developing. He would have to be careful when he undressed. Parts of his body still throbbed. He would try not to show pain in his movements.

He sat on the bed exhausted. He switched to the local news on TV. He did not expect any report yet from the San Bernardino flats. The police would certainly go out there at some point, following the discovery of the cars. They would find Wildman's burned body. They would examine the cars. If they did take finger prints from the Oldsmobile they'd be useless. Hammond had no criminal record, not even a parking fine. He had removed the serial number from the car, so both he and the Olds would be untraceable. A dead end.

'I've a confession to make,' Pandora said at dinner.

'Serious?' Hammond's skin prickled.

'I've arranged to go home for the weekend. Daddy hasn't been well and I just feel –'

'Of course, go. That's fine.' Hammond tried not to sound too pleased. The idea of being alone for a couple of days was refreshing, a cool breeze to come.

'Are you sure you don't mind?'

'No, I'm not sure, I'm certain. Maybe I'll take Paulette fishing on Sunday.'

'You can't.'

'Why not?'

'Don't you remember? She's going to stay with the Balfours this weekend. They're having a kids' party Saturday night and a couple of them are staying over. Paulette's looking forward to it.'

'Yes, I remember. Well, that's fine too. I can amuse myself.' He told himself to beware of being forgetful. He mustn't appear self-absorbed. She'd start to ask questions. He wasn't sure Dora really bought the washroom story.

'I'll pick Paulette up from school. No problem. Now relax. Is your father sick?'

'Not really sick. It's his eyesight. It's really bad now. And I think he's a bit scared.'

'He'll enjoy seeing you.'

Pandora didn't reply. Hammond knew that it wasn't just her father she wanted to see. She had periodic bouts of homesickness. She loved her farm, the land, the restrained opulence of her growing up. She never complained about her life in Southern California, but she needed sustaining fixes of New Hampshire from time to time. Hammond never tried to stop her going home.

'I married an angel,' Pandora said.

An angel? An avenging angel, Hammond thought. What would she think if she knew what he had just done?

'Daddy, do you believe in UFO's?' Paulette suddenly asked in the middle of dinner.

'I don't know. I don't think so. Why? Have you seen one?'

'No, but a boy in our class says he saw one.'

'I believe in them,' Pandora said. 'There's too much that's unexplained.'

'Because things are unexplained doesn't mean there isn't an explanation,' Hammond said. 'It only means we don't yet know the explanation.'

Pandora experienced a wave of dizziness. The unexplained. Images from her nightmare forced themselves into her mind.

'So you don't believe in them,' Paulette insisted.

'I guess not.'

'Didn't you design one once?' Pandora asked. 'I seem to remember you made a model of a UFO.'

'You're right, I did,' Hammond recalled. 'It was rejected.' The project was called *Zone of Silence*. 'I'm not very good at fantasy,' he said.

Zone of silence. Pandora wanted to leave the table, shut herself away where the images couldn't reach her.

'We're going to have to write about it,' said Paulette.

'Well, there's a lot of books on the subject,' Hammond said. 'Maybe when I pick you up on Friday we could go and look one or two out. There's a good shop for that kind of thing in Santa Monica.'

The dizziness subsided. So did the flesh of her thighs. Suck back the liquid, Pandora ordered herself. Go on. Do it. Talk about flying saucers. You're on a quiz show. Start now.

'Jung wrote a book about flying saucers,' said Pandora. 'He said that they were always circular because they were like visions of the soul and the soul was like a miniature of God. In the ancient world God was represented as a circle or a sphere.'

'Very good, Mom.'

Hammond loved his wife's pieces of erudition. He found them

64

oddly sexy. It was attractive, the way she never ran out of things to say.

'Someone once defined God as a circle whose center is everywhere and circumference nowhere.'

Her feelings of arousal ebbed. Thank God. The images had gone. God was merciful.

The phone rang. Paulette jumped up to answer it.

'How do you know it's for you, young lady?' Hammond asked.

'I don't,' Paulette said, running out of the dining room.

'She just loves answering the phone.'

Pandora had not gotten over her phone-fear while Hammond had been away. She was still scared the man might call even though he didn't know her name, let alone have her number. It was irrational, but so was what had happened.

'Jung also said that flying saucers were projections of our fears and hopes,' Pandora said.

'Interesting.' Hammond's fears over the past weeks hadn't needed flying saucers to project them.

'Dad, it's for you,' Paulette slumped back into her chair. She had been hoping for a call from her friend, David Wing. Paulette was in love with David Wing. That was her secret. Her mom didn't know. No one knew. Except David.

Pandora relaxed. The tension, the memories and imaginings vanished. It was like a fever passing. She felt safe for the time being.

Hammond went out to take the call. His legs were stiff. He flexed his shoulders. Fearfully, he imagined the police had somehow traced him. Stay calm. It wasn't the police. The meeting he was supposed to take the next day had been canceled. It was the one he'd lied about to Dora. Hammond came back to his dinner. He knew he was in for a period when his fears would come and go like memories.

After dinner Paulette went to her room to play with her computer. She was far more adept with electronics than either of her parents. Hammond himself had been only an average student in school with the exception of design and architecture. He worried that Paulette was precocious. He worried about her school life. He didn't think much about her emotions. 'Just as long as she stays away from drugs,' he said.

Pandora never talked about her drug stage. She believed that the early years of life were a poor indicator of future development. She often cited her own childhood. She did admit to having run away from two schools.

'And look at me now,' she said, as she and Hammond finished the washing up. 'A model housewife.' No hint of irony. No secret meaning this time.

Pandora always washed and dried the good china herself, never leaving it to the maid or to the aggressive dishwasher.

'I feel tired. I think I'll have a dip. Get the circulation going.' Hammond stretched his aching muscles.

'I'll join you.'

'That's what I was hoping.'

Taking a dip at night with Pandora was one of his homely delights, along with Sunday lunch and the occasional afternoon's lazy fishing in the waters off Catalina Island.

He turned on one of the patio lights but not the lights underwater. He didn't want her to see his bruises. The pool was shielded by trees and trellis work from their nearest neighbors. He loved to swim naked at night in the dark. He saw Pandora coming his way like a fish. Her hair swirled in an arc behind her. She swam between his legs trailing her hand across his genitals.

Hammond never failed to respond. He turned and brushed her breasts with his hands. For a few minutes they swam around each other in a water dance on the surface and beneath it. Soon they were both gasping, holding their breath, holding each other's flesh.

Pandora swam to the end of the pool and folded her arms over the green tiled rim. She threw back her head and waited, her shoulders out of the water. She listened to the cicadas. She felt Hammond's hand on her thighs, moving from one to the other. She spread her legs slightly underwater. It was a gentle ritual between them.

Buoyed by the water, Pandora's body rippled with pleasure. This was the kind of sex she really liked. Hammond pulled her legs back so she was floating full length. His left hand circled slowly inside her. This sex was kind. He put his face to her buttocks and gently bit the tightening flesh. She felt no threat. Her bottom rose to his face and fell away and rose again. This was an exciting moment for him, when he felt his wife begin to lose control. Her body shook. He held her tightly now as she half-struggled to be free. Her release would be comfortable, safe. No dangerous silence to scare her now.

In these moments Hammond thought only of his wife. He ignored himself, knowing his pleasure would come in a few minutes. He turned her over in the water, pulling her away from the edge of the pool. Pandora lay on her back, held by his arms. Hammond gripped the flesh between her legs with his left hand, holding her like an excited fish. He put his mouth to her wet blonde pubic hair and nuzzled her.

Involuntarily Pandora started to stroke her own nipples. Her hands seemed not to belong to her. When he pushed his finger between her buttocks she gave a groan. Her body splashed. She was on her own. When Alec made love to her like this she felt free. She floated, in love with her own feelings, unpossessed.

Hammond trod water and held Pandora's shaking body, one of his arms under her shoulder blades, the other under her thighs. He watched her come, her eyelids closed and flickering. Suddenly, he became aware of a strange, unfamiliar whining sound. It was like a drill. And it got louder, closer. Hammond held Pandora lovingly. Her body was relaxing as the sound became more insistent. Now she was aware of it too. It was on them.

There was a splash, a fizzing sound, a spluttering, then silence. Something had crashed into the pool a few feet away.

'What is it?' Pandora whispered.

'It's a plane. A model plane.'

Pandora eased herself from Hammond's arms. She kissed his shoulders. They both swam towards the fallen model. The wingspan was about two feet. There was a radio aerial and a single engine propeller.

Hammond picked it out of the water and examined it. He looked around in the darkness and up at the starry sky.

'Where did it come from?' Pandora asked.

'God knows.'

Pandora took the plane from his grasp and examined it.

'It's a UFO,' she said.

'I don't think so. Someone will come looking for it.'

'It's weird though, flying the thing at night.'

Hammond agreed. It was weird.

'I'm feeling cold,' he said.

Pandora put her arms around his legs and hugged them. His erection had gone. He shivered.

'Do you want it here or shall we go upstairs?' Pandora stroked his bottom. The muscles were tense. She didn't notice the slowly developing bruise on his upper left thigh. She brushed his testicles with the back of her hand.

'Let's go up.'

They pulled on their robes and went inside. At the patio door Hammond, holding his wife's hand, looked at the pool for a long moment before he turned off the lights. His dream still scared him.

Pandora, her skin damp from the pool, waited for him in bed. Hammond dried his hair in the bathroom. He stared at the plane which he had put in the tub to dry out. It meant nothing. Yet it disturbed him. It looked like a weapon.

In the next hour she did everything to Alec that she knew he liked. He just couldn't come. In some obscure way she wanted to make it up to him. It was guilt. She cursed the man. She despised his scar. She realized now that she was waiting for the silence. She wanted the sound to cut out. She couldn't help herself. She wasn't satisfied. She wanted more. Now. She longed to be shattered, blown apart by lust. Overwhelmed. Possessed.

'You're too tired,' she said.

'I guess.'

Pandora's hands shook as she turned out the light. 'If you want me, I'm here. Just wake me up.'

That night Pandora dreamed another silent dream. Hammond couldn't sleep. Now Wildman, not Betty May, filled his mind. Eventually he dozed. When he woke it was two in the morning. Wide awake, he was plagued with a new thought that wouldn't go away. I shouldn't have done it. I shouldn't have done it.

The next day was dominated by the broken dishwasher. In the morning, after breakfast the kitchen became flooded. Hammond tried to stop the flow of water, but eventually had to turn the whole thing off at the main. The repair man didn't appear until after lunch. Pandora stayed in to wait for him.

Hammond left the house having nowhere particular to go. He drove aimlessly down Hollywood Boulevard. He went into a bar for a beer. He drank a vodka martini instead. Sex filled his brain. He was betraying Dora with every thought. He looked at his face in the patterned mirror behind the bar. He saw the enemy.

There was a girl alone in a booth. Hammond wanted to go over to her. She seemed like a hooker, drawn, sick-looking. He wanted to offer her money. He felt like a rapist. He did nothing. He went to the payphone to call Rosie. He wouldn't try to seduce her. He just wanted to be with a woman, any woman. He got Rosie's machine. When he got back to his second martini he saw that the girl in the booth had gone. He was all violence and no courage. He did nothing. He drove home two hours later weak with despair. Later, he sat by the pool waiting for the sun to go down. The dishwasher had been fixed.

In the evening Pandora and Hammond watched the news on TV. There was a storm warning for the Los Angeles basin. Heavy rain was expected during the coming night, one hundred per cent humidity. The weather predicted for the East Coast was very good. Pandora was pleased. In her years living in Southern California she had grown used to the perpetual warmth and she had stopped complaining about the absence of seasons. The threat of earthquakes didn't bother her half as much as the destruction of the ozone layer.

Hammond waited through the tedious weather reports for any news of wrecked cars on the flats in San Bernardino County. There was none. The news silence was beginning to irritate him. Hadn't the cars been found? It seemed for a moment as if all he had done and gone through in the past weeks somehow hadn't happened.

That was real criminal thinking, he told himself. Wasn't that the mark of a sick mind, the desire to see your crimes reported in the media? Crime as an expression of a lack of self-esteem. What the hell did he want? It was crazy. Did he want the whole story to come out? Did he want to be discovered? Shit, the best thing that could happen was nothing.

'Look at that,' Pandora said, cutting into his introspection.

'What?'

'That.' She pointed at the pictures of a crashed helicopter on the TV screen.

There was an account of an accident that had happened on a film location earlier today. Two people had been killed in a stunt. Hammond didn't know either of the dead people, a stunt man and an actor. But he knew what Pandora was going to say next. He had told her about it in the briefest way when he returned from Arizona.

'What happened about that girl?'

'What girl?'

'The girl who died on your film?'

'The company paid compensation to her father.'

'How can you compensate for a person's death?'

'You can't, I guess. It was an accident.'

'Poor girl.'

Betty May was going to haunt him for a long time to come. He could see her face now, smiling at him after they had made love. And he could see her unconscious on the floor of the shack, dying. And he could see Wildman in the burning car, dying.

He was glad he had fought and killed Wildman. That was good and just, he told himself. But it bothered Hammond that his sexual passion for Betty May had released another kind of violence in him. It was possible that uncovering of his unsuspected ability to hit a woman while making love to her had unleashed a desire to fight another man to the death. And unchained another man in him.

The front door bell rang. It was eleven fifteen. Pandora was in bed reading *People* magazine. Hammond was in his pajamas.

'Who can that be?'

'Somebody's come to the wrong house,' Pandora said.

'I'll go down.'

The bell rang again before Hammond reached the door. He unlocked it. For a moment he didn't recognize the woman standing there. Beverly's hair was untidy. Her face was drawn and blotched with tears.

'I'm sorry to wake you up, but I must talk to Pandora. I'm terribly sorry.'

'Come in Beverly.' Hammond recognized her now. Her voice helped.

'What's the matter? What's happened?'

She was crying. Hammond turned on the lights in the living room. They both blinked at the brightness.

'She is here, isn't she?' Beverly was desperate.

'I'll get her.' He turned off two of the lights. He could hear her gasping sobs as he went upstairs. Pandora pulled on a gown, glanced at herself in the mirror. Hammond stayed in the bedroom when she went downstairs. He didn't know Beverly very well. He had nothing in common with her bonehead husband Jimbo, who once expressed indifference to classical music.

'And as for opera,' Jimbo had said, 'the stories are so dumb. There's nothing real about it when they screech like that at the tops of their lungs.'

Hammond was happy to let Pandora deal with the crisis. He didn't find Beverly attractive at all. Too domineering.

Pandora guessed right away what it was about. She poured Beverly a scotch, gave her some Kleenex, and listened.

'I should have called I know, but I had to be with someone. And you're so sensible you'll know what to do.'

71

'I don't know about that.'

'What happened was just beyond . . . it was horrible. I mean
I told you I found out he was having an affair with my cousin.
She's ten years younger than me, seventeen years younger than
him. She's young enough to be his daughter. Our daughter!'

Beverly started to gasp, controlling her crying. It was the
wounded sound of animal pain. Pandora was affected. At this
moment it was happening to her. Beverly didn't use any names
either for her husband or her cousin. Anonymously. It was him
and her. The objectivity of Beverly's language increased Pandora's sympathy.

'I followed him when he went out. I know it was stupid but
I couldn't help myself. I had to find out. See them together,
I suppose. Grotesque, isn't it? They met in a motel off Wash-
ington Boulevard. I saw them leave together. I wanted to
go up to them, confront them right there. But I didn't have
the courage. I didn't want to lose him, you see. What would
I do if he left? What would happen to Lisa? She loves her
father.'

'Where's Lisa now?'

'She's at home.'

'Not with him?'

'No, he left. I threw him out. You know what he said? Thank
God I can go now. That's what he said.'

'Wait a minute, Beverly. Maybe he didn't really mean
that.'

'Oh yeah. Then let me tell you what he did. I took Lisa to
my mother's for the day to visit. But she suddenly got sick. I
don't know what it was, a bug or something, and I decided to
drive back home. They were there together. In our bed. In my
bed! Can you believe that?'

Yes, she could believe it. If Jimbo had wanted Beverly to find
them. Otherwise, why take the risk? OK, Lisa getting sick was
an accident, but Jimbo's desire to be discovered must have been
there. It was awful. The idea of Alec bringing someone back to
the house was inconceivable.

'When I walked in, they were fucking. I can't get it out of

72

my mind, Pandora. It was disgusting. She had her fanny in the air and he was . . . inside her ass. He was fucking her in the ass. And he won't even fuck me when I have a period. I'll never forget it. It was vile.'

'Did Lisa see it?'

'No, thank God. I'd put her straight to bed.'

'But now she knows something happened.'

'I just told her he was going away for a while.'

'She must be devastated.'

'She is.'

'Shouldn't you go back to her now?'

'Yes. I shouldn't have left. I don't know what to do.'

Beverly got out of the chair and flung her arms around Pandora. The two women held each other tightly. Pandora could feel everything Beverly felt. She wanted to say, 'Don't you see, they were waiting for you to walk in. They must have heard you come in. But still they went on fucking. Don't you see?' But she didn't say it.

'Would you like me to come over with you tonight? I will if you want. You mustn't leave Lisa alone.'

'Could you do that?' Beverly looked at Pandora. 'Would you do it?'

'Of course I will. Give me a moment. I'll throw on some clothes.'

'You're wonderful.'

'No. I'm not.'

Pandora went upstairs. She told Hammond only that Jimbo had walked out on Beverly.

'He's a bastard, that guy.'

'You don't mind if I go?'

'You go. That's all right. I mean it. I'll take Paulette to school tomorrow.'

'I love you,' Pandora said, and gave her husband a long, lingering kiss. She felt lucky and strong.

Pandora drove Beverly's car to her home in Westwood. The streets were easy now. At one in the morning. The world was quiet. Beverly said nothing as they drove. She wasn't crying now. Pandora guessed that she was still seeing Jimbo and her cousin. Seeing them over and over. Pandora understood that completely. She was expecting the silence to engulf her at any moment.

8

The model plane worried Hammond. It was now hanging in his studio, turning slowly on the wire he had cut for it. Hammond was not a model-maker, except in architectural designs, but he could see that this plane was extremely well-made. Where had it come from? Under his magnifying glass he discovered some minute writing on the lower fuselage. He hadn't noticed it before. The tiny waterproof letters read: IACTAALEAEST. He wrote the word down on a clean sheet of paper. He wondered if it was a form of identification, either personal to the owner, or perhaps representing a model aircraft organization or club. But there were no numbers of the kind you expect to see on aircraft. So the letters could be a code. Or an anagram. Hammond wasn't adept at puzzles.

Frustrated, he picked up the phone. He called Jeff Welsh, a model-maker he had employed on a movie a few years back. Hammond had needed model boats, planes and trains to decorate the apartment of a character, representing a man who couldn't grow up.

Jeff hoped the call was a job offer. Hammond could hear the disappointment when Jeff realized he only wanted information. Jeff gave him the addresses of two clubs in the Los Angeles area. He was on the point of calling them when he heard Pandora come in.

'How's Beverly?'

'She's tougher than she knows.'

'I guess if you're going to have an affair you have to be completely secretive,' Hammond said.

75

'Either way, it's a killer,' Pandora said.

Hammond let the subject go. He felt incriminated, guilty. Yet he would never have left home for Betty May.

'What time is your plane tomorrow?' he asked.

'Morning. Ten thirty, I think.'

'If you have things to do, I can pick Paulette up this afternoon.'

'Would you, darling? I feel guilty. You drove her this morning. And you'll have to take her tomorrow to the Balfours'.'

'Yes. And I'll have to pick her up from the Balfours' again on Sunday. You'll still be in New Hampshire.'

'I'll make it up to you,' Pandora said. 'I'll buy us all dinner tonight. How about The Imperial Gardens?'

'You don't have to compensate me. Paulette's my daughter too, you know. I love doing things for her.'

'I know you do. You're a wonderful father.'

Pandora drove into Hollywood. She went to Book City looking for a present to take her father. A book was the only gift she could conceive of buying him. He had everything else. And anything he didn't have he rejected. She was aware that his eyesight was deteriorating. So perhaps a book of pictures.

All her life Pandora had had a love-hate relationship with things classical. She had never managed to master Greek, but her Latin had been passable. Understanding Latin, her father said, was what distinguished men from animals. To know a language that was no longer spoken, which had no practical value, was the proof that a man was capable of resisting the material world.

She came upon *Sculpture of The Classical World* on one of the dark shelves. She couldn't resist touching it. She paged through the book. She saw herself in the naked forms of the marble statues. The models for these statues must have had the same experiences as she. Yet they were embodied in images of harmony. There was no anxiety or madness in their subtle, erotic presence. If she were an artist, how would she go about representing her recent sensations in poses like these? It would be impossible. The one thing they had in common was a surrounding silence. The Mediterranean silence was peace. Her Californian silence was violent. Pandora bought the volume thinking about the books in the man's bungalow.

Hammond saw his daughter in the crowd of kids in the school yard. She was holding hands with David Wing. She let go when she saw Hammond. He smiled to himself. So my daughter has a boyfriend. Well, why not. David was the son of a successful banker who was originally from Hong Kong. She had mentioned him once, casually. He was the brightest boy in Paulette's class. They were geniuses together. David was also very good-looking. And Chinese. Hammond wondered if Paulette was drawn to the boy because he was exotic.

On the drive back she took the plunge: 'Can David Wing come to stay?'

'You're going to the Balfours' this weekend.'

'I meant another weekend.'

'Sure. But we must ask David's parents.'

'Would you write to them?' Paulette was very formal.

'Is that the way to do it? Maybe Mom should just call Mrs Wing.'

'I think it's better to write.'

'I'll talk to Mom.'

Paulette said nothing more. Hammond could see that she wasn't satisfied.

The Hammond family had an early dinner at The Imperial Gardens. Paulette had to go to school the next day. Pandora had to get to the airport. Hammond had his own plan.

During dinner they encountered two lots of people they knew, an art director and his Japanese girlfriend, and Pandora's hairdresser who was with his drug-dealer friend. The family conversation however was dominated by Paulette who insisted on trying to order Chinese food.

'This is a Japanese restaurant,' said Pandora.

'The Japanese were horrible to the Chinese,' said Paulette.

'What's that got to do with it?'

'She's got a Chinese boyfriend,' Hammond said.

'I'm going to learn Cantonese,' Paulette was emphatic.

'You mean David Wing?' Pandora remembered the Chinese boy from school. He was very pretty, she had thought.

'Look, you don't have to eat if you don't want to,' Hammond said.

When Paulette saw the first food arrive, she gave in, asked for some *tempura* noodles in soup. She couldn't deny her hunger.

Halfway through the meal Hammond took out a sheet of paper. On it he had written out the letters from the model plane. He handed it to Pandora.

'You like crosswords. Is this an anagram? It was painted on the undercarriage of that plane.'

Pandora looked at it as she ate. She was easily intrigued by puzzles. IACTAALEAEST.

'I've tried it backwards. It doesn't make sense.'

Paulette looked over her mother's shoulder. A Japanese waitress came into their private *tatami* room.

'Mr Hammond. There's a call for you.'

'For me? How does anyone know I'm here?'

'I switched the phone to the service and gave them this number,' Pandora said.

Hammond got to his feet, put on his shoes outside the sliding door and crossed the main restaurant to the desk at the entrance. The hostess handed him the phone.

'Hello.'

'Mr Hammond?' It was a woman.

'Yes. Who is this?'

'I'm enquiring about a model aircraft. I understand that . . .'

The line clicked three or four times and went dead. Hammond had no alternative but to hang up. He waited by the phone for a few moments, hoping that the woman would call back.

'We were cut off,' he told the hostess. She smiled in the Japanese manner. He was uneasy. That plane. How had he been traced? The only possible link was Jeff, but he hadn't told Jeff about the crashed plane, only that he wanted to know about model clubs. He waited helplessly. A call came through. It was just a reservation. The woman didn't call back.

The girls were still puzzling over the line of letters when Hammond came back into the room.

'Dora, did you tell anyone about the model plane?'

'No, of course not.'

It was spooky. Who was the woman on the phone? He had had a suspicion that there was more to the crashed plane than sheer accident. Had it been sent deliberately? If so, why? And by whom? Maybe there was nothing sinister in it at all.

'Who called you?' Pandora asked without looking up.

'It was just someone wanting to know my availability for a meeting. You remember, the one that was canceled yesterday.' Why did he lie? He had nothing to hide. Not about the phonecall.

But Pandora wasn't really listening to him.

'I've got it. I think I know what it is. It's not a code at all. It's Latin. Three words. *Iacta Alea Est*. It's a famous quotation. Julius Caesar said it when he crossed the Rubicon. It means "The Die Is Cast".'

Hammond shivered.

'See what a good Sarah Lawrence education can do for a girl?'

9

It was raining heavily when Hammond kissed Pandora goodbye. She clung to him for a few moments. He had a sudden, irrational fear he wasn't going to see her again. Paulette gave her mother a bear hug.

'Have a wonderful time,' Pandora said.

'Give me a call when you get there,' he said.

'I will. I'll miss you.' She held a few tears back.

Pandora waved in the rain as Hammond drove away to the school. He was driving the Honda, their runabout. For a moment she wondered why he hadn't taken his Mercedes. Perhaps he didn't want to drive it in the rain. He looked tense, she thought. She hurried back into the house and called a taxi to take her to the airport. Then Pandora started thinking about her father.

In the car Hammond listened to the news. There was nothing about the discovery of Wildman's body in his car. Maybe this unexplained one-off event didn't rate news attention. Not when there were serial killers on the loose. In the end it was probably a local matter for the San Bernardino police.

Paulette took her overnight bag from the back seat. Hammond walked with her across the schoolyard. He carried an umbrella. He noticed the Chinese kid. Paulette had already seen David. She turned to Hammond to be kissed goodbye.

'Don't forget to pick me up.'

'Give me a break.'

'And the UFO books.'

'I don't forget things like that.'

Hammond watched Paulette as she talked out of earshot to her friend David.

The rain drummed on the car as he drove homewards. In his head there was a pounding impatience for some kind of reassurance. He didn't like the idea of going back to the empty house. Now the wet day stretched before him. He had to do something. He ought to go check out those model flying clubs. But what was the point? And the lousy weather took away any incentive. As he listened to the classical music on the radio, he had a thought. More than a thought, an impulse. He knew what he wanted to do. By the time he got onto the Hollywood freeway the impulse had become a compulsion.

He wasn't driving to the flats out in San Bernardino. He was being driven there. What had been a necessary ride before was now a trip of obsessive curiosity. He had to return to the flats. The scene of the crime. What did he expect to find? The burned out wreck with Wildman still in it. Maybe his Oldsmobile had been stolen, broken up for spare parts. No. He had to see the body.

As he drove out on the desert highway the rain stopped, probably gradually but Hammond noticed it only suddenly. He switched off the wipers. The hood steamed under the fresh, hot sun. The black top surface became slippery. He felt the sliding in the Honda. Hammond wished he had brought his car, or better yet, Pandora's BMW. But instinctively he didn't want to be recognized. Now he was nervous of getting stuck out on the flats with all the rain that must be lying there. He remembered his warning to Wildman. No purchase for the tires after the rain.

An oncoming car, way over the limit, slid out of control. The driver braked. The car came broadside towards Hammond. The car couldn't stop. Hammond swerved as the car glided past. He breathed a sigh of relief and looked in the rear-view mirror. Other cars following honked their horns at the guy. More than ever he needed to return to where it had happened, to see whatever had to be seen.

He turned off the highway at the same exit and headed out to

81

the flats. The windshield steamed up. He wiped the glass with his sleeve. The place was different after the rain. The surface of the land was glossy like a lake. It reflected the sky, the bright and dark clouds. It was a painting under glass. Everything was made double. The real and the unreal mirrored each other.

Hammond couldn't drive as fast as he would have liked. The Honda was decidedly insecure on this ground. He stayed in second. Two thin lines of hypodermic spray came from under the back wheels. In this illusory landscape, faced with this *trompe l'oeil*, Hammond wondered if he'd come too far. He couldn't see the cars. Perhaps he'd gone the wrong way altogether. Maybe he hadn't driven far enough. He looked around. He was mapless.

Then he saw what looked like a boat in the glassy distance. He knew it must be a car. He carefully accelerated towards it, skating alone on the surface of the mirror. It was a car. Just one car.

He approached the becalmed wreck. He could see that it was his Oldsmobile. So where was the Bentley? He knew that it had been maybe two hundred yards from the Olds. But which way? He looked round. It didn't matter which way. He could see for five miles in every direction. The Bentley wasn't there.

This is ridiculous. He said it to himself out loud. Ridiculous maybe, but fact. He drove in a silly circle around his ruined car, abandoned in the shallows. There was no sign, no evidence, no clue to the Bentley. Or to Wildman.

Hammond was alone and unnerved. He needed Wildman. He needed to see him. To know. Alternative scenarios began to unfold in his head. The police had found the Bentley, removed the body and taken everything away. Or some kids had taken it. After all, it was a valuable antique, even smashed and burned out. Kids could always do something with automobile parts. How could he find out? He thought of stopping and getting out to look. But what would be the point? He had simply to accept it as something unexplained for the time being.

There came a new rumble of thunder. It threatened more rain. Hammond had no alternative but to head back the way he came. His anxiety became a dreamy fear. It was as if none of it had happened. There had been no Bentley. No duel. He half-wished he hadn't returned to the flats. He should have stayed home.

Hammond drove back along the highway, faster than was safe. He didn't switch the radio on. His head was buzzing with inconclusiveness. He drove. Then he saw her up ahead. Impossible.

She was standing at the edge of the wide, deserted highway, beside her car. It couldn't be her. This was crazy. She was wearing the same dark glasses, her dress was different, red instead of black. The woman who had given him a ride after he had killed Wildman was back like a ghost, standing where he had stood.

She waved him down. A voice in his head said: 'Don't stop. Let her be. Don't stop.'

Hammond stopped. The woman looked relieved.

'Hello,' he said.

'It just stopped,' she said, explaining why she was hitching. 'I don't know why. I guess it's just old.'

Her red dress was stained dark with rain. She must have been standing in a shower.

'I'm not a mechanic,' Hammond said in a daze, 'but I can give you a ride.'

'Thank you so much.' She smiled, or at least her red lips pouted, and she pushed her dark glasses back on her head. Her dress stuck to her body like a swimsuit.

He wasn't sure whether he had smiled or not. Her eyes were as dark as her glasses. She might as well have been naked, except that the wet folds of her dress were at odds with the natural folds of her flesh.

'There's a filling station about two miles down there, I'd really appreciate it.' Her voice was the same as before, but there was a lightness in her manner, unselfconscious. When she raised her arm to push her wet hair away from her forehead he could see the pull of her breasts.

Now Hammond was perplexed as well as dazed. Fearful and

also aroused. This was definitely the woman who had picked him up two days ago. It was her car. But what had happened to the silent mystery? Now she talked. This time she was, well, ordinary. But not really ordinary. Just available. But not really. In the hot sun her wet dress steamed as it dried. For a few minutes Hammond forgot Wildman, forgot the missing car.

She climbed into the Honda. Her dress stretched and folded across her thighs as she sat down. He remembered she had said she was a dancer.

'I love storms, don't you?' she said.

'I like the skies.'

'I guess I should get a new car, but I love that old bus.'

At the mention of her car Hammond reeled again with worry about the Bentley. Sitting next to the woman again, their driver-passenger roles reversed, Wildman again invaded his memory. She would always be connected with him. He hardly took in what the woman said. Whoever she was, clearly she made this trip frequently. But why didn't she remember him? It was crazy. Wait.

'If anyone asks, I didn't pick you up. You were never in my car.'

That was the last thing she had said to him. Maybe she was still holding to that. And that was why she pretended not to recognize him. Fair enough. He was vaguely relieved.

When they got to the filling station she slid out of the car. The muscles in her bottom stood out under the dress.

'Thank you so much.' She smiled.

'You're welcome.' He smiled.

She looked up at the sky. He looked up at the sky. It was getting dark again.

'I think the storm's coming back.'

'Maybe.'

'I love the darkness. It's so dramatic. Especially when you're driving in it.' She put her dark glasses on again.

Hammond nodded but didn't say anything more. Watching her covered thighs level with the car window he saw that the dress she was wearing was similar to the one Dora had bought

84

while he had been away in Arizona. A coincidence, that.

He put the Honda into gear. The woman didn't seem to need any more help. She waved to him as he drove on. He saw her begin to talk to the pump attendant at the station. She pointed back along the highway, towards the flats, presumably explaining what she thought might have happened to the engine of her twenty-five year old Mustang.

10

By the time Hammond got back to his home the storm had cleared completely. But his mind was clouded and thundering with confusion. What had happened to the Bentley, to Wildman's body? There was no illuminating flash of lightning. Maybe Wildman had arranged with a friend to take the car after the battle, whatever the outcome. Perhaps he had had a second. When a man fought a duel in the past with swords or guns he always had a second. Hammond hadn't considered finding a second. And who the hell was that woman?

In the kitchen he found a note propped up against a bottle of Russian vodka. The note read: 'I love you, love you, love you . . . your Dora.' Hammond was suddenly moved. The way Dora loved him was so simple, so direct and so uncomplicated. It was irreplaceable. He wished he had never bothered with Betty May. Suddenly, that whole affair seemed crazy and pointless. What had he achieved? It had cost Betty May her life and turned him into a killer. How could he have let that happen? But it had happened. Now his life was totaly unbalanced.

He opened the vodka and sniffed it. The quietly pungent smell of dried grass from the steppes of Russia crept up his nose. It reminded him of his days of drinking, his moments of anger, and those occasional scenes of violence. Wildman had had that same effect on him, releasing the other man, like a genie from a bottle.

He screwed the cap back on the vodka and poured himself a Miller Light.

There was a message waiting for him on the machine. An

invitation to a screening of a rough cut of *Ghost Town* at a laboratory in Hollywood. He was intrigued to see it, tempted to go, but afraid also. He was scared of watching it now, especially that scene. Watching Betty May's stunt would be rubbing salt into the memory wound. Or pouring alcohol over the past. Then setting light to it.

The screening was at two o'clock. He was there on the dot. He knew he wouldn't be able to stay for the whole movie. He had to pick up Paulette at three thirty and take her to the Balfours'. He could watch an hour of it. The screening was for Peter Anders, the cameraman, the lab color timer and the post-production supervisor. Hammond exchanged a few words with Peter before the film started. It was Peter who had invited him. Neither of them said anything about the death that had over-shadowed the second half of the shoot. Hammond knew it was on Peter's mind as well.

As usual he could see the script typed on the page as he watched the movie. His sets looked good and real. Peter had lit them atmospherically. The interiors were dark and deeply shadowed. The exteriors were bleached and you could feel the dusty heat of the desert. The lostness.

Hammond slumped in the screening room waiting, only wait-ing for scene No. 103. He had blotted out the scene which preceeded it. 102 was a night love scene between Bobby and Helga in the shack. He remembered it being shot.

Hammond had built the set not outside, but in a small com-mercials studio on the outskirts of Scottsdale. He now remembered how strange it had all felt, doing the scene which came before the death of Helga in the story after the real death of Betty May. Never had the film technique of shooting out-of-sequence seemed so poignant to Hammond. It was as if the dead girl had been brought back to life.

He remembered that the young actress playing Helga, for whom Betty May was the stunt double, had suddenly broken down in tears during the shooting of the love scene. She told Hammond afterwards that she couldn't erase the idea from her head that Betty May had actually died for her, in her place.

There was a deathly eroticism about it. Helga was making love for the last time. It was to be her last night on earth. When she came out of the shack in the morning light she would be shot to death. As he watched the night scene he could see himself as if in a mirror, making love to Betty May on what was to be her last night on earth.

He saw the machine-gun fire, the bullets thudding into Betty May's clothing, her backwards trajectory, with Wildman's unseen wires taut, yanked out of control through the soft balsa wood door he had constructed. Hammond was close to tears.

'That's a nice stunt,' the admiring voice of the post-production supervisor came out of the darkness. He hadn't been present during the shooting.

Hammond got to his feet, tapped Peter on the arm and excused himself. He knew Peter would understand. It was so fucking sad. He hated Wildman with a renewed passion. Wildman had deserved to die.

Hammond drove along Sunset from Hollywood towards Beverly Hills. Images, words, came back to him like projections onto a screen.

Paulette, his mother, had suffered his father for years, with all his financial craziness, all his promises. But when he began to drink with two hands, she left. No one would blame her. Hammond had been seventeen then. They lived in a large white wood house outside Saratoga, New York. When the money went finally Hammond moved with his father to Albany. He wouldn't go with his mother. He didn't like the guy she was seeing. And he wanted to stick by his dad. He was at that age. For all his faults his dad was a man, and men should stick together. Hammond stuck it as long as he could. He left home when he went to college. His father's violent rages made it impossible to bring friends back. Girls were out. His father was jealous of them.

Hammond found that he himself had started to drink, probably to keep his father company. A few beers in the morning led to a couple of scotches in the afternoons. Vodka at night.

88

He was on track to becoming a teenage drunk. He stopped just in time. Thank God. Shit. He hadn't called Dora. He'd promised to. He wanted to thank her for her note and the vodka. It meant she trusted him.

Hammond was a few minutes late arriving at the school. Paulette was waiting in the yard near the gate with David Wing and with her bag for the weekend. She was clearly excited. She said goodbye to David. She ran to the car before Hammond had time to get out.

'Let's go,' she said.

'David not coming?'

'He wasn't invited. He's not really a friend of Clarisse.'

Clarisse Balfour's parents were hugely rich. Obscenely rich, Hammond thought. They had three Rolls Royces. They lived in a ten bedroom mansion on Bellagio Drive in Bel Air. Not far from where Alfred Hitchcock had died, Dora told him. Hammond didn't know what Mr Balfour did. Maybe the money was inherited, or belonged to Mrs Balfour. He wasn't envious. After all, Dora had provided him with a lifestyle he could not have afforded at the beginning of their marriage. But he did wonder what the Balfours did with their freedom.

'Did you get my book on UFO's?'

'Darling, I didn't forget. I've had kind of a busy day.' He had forgotten, of course.

'Dad, you're a flake.'

'Well, you're not going to be doing any homework while you're staying with the Balfours, are you?'

When they drove up the cypress-lined drive to the tall white Southern mansion Hammond thought that this was probably the kind of home his father had envisaged. In fact, his father ended his days and nights, which became the same to him, in a one bedroom apartment in a slum in Queens. His father never saw Paulette.

Clarisse Balfour greeted Hammond and Paulette in front of the steps to the house. She was a rather domineering woman in her forties from an old San Francisco family. She owned a winery in the Napa Valley, Dora had told him.

'When shall I pick Paulette up?' Hammond didn't want to mess that one up.

'Around five o'clock on Sunday. Is that OK?'

'I'll be there.'

Hammond kissed Paulette goodbye. She joined a noisy group of children at the paneled door of the house. Looking at the young, chattering, bird-like girls, Hammond thought about Penny. Penny Turner, twelve years old, auburn-haired, a good arm-wrestler, and his first love.

The memory of Penny persisted as he drove home through Westwood. She had been Paulette's age when they were in love in school at Saratoga. Penny didn't look anything like Paulette, but in her physical toughness she did resemble Betty May. Hammond hadn't thought of it before. Now that he did, he was moved. Suddenly, all around him on the streets of Westwood Village, Hammond saw young girls, students at UCLA, all of them Betty Mays and Penny Turners. It didn't arouse him at all. It chilled him. Penny had died, aged nineteen, of leukaemia.

When he got home Hammond found a package waiting. He opened it. It was a screenplay sent over by hand from George Elliott and Associates, a talent agency in Beverly Hills. There was a brief note enclosed asking him to read the script over the weekend. The director, represented by Elliott, wanted to know if Hammond was interested in the job of production designer on the project. He'd like to know, by Monday if possible, Hammond's reactions to it. Hammond was pleased at the offer but in no mood right now to read. He glanced at the title page. It was called *The Box*.

He went into the kitchen, opened the fridge, threw some ice cubes into a glass, and poured himself a triple vodka. He wasn't hungry. He sat down in front of the TV in the living room. He watched news programs as if they would provide clues to what happened. They didn't. And by nine o'clock Hammond was drunk.

By ten he was dozing fitfully in his chair, the TV still on, but with the sound low. He awoke to find himself watching a beauty contest. The sight of girls in bathing costumes aroused in him vague longings for sex. He wanted Dora. He wanted to be in bed with Dora. He rubbed himself lightly, but he was too depressed to concentrate on any specific sexual images. He drank some more vodka and hauled the clinking tumbler of ice and alcohol to bed.

Hammond undressed down to his shorts and lay back on the bed. He switched to the classical station on the radio. It was a familiar orchestral piece, but the drink prevented him from remembering what it was. He was aware that there was someone he said he would call, but he couldn't remember the person's name. Was it male or female?

The last thing he remembered before falling asleep was a plan to go down to the kitchen and freshen his glass. With the musty taste of lemon grass on his tongue he fell into a confused sleep, his mouth open, like an old man.

Hammond woke with a start in the darkness. There was a crackling sound from the radio. The station had closed down. But that wasn't the noise that had woken him. He had heard someone in the house. He got off the bed, stood unsteadily, pulled up his shorts. There was the sound of a door closing. Shit. It was quite clear.

'Dora!' He called out as he stumbled out of the bedroom and started down the stairs. Dora must have come back. Something was wrong. He switched on the lights in the hall. But he knew it wasn't Dora. He was getting scared. Where did Dora keep her gun? The vodka blocked his memory. Hammond shook.

Sweat dribbled down his naked back. He went slowly towards the kitchen. The soles of his feet stuck to the oak floor. He could see the light was on. The door to the kitchen was ajar. He listened. Should he go into the kitchen or not? He was sweating heavily now. Alcohol. The vodka hadn't helped his bravery. He could hear his own breathing, his own heart pumping, his scalp was stinging.

His forehead was cold with dripping sweat. He thought, no burglar would go into the kitchen. Pathetically, he called out

'Dora'. Hammond's courage ran out. He couldn't make it into the kitchen.

He started to tell himself it was nothing. Nothing. No one. He had dreamed the sound. He had imagined that someone was in the house. Far in the distance there came the sound of dogs barking. Scores of them, it seemed. Dogs. A pack of hounds in pursuit. He was the fox.

Hammond crept back upstairs to the bedroom. He closed the door behind him and locked it. He had never done that in his life before. The brass key was cold as ice. He got into bed and pulled up the covers. He shook with fear. What the fuck was the matter with him? The killer of Wildman was tonight a cringing coward. What had happened to the other man inside? He needed him. The angry beast, capable of destruction when roused, where the fuck was he?

Under the covers Hammond was in a cotton sweat box powered by his own body heat. He was liquid fear. Waiting for someone to smash down the bedroom door with an axe, he faded out.

When Hammond woke daylight was streaming in through the window. He hadn't closed the drapes. The phone rang. He jumped. He grappled for the receiver. It had to be Dora.

'Hello.'

There was a long pause.

'Did you have a good night?'

It was a woman's voice, but not Dora's. He couldn't think who it was.

'Who is this?'

There was a click at the end of the line. She had hung up. The woman's voice . . . It was the woman's voice from The Imperial Gardens . . . The plane . . . The model plane . . .

Hammond leapt out of bed. His head throbbed. He almost fell down the short flight of stairs which led to his studio. He kicked open the door with his bare right foot.

The model plane had gone. The curling wires were hanging limply in the morning sun. Hammond was transfixed. No such thing as a nightmare. There had been someone in the house.

He'd been in the kitchen. The plane had gone. Someone had taken it. The person who sent it had taken it back.

Wildman was alive. Alive.

11

I had no idea how he'd done it. Escape from that burning wreck seemed impossible. Yet somehow he must have achieved it. He was alive. I knew it. Now he'd broken into my house. He could get out and he could get in. The fucker was laughing at me. Wildman and his second, probably the woman who called me. I knew he had women. He'd had Betty May.

I was nauseous, hung over. I was so shaky I cut myself shaving. Every little sound sent me looking for its source. With the refrigerator switching itself on, I ran to the kitchen. Squawking birds on the patio drew me to the pool. At the sound of a car I looked out front. He was playing with me and I was his toy.

I will not give in. I will not submit. I went into the kitchen for water, iced water. My mouth was blotting paper. My whole body was dehydrated. I must have drunk a whole bottle of mineral water. I looked at the vodka bottle. Shall I? Hair of the dog. I knew from my drinking days it was dangerous. Don't touch it.

I poured a triple shot into the glass of ice from which I'd drained the San Pellegrino. Dora's favorite water. I needed her. Yet what could she do? The vodka burned my throat, tickled my stomach lining.

Don't back off. Think. That's what he wants. Think. That's what he expects. So don't be defensive. Don't be a moron. Attack. Attack!

I didn't expect him to answer the phone. He didn't. The operator picked up.

'This number has been temporarily disconnected . . . this

number has been temporarily . . .' I hung up on the mechanical female voice. It was mocking me like the Latin quotation on the model plane. The die is cast. Did it mean he was out to get me? To finish me off? Well, Wildman would have a fight on his hands.

I still felt sick, but I had gotten over the fears, the cowardice of last night. To prove it to myself I drank some tomato juice with Worcestershire sauce and no more vodka.

I left the house around eleven thirty. I took Dora's BMW. I don't know why. Maybe it brought her closer to me. I needed her strength. I didn't care where she was now. My thoughts were all Wildman. It was a long ride to the north Valley. I took the first address given by Jeff Walsh, not because it was the first of two, but because it was in the Hidden Hills area. Hidden Hills was the home of Betty May. I had a strong feeling about it.

I wound down the car windows, despite the increasingly oppressive heat. I could've put on the air-conditioning but closed in I felt like a prisoner. I accepted the hair-dryer effect as I drove fast on the freeway.

When I reached Hidden Hills I stopped to check the map. I was exhilarated now, tracking him once again. I had a vague feeling that Wildman might be waiting for me at the Wide Wings model aeroclub. He couldn't know I was coming right now. But he must know that I'd be looking for him. Unless he thought I was too weak or scared to bother.

The club was like a small private airport. The buildings were at the end of a street. Beyond them was ranchland, the open space of an older Southern California. I parked on the lot. I could hear the sound of the model planes' engines whining and buzzing, mechanical insects in the thick white air. The pool at night. The first warning. I knew their owners were obsessive types. I knew Wildman well enough to see that being one of them would fit his personality.

The club room was chill with air-conditioning. The sweat on my face and body began to dry. I went up to the bar and ordered a soda.

'You are Mr . . . ?' said the barman, a white-haired man who couldn't be more than thirty-five.

'Wildman. I'm trying to trace Mr Charles Wildman.'

'But your name is?'

'Hammond.'

'Are you a member here, Mr Hammond?'

'No, not really.'

'I shouldn't really serve you if you're not a member.'

'Oh.'

'But if you only want a soft drink, I guess it's all right.'

I tipped him fifty cents.

'Do you know Mr Wildman?'

'I'm afraid not. Is he a member?'

'Gee, I don't know. All I know is he's a model plane enthusiast.'

'Sorry. Can't help.'

The barman went to serve someone else. I turned away looking for a place to sit and get my energy together to go on to the second club. It was right out beyond Pasadena. Another long drive.

I saw that there was a whole wall of the club room devoted to photographs of men and their little planes. Some of the framed photographs were signed. I examined them. The men, like their models, came in many shapes and sizes. I guessed that they were stars in their field. Most of the photos were in color. I was impressed by the look of one or two in black and white. They had that proud, pioneer feel of the early aviators with their machines, their follies.

Then I saw him. I moved closer to the image to make sure. No question. It was Wildman. Some years ago. He was smiling youthfully at the center of a group of admiring enthusiasts. He was holding a large model with an exceptionally wide wing-span. There was an inscription on the fuselage. I couldn't make it out. It was probably in Latin. Wildman was smiling. At me.

At home there was a message waiting for me on the machine. I paused before playing it back. I could hear Wildman's heavy voice.

'OK Hammond. It's your call. I'm waiting for you. This time you won't walk away.'

I pushed the button fearfully.

'Darling, you didn't put the machine on before. Are you all right? I called to tell you that I'm staying with friends for tonight. I should be back Sunday late, or maybe Monday morning. Don't worry about me. I'm just fine. I just didn't want to stay in the house any longer. I'll tell you all about it when I get home. It's not serious, so don't worry. How are you, my darling? Did you drink the vodka? Don't forget to pick up Paulette. No, I'm joking. I know you won't forget. I love you.'

I felt better. I decided to get Wildman out of my mind. Force him out just for a while. Think of something else.

I took the script that had been sent over, *The Box*, picked up a sketch pad and a couple of pens, and went out onto the patio. I sat under an umbrella by the pool. I imagined I could see Dora swimming underwater. I heard a dog barking. Then I opened the script.

EXTERIOR. DOWNTOWN AREA. SUNSET

Deserted Sunday streets. A patrol car passes, radio talking. The window of a tall industrial building reflects the cityscape at the end of the day.

INTERIOR. BUILDING. SUNSET

A dark loft, cavernous, echoing, lit by photographic lamps on stands.

An elevator cage climbs to the top floor. It stops with a clang. The rusting see-through iron doors open. A MAN steps out. He looks around and sees two Dobermans lying asleep beside each other. They do not stir at the sound.

The Man pulls the limp body of a second man out of the elevator cage where he has been lying unconscious on the steel plate floor. The Man hauls his victim across the hard wood loft flooring.

In the center of the raw space stands a Box. The Box is about nine cubic feet, is made of wood and metal, has obviously been carefully constructed. Tubes and wires come out of the Box and lead to a large control console. Beside the hand-crafted console are two steel cannisters containing oxygen.

The Man opens a door panel into the Box by means of a remote control unit, like an infra-red TV remote. He begins to undress the unconscious guy, taking off all his clothes.

When the victim is naked, the Man begins to attach diodes to the nerve spots and vital organs of his body. The final diode is attached to his genitals, held in place like the others with surgical adhesive tape.

All the wires from the diodes end up in a small black metal device the size of a pocket cassette player. The device itself has two small antennae protruding from it.

The Man eases the unconscious victim into the blackness of the Box interior. When the body is inside, the Man closes the Box door by operating the remote control.

INTERIOR. LOFT. NIGHT

The elevator doors slide open and a WOMAN appears. She is dressed in a red

I stopped reading. I looked back to the title page. Strange, there was no credit for the writer. It was an interesting opening scene. Interesting anyway from the design point of view. I put the script down, picked up my pad and Rotring and began to sketch an impression of the box. Maybe I could change it a little. Perhaps the box could be made out of other materials as well. Give it more interest, more presence. After all, whatever the story was going to end up being, the box had to be a character on its own. It ought to have a personality.

I thought I heard a movement behind me. I looked round. I could hear a slapping sound. Like feet, but I couldn't identify it. Maybe it was the pool guy come to check the filters. As I picked up my drink I felt a heavy thud between my shoulder blades.

I guess I shouted. Suddenly I could see the blue-green water coming towards me as I plunged. My mouth was open as I hit. Water flooded in. I panicked and choked. I could taste the sour chlorine.

Blue water, bubbles, sunlight, dull echoes, I struggled to the surface, closing my mouth, too late. I caught sight of a figure diving at me, all black and shiny, a shark. Someone in a wet suit.

The creature grabbed me around my chest from behind. Now I was in terror. I kicked, fought, my legs were helpless, slow in the water, my hand grasped at nothing but bubbles. I was going deaf. In a pool of clear glue I could hear my heart pumping blood against my ear drums. Drowning. No. It couldn't be, mustn't, mouth open, throat contracting, choking, fighting like a madman, pulled down deeper, wrong way, eyes stinging, water pouring into my throat, muscles useless, streaming sunlight, eyes closing, dark, kicking, kicking, the first blackout, Dora, no giving up, the center of nothing, beginning weightless, fight against the black, sudden cold, loss of desire, helpless, water like blood, thrashing, limping in cold space, mindlessness, terror of . . . nothing to do . . . and how . . . lungs of water, second blackout, dizzy, loss of control, a final fight, knowing it was the end, to the end, trying to count, five, eight, ten, death wish, spasms of fear, endless, hopeless, Dora, no point, less and less and less . . . dark, darkness, black, nothing, nothing more to . . .

FADE OUT

Part Three

1

As he watched her yellow dress burning in the grate he knew he would see her again. He had to. This wasn't the end of the affair. He would let her go now. Later he would find her. Or she would find him. She'd have to.

He loved hotels, hotel rooms, bungalows. His loft, downtown Los Angeles near the art museum, was his base but hardly his home. He spent as little time as possible there. When he wasn't away working he stayed in hotels for two or three days at a time. He didn't just go for the best hotels. Sometimes he would select a sleazy place in Hollywood or a touristy motor hotel along the Pacific Coast Highway. This brought him into contact with all kinds of women from everywhere. Women were relaxing for him and stimulating at the same time, better than going to the movies. He was writing his own scripts. And playing the male lead.

When he first saw her earlier in the week she seemed ordinary, a typical rich Beverly Hills housewife. But watching her eat her Eggs Benedict changed his impression. There was sensuality in the way she ate. She ate hungrily and quite quickly, finishing while her friend was only half way through her California fruit plate. She hadn't caught the local disease of counting the calories. She didn't immediately wipe the cappuccino foam from her lips. She was unselfconscious about her body. He wanted her.

Laura arrived right on cue, gun in hand. He could see the lady in yellow found the scene irresistible. None the less he was surprised that she went with him quite so easily. There was no stiffness in her manner. He liked the fact that she wasn't automatically on her guard. There was no feeling of inhibition in her behavior. There was no scent of sexual fear about her.

Her heel catching in the wooden bridge on the way over to his bungalow was the clincher. He knew she was his when he touched her ankle. There was no shiver of resistance in her leg. He liked her paleness. It wasn't bloodless. Her scattered freckles made her youthful. She must have been about thirty-five, he guessed. He could imagine she had seen things, done things with men, but they had left no outward trace.

When she unhooked her bra her breasts revealed another woman to him. They had an unexpected sensuality, maternal in their weight, eternal in their seductiveness. They reminded him of a classical Roman statue he had seen in the Louvre in Paris. Like that marble, this was a woman in whose body you could see anything and everything you wanted.

There was an incredible balance in her form. She belonged in a bedroom and at the same time in a landscape of cypress trees and mountains. He could see her running naked along an island shore, swimming in green Mediterranean sea, dancing a waltz in Vienna, glittering in red satin and gold, sitting in a black and white dress in a cafe on the Via Veneto in Rome. Most disturbing of all, he saw her asleep in bed beside him. He had seen a thousand women naked, but only one had ever aroused his aesthetic sensuality to this degree. His sister.

Every part of this woman was sexual. Her salty fingers in his mouth stroking his tongue, her pale beige nipples that softened at his touch instead of hardening, giving instead of resisting, her truly yellow pubic hair that grew naturally, evenly from her white skin and did not seem darkly stuck on. And then there was her mouth.

As the fresh coating of her pink lipstick dissolved through their kissing he saw that the skin of her unpainted lips was darker than he imagined. They didn't quite belong to her. They were the lips of another woman altogether, almost Latin. They behaved differently too. The passivity of her limbs in accepting and responding to his caresses was countered in the purposeful aggression of her mouth. He wasn't accustomed to a woman's

104

lips taking charge of his body. It was a surprise to have his nipples manipulated as if he were a woman. Her lips caused him to suck in breath as they controlled the responses of his cock. This woman could bring him to orgasm with ease.

There were moments with her when he was in danger of losing control of the scene. He had consciously to resist her mouth or he would be lost. The game would be over. He carefully kept her tongue away from his balls, and prayed she wouldn't notice. He didn't want her to think that he was reticent. And he didn't want her to realize the power she had. After all, who was doing what to whom?

As his cock hardened, his heart softened. He wasn't supposed to have a heart in the romantic sense. A heart was a muscle. Nothing else. Nothing more. He lost his heart inside her mouth. She was probably unaware of it. But he despised himself for allowing it. He would have liked to have hated her. But he couldn't. After he exploded with joy, the chemistry of his body produced a feeling of death by absorption. Then an even greater, a broader sensation enveloped him. He was alive, a quaking living being, led through desire and then lust to fulfilment and then need. Need. It was crazy. It was female.

His response to needing her, natural and unnatural at the same time, was revenge. He wanted to pay her back for having done this to him. She had given him something. He knew that. And he had treated her as if she'd robbed him. Why?

She had welcomed his hard and purple penis between her sand-colored thighs. Now her buttocks embraced him. The muscles stood out under her flesh. He pushed into her. She rose to accept him. Her veins swelled with passion. This woman was crazy. Crazy. Didn't she understand? He was violating her. Why didn't she squirm away, get off that chair, yell, anything. She wasn't a prostitute. He wasn't paying her, for Christ's sake. So why did she want him?

He streamed into her. For several minutes he forgot the question. She was silent. Still inside her, he put his arms around her ribs below her dipping breasts and pulled her up. She leaned her head backwards towards him. He smelt her blonde hair, the small secretion of oil from her scalp, the almond scent of her underarms. He held her tightly. He couldn't see her face, but he knew she was smiling. He was intoxicated. When she lifted her smooth leg to stroke his leg and its sticky hair, he was overwhelmed. He pressed his face between her shoulder blades, hiding, not wanting to show his emotion.

He relaxed. His cock drifted out of her. She sighed. The muscles of her rectum twitched. He turned her around. Her face was fuller, more fleshy. Her eyes were soft, liquid. She was wonderfully tired. Her knees were weak. As she relaxed he set her gently on the carpet. She turned into a wonderful nude. A sculpture of a woman on her back.

For the first time in ten years he was consciously sorry for something he'd done. As he washed himself lightly in the bathroom there was a stab of guilt. He shouldn't have taken her in the ass. It wasn't the act that was wrong. It was the motive. He had done it in anger and in revenge. She had wanted it, but that didn't make it right. Her enjoyment had spurred him on. The taste of rape in sex that always excited him had eluded him with her. It wasn't necessary.

When he came back to her he wanted to ask all kinds of questions. How she felt. But he didn't. That wasn't part of their unspoken pact. He decided to give her something. She could make of it what she wanted. One of Laura's dresses. The red one was perfect.

He wanted to delay her departure, keep her here with him. But she was a married woman with one or more children, probably too old to change her life. He was being childish. He was thinking like a lover. Let her go and forget it. It was only a fuck. Just a fuck.

He had to kiss her breasts before she left. She understood it and responded by holding out her hand to say goodbye. The mid-morning meeting was over. He let her go.

'Something's burning.' That was the first thing Laura said when she came in.

'I burned her dress.'

'What did she say to that?'

'I gave her one of yours.'

'The red one. I saw it.'

He had never done that before. It disturbed Laura. They had developed an understanding in the last two years. Having other women made her need him more. But she couldn't help wondering about the dress.

Laura enjoyed helping him pick up women. It was a neat and resourceful game. But with fairly strict rules.

1. Select the target. He would choose the woman. She never argued with his choice. She never opposed anything of his.

2. Devise the game plan. That was her department. She could be as inventive as she liked. He never opposed her plans.

3. The hit. He took care of that. She would wait somewhere nearby and imagine what was happening. She could invent the sex in her mind. That was her territory.

4. The aftermath. He would tell her what happened. Together they would compare notes, her imaginings with his factual account. You didn't lie about either. The most successful hits were those in which her guesswork most closely matched what had actually happened.

5. The conclusion. This was the sex between them immediately after the hit. Sometimes this consisted of an exact recreation of what happened. Sometimes it was ritualized submission on her part. He would decide which. She enjoyed both.

In this case, the Bel Air Hotel, he had selected the woman, the hit, and Laura had come up with the idea of the gun. Drawing a gun in public was the most dangerous game plan she had yet devised. It worked. It excited her.

All the time he was with the woman Laura sat in her Mustang in the hotel forecourt and waited. It seemed an eternity. In fact, it was two hours.

Laura hoped that her gun would play an important role in the sex. She imagined him touching the woman with the cold steel barrel. She could feel the shivers herself. The woman would be frightened, perhaps for her life. Good. Laura got a special, acute thrill from fear. That was why she was with Wildman. He had a frightening aspect. He was capable of anything. Even murder.

She had an obscure feeling that one day he would murder her. He talked very little about his past. She was sure there had been a killing in it. He had never explained the scar that dominated his body.

She made it a rule never to touch herself while imagining him with another woman. Sometimes it was difficult to resist the tightness between her legs. But she refused to cross them or clamp her thighs together. There must be no relief of the tension. Instead, as she became wet, she opened her legs slightly. Let things breathe. No part of her body must touch another part. She kept her hands on the steering wheel.

As imagined pictures of the woman's body flowed into her mind they multiplied as if they were reflecting themselves in a maze of mirrors. Laura became rigid. She had never had a lesbian experience, but she responded intensely to conjured images of women. She wondered at times if she was evading something in her own nature. Was she a closet gay? Was that why Wildman was fascinated with her? Her taut muscles and well-toned dancer's flesh, her addiction to exercise, her obsession with watching herself in mirrors, were all these symptoms of homosexuality?

It was not something she could discuss with Wildman. She had no friends she dared talk to about that. Her creature aloneness was the root of her sexuality. Laura achieved pleasure and satisfaction through people, rather than with them. The woman who had been with Wildman, was a catalyst, a conduit for Laura's own sensations. When Laura pressed her breasts into Wildman's groin she could imagine the woman doing the same thing. When his hand opened Laura's vaginal lips and her small tongue quivered, soft and hard at the same time, she felt what the other woman had felt.

To stop herself coming Laura slotted a music cassette into the car stereo. Romantic movie music filled the car like bath water. She sometimes played it as background to her dance exercises when she got too tense. The sound was vulgar and lush and took her mind off the white and pink images that were getting far too compulsive. This music, like the movies they came from, was a generalisation about love and feeling. It was so far from the sharp, specific moments of sexual excitement that it dissolved Laura's erotic thoughts in a lukewarm bath, its temperature just below 98.4, at which no passion can survive.

She had played both sides of the cassette twice when the woman appeared in the hotel forecourt and got into her car. She had changed her dress. Laura wondered why. She watched the BMW leave, then got out of the Mustang and made her way to the bungalow for the inquest.

Wildman did not want sex with Laura. He wanted solely to exist in the immediate memory of the woman who had just left. Usually, a scene like that would have provided Laura and him with an intense sexual dialog. This time he wasn't up for that. But he did not want Laura to realize it. So he forced himself to go through with their formal devices.

Laura sat in the armchair over which he had draped the woman's body an hour before. She started to take her clothes off sitting down. It was a favorite trick of hers. Until now it had never failed to arouse him. As she twisted her feet out of her black patent leather shoes, Wildman wanted to shout at her: 'For Christ's sake, don't do that!' He had picked up the woman's shoes after she left and put them in an overnight bag wrapped in a red silk square.

During the question and answer session which followed he lied over and over again. He had to protect himself.

'Her tits were overweight.'

Laura pulled her black dress down to her waist exposing a tight sheer black bra underneath.

'Very,' he said to confirm it.

'And her nipples were lipstick pink and too big?' That was Laura's guess.

'But she had made them up. They were painted dark red. Done with a brush, I'd say. Not with a lipstick.'

'She was waiting to get picked up, then,' Laura said. 'That surprises me. I'd never have figured her for a whore.'

Laura pulled her dress all the way down to her thighs. She left her bra on. She wasn't wearing panties.

'You didn't give her any money?'

Wildman hesitated.

'You did?' Laura was surprised. 'How much did you give her?' Laura's guess was two hundred bucks.

She opened her legs and leaned back in the chair. Her dark hedge of hair, which he himself had carefully trimmed two days ago using her curled golden nail scissors, now seemed too definite. Next to the woman's bed of yellow flowers. Laura was waiting for him to speak or move towards her.

'Not much. A token hundred.'

He moved towards her, glad she was buying his story. It made him cringe, describing the woman as a whore. Anyone less a whore than she would be hard to imagine.

Laura reached her hand forward and slipped it inside his underpants. He wasn't hard. What happened with that other woman? she asked herself. Something had gone wrong. She knew it now.

'Did you make her come?' Laura tugged his penis, pulling the head out of the shorts.

'Yes. She came.'

'Ah, but you can never tell with whores, can you? They fake it all day long.' Laura thought a little dig at his prowess wouldn't hurt him.

'I can tell.'

'How?'

'The same way I do with you.'

'Oh, and how's that?'

'You sweat down the back.'

'You can get worked up without coming.'

'But not afterwards. If you sweat afterwards, sweat for a good ten minutes, then you weren't faking. No way.'

'Maybe.'

Laura sat up. She was worried. She couldn't buy his story about the woman being a whore. She may well have come. But maybe, just maybe, he didn't. And that's what the trouble was.

So why didn't he? Why invent all this? Why lie? He didn't have to. He knew that. Between them there was no need to lie. As far as Laura knew he never had. She never had.

She put her arms around his buttocks and without removing the undershorts, she pulled him, now half-erect, into her mouth.

Wildman looked down at Laura's raven head. He had lied about the woman and broken his pact with Laura. Dumb. He should have told her straight out. 'This woman had an incredible effect on me. Period.' And let it go at that. Shit. He wouldn't go back on it now. Pride. He'd stay with the lie. She'd never know.

Laura wasn't going to let him get away with it. Wildman felt the sensation that only she gave him. Laura used her teeth. Most women were afraid to do that, afraid of putting the guy off. Men scare easily with women.

He was on the brink of exploding when she took her mouth away. She heaved herself up, out of the chair. She took him by the waist and pulled him sideways. They slid down on the floor. Because of her strength it was a soft landing. She tugged his shorts down and climbed on top of him. The certainty and grace of her movement was like a dance. Sexually aroused, Laura was all strength.

She whispered, 'I want you inside me. Inside. Where it counts.'

She folded herself over him. Her concentration was intense. She pressed herself down twice and waited for him to come. As he put his fingers inside the black silk of Laura's bra, he saw the woman's blonde hair fall onto his eyes. Her past cry merged with Laura's gasp. He merged with both of them. He felt himself spinning. He was the center of a whirlpool. He was going down, taking them with him.

Laura felt the fire. She started to cry. Tears streamed down her face as she lowered her lips to his mysterious scar. Wildman shook. The shaking made her come. He was hers. And no one else's.

They lay on the carpet, slowly catching and controlling their breathing. After a while she lifted her body from him. He was still hard. She smiled and lay down beside him. There was a knock at the door. Wildman groaned.

'Come in,' Laura called.

The door opened. A young Mexican maid looked in. She was startled by the two people lying on the floor.

'I'm sorry,' she stuttered, but couldn't look away. Laura was smiling at her. Wildman lay still, on his back.

Laura lifted his penis in her hand.

'Isn't he beautiful?'

'Excuse me,' said the maid. She closed the door behind her. Laura turned to Wildman.

'Look at me,' she said.

He opened his eyes.

'You're so sleek. You know that,' she said.

Half an hour later they were both dressed. Wildman seemed preoccupied. Laura's anxiety returned.

'You're not checking out today?' she asked.

'No, tomorrow.' He didn't want to leave the place where the woman had been.

'Maybe I should go back to the loft.' Laura was as keen to leave as he was to stay.

'I'm waiting for a call.'

'What about the dogs? Shouldn't they be fed?'

'There's plenty of time. They'll still be asleep. In any case I left them a good bowl of rabbit meat.'

Laura was puzzled by his habit of drugging his pair of Doberman Pinschers. He claimed that in sleeping long hours they could enjoy dreaming without the constant compulsion to be on the alert, either to defend or attack. She thought it was cruel but she couldn't prove it.

'I know her name.' Laura suddenly wanted to upset him. That would do it, she knew.

'I'm not interested.'

The rule was no follow-ups, no subsequent involvement.

'It's Pandora.'

'Forget it.' He was angry with her. She was interfering in his memory. 'What's the matter with you?'

'I saw her car license plate. It's Pandora.'

'Look, why don't you go home. Your own place if you want.'

Ever since she had known him she had kept her small apartment in the Valley. He didn't mind. He had a key. And a machine for messages which he picked up by remote. It was fair. She had a key to his downtown loft. He'd installed a mirror in the huge space so she could do her dance exercises. He liked to watch her.

Right now he was irritated. Why had she told him the name? Did she suspect his interest? Maybe. Laura was very intuitive. That was one of her most seductive features. This hint of telepathic communication kept them together. He wondered if she, Pandora, was telepathic.

'You go ahead,' he said. 'I'll wait for my call.'

'Shall I take my clothes? The ones that are left, that is.'

'No, I'll bring them.'

He wasn't going to respond to Laura's dig at him. When he thought about it, giving the woman that dress, it seemed an odd thing to do. But it was quite natural at the time. Even essential. She couldn't very well leave the bungalow without any clothes.

There had been occasions in the past when he had refused to allow Laura to wear a dress. In the days when he set her tasks, the one she responded to best was arriving somewhere to meet him in a public place, dressed only in her underwear. Her challenge was to think of ingenious cover stories to explain her undress to other people.

With Laura's lean dancer's figure being undressed seemed almost natural. She could carry it off. He loved watching men watching her. She was clever about it. She would wear a bra through which everyone could see her dark aggressive nipples. She rubbed them with an eraser before appearing. One time she wore panties, one size too small to emphasise her pubic mound and show off little tufts of black hair. At the same time she wore her dark glasses. Laura was a doll. He was lucky to have found her.

After she left he sat back in the armchair. Pandora. Incredible name. It was perfect for how he felt about her. Even now he could see her lying on the rug in front of him.

The phone rang. It was the hotel operator.

'Mr Wildman, there's a call for you. A Mr Elliott.'

'Put him on.'

George Elliott was his agent. He'd been negotiating for a job in Arizona, a movie called *Ghost Town*.

'Charles,' said George. 'OK. Your deal's cut. The movie starts shooting in four weeks' time. In Flagstaff.'

After Wildman hung up, his mind went racing back to the woman. She was a living ghost, there in the bungalow. During the afternoon Wildman did mundane things. He re-read the script of *Ghost Town*. He checked his messages on the machine in Laura's apartment. He made notes on the stunt requirements for the movie. He called the producer's office to set up a meeting with the director to discuss the project. And he called the Southern California Department of car licensing to check on the name and address of the owner of the plate 'Pandora'. Wildman knew going in this was a bad idea. He was breaking the rules of his own game. He knew he was rousing a sleeping dog.

Pandora. He was about to open her box.

2

It would have been easy for Wildman to contrive to meet her again. From the license plate he had traced Pandora's address. He went over to her house. He watched her come and go, alone and with her daughter. He didn't see her husband. Maybe they had split up. It would have been easy to talk to her, at the supermarket, in the school yard, at her favorite lunch place in Beverly Hills. Yet he held off. She might not want to be reminded so soon about what happened.

Wildman's feeling for Pandora had increased dramatically in the days following the Bel Air Hotel. If it wasn't enough that he couldn't get her out of his conscious mind, she had started to enter his dreams. That had never happened before with any of his casual hits. Pandora had invaded his life. He felt an acute sense of danger.

Wildman began to prepare for his upcoming movie. From his point of view as the stunt co-ordinator it was a run-of-the-mill project. He wanted to spend more time on his own writing. He had spent weeks working on his screenplay. Wildman had caught the movie business disease: he had become a frustrated writer.

He ought to have kept away from her house in Rancho Park. But he couldn't. One Saturday night he drove past just before midnight. He could hear the sounds of a party in progress. Classical music and romantic laughter came echoing from the back of the house, from around the pool area. It was irresistible. Wildman parked his car and went to look.

He walked around the back of the house next door which was in darkness. He could see the people were out, maybe away for the weekend. He made his way through a Japanese-style water garden to the line of tall thick interlocking bushes that divided and shielded the back yards of the two houses. He found a position where he could see the pool.

There were five or six couples sitting or standing around. The blue watery light of the illuminated pool made them look as if they were on a stage set. Wildman saw Pandora. She was laughing, waving a drink, perhaps even slightly drunk he thought. Then his heart pounded. She was wearing the red dress. And she was happy. Wildman concluded that the dull-looking man who was talking and pouring champagne among a group apart from her was her husband. What was she doing married to him, to a man who wore a tailored western shirt?

Pandora was sharing a joke with some moron in a striped jacket. The guy put out his hand and touched the scarlet chenille material. Take your hand off her, you cunt. Wildman received a stab of jealousy. Jealousy. That word wasn't in his vocabulary. Until now.

He stayed watching her, and only her, for almost an hour. People started to leave, couple by couple. This was what he had been waiting for. He wanted her alone. To himself. Why couldn't the dull husband take off with the rest of them? The striped moron had gone, so why not him?

Hammond went into the house. Pandora started putting the wine glasses onto two trays. For a few minutes he watched her walk round the pool back and forth, tidying up like a maid. Hammond reappeared and took the tray she was carrying from her grasp. He smoothed his hands over her dress.

Wildman watched as Pandora threw her head back as Hammond kissed her neck. He felt sick with desire. Hammond lifted the dress and ran his hand under the material across her thighs, it seemed to Wildman. They were just too far away for him to see the detail. But close enough for him to imagine it, to feel it as intensely as if he were Hammond.

She put her hand on Hammond's pants. Wildman twitched in response. Was it possible that she was thinking of him, remembering him?

When Hammond tried to lift her dress, Pandora stopped him with a kiss. Wildman could imagine her tongue in his mouth. Their mouths, Hammond's and his. Hammond. How could she put up with this guy? Habit, probably.

As they became more passionate, Pandora pulled away. She looked round, momentarily in Wildman's direction. Then she took Hammond's hand and pressed it to her breasts. Hammond went to turn out the patio lights. Pandora picked up one of the trays and went inside. Hammond took the second tray and followed her. Another light went out. The pool shimmered. Wildman took several deep breaths. He knew that was it. They weren't coming back outside.

Laura was asleep when he arrived at her apartment. He woke her up.

'What's the time?'

'Time for a dip.'

'What?'

'In the pool.'

'Are you crazy?'

'Yes.'

Laura slept naked even when she wasn't expecting him. She liked the feel of the bed sheets on her skin. She would wrap herself up sometimes, a living body in a white shroud. Wildman liked her sleeping naked, liked her available.

She yawned and opened a drawer, looking for a swimsuit. Wildman held out the red dress he had bought her to replace the one he had given to Pandora.

'You want me to wear that?'

'I do.'

'I've never swum in a dress.'

Laura went into the bathroom and removed her tampon. Wildman waited, controlling his impatience while she tied her hair back with a band.

The communal pool area for Laura's apartment building was surrounded by a high fence. The gate was locked at night. Each tenant had a key.

During the day the pool was uninviting, a rectangle of water surrounded by miserable white plastic chairs and rusting metal tables. Hardly anyone in the building used it. It was too exposed. There were no umbrellas, no vegetation, no shade from the baking Valley sun. At night, deserted, lit only by the moon and a single naked security lamp on top of the fence at one end, the pool area had the sinister aspect of an empty parking lot. The night breeze ruffled the surface of the water as it caught Laura's dress. The dress was dark blood red in the artificial light. The setting looked like a location for a murder in a B-movie.

But Wildman saw only the elegant patio of Pandora's house. When he touched Laura through the cool material of her dress he was close to Pandora's body. When he kissed Laura he was sucking Pandora's mouth, the unconnected free floating lips of a surrealist painting.

Laura did not know what was expected of her. Wildman gave her no instruction, nor did he describe the sexual encounter she assumed he had just experienced. With his lips still on hers he put his hand between her legs. His fingers pushed the chenille into her, gently pinching the flesh of her vulva. He could see the lips parting, Pandora's delicate yellow hair. As he felt the dampness he could smell the crushed hazelnuts, the unforgettable scent of her opening thighs.

Wildman's free hand grasped Laura's hand and drew it to the buttons of his pants. She began to undo them. This was familiar to her. Laura started with the lowest button and worked her way up.

He pushed his cloth-covered fingers deeper. Her vagina became dry as the material absorbed the liquid. He seemed in a daze, a dream. There was no familiar urgency in his pressure. Instead there was a passive tension in him she hadn't felt before, a stillness, a state of feeling that wasn't thrusting for release. Something that just wanted to be. For a moment Laura was with another, unfamiliar man.

Wildman pushed his penis into the dress and into Pandora. He knew Laura wanted to take the dress off. But that was impossible. He didn't want to see her body. He wanted only Pandora. The red dress was an essential mask for the body. He clasped Laura to him and felt the subtle fleshiness of Pandora. He put his hand on her shoulder as he began to come. She couldn't see his face.

A girl on the third floor of the apartment building was watching them from her bedroom window. She was young, fifteen years old. She had drunk coffee too late and couldn't sleep. Watching the scene below had aroused her. After a fight with her father over poor grades in her schoolwork, she felt suddenly and violently alone. She wanted company. She wanted sex. And she wanted revenge. All abstract.

She left the window for an agonising moment and rummaged through her underwear drawer for her swimsuit. She pulled her nightgown over her head and put on her white lycra one-piece. She went back to the window and looked down. They were still there. She hurried out of her apartment, shoving a door key into her suit, and jumped barefoot down the cold alabaster stairs.

Wildman didn't react to the sound of the splash. Laura saw the girl swimming underwater, past them. She was faintly nervous. Wildman had come into her, into her dress inside her. He felt huge. She wanted him to make her come, soon, now.

The water was cool. The girl in it was hot. She swam the length of the pool again, side stroke so she could see them. She half-expected them to move away. They didn't. The man moved out of the woman. His cock stuck to the woman's red dress. Neither of them seemed concerned by being watched so blatantly. The girl had heard about threesomes. She wished she had had the guts to dive into the pool naked.

Wildman ached. Ached for Pandora. He had held off long enough. He had to see her again. He turned to the pool and watched the girl for a moment. Who was she? What the fuck was she doing? Spying on him.

'Hey you. Get out of the pool.'

The girl was terrified.

'Let's go inside,' said Laura. She detached the dress from Wildman's cock. He gasped as if she had dug a nail into him.

The girl reached the end of the pool under the security lamp. She hauled herself out with a single movement.

'Come here,' said Wildman.

The girl stared at him. She looked at Laura. She wanted to run away. She wanted to obey. Wildman saw that she had short dyed blonde hair. Even in the distorted light, he could see the terror and also the curiosity in her eyes.

'Come here,' Wildman repeated his order, but quietly.

Laura felt uneasy. Waking her in the middle of the night. Bringing her down to the pool. Fucking her in the red dress. And now talking to this unknown girl. It added up to something strange. Something to do with the red dress he had given the woman at the Bel Air Hotel. The next day Wildman had gone out and bought a duplicate. Why?

The girl came up to them.

'Listen, sir, I'm sorry. I just went for a swim. I'm sorry, I wasn't spying.'

'Of course you were.'

The girl looked helplessly at Laura.

'You live in this building?' Laura asked, worried now about Wildman's mood.

'Yes. Up there.' She pointed to her bedroom window.

'How old are you?'

'I'm eighteen, sir.'

'Go back to your apartment,' Laura said. She touched the girl's arm. It was quivering. 'Come on, let her go to bed.' Laura was as scared as the girl. The look in Wildman's eyes frightened her. A savage intensity. The girl was held in that look. A fluttering bird stilled by the hypnotic gaze of an erect snake.

Wildman was in a dangerous trance. And he knew it. He suddenly realized that this girl was a mirror of his sister twenty years ago. He could see his sister in her. More than that. He could now see that it was his sister who inhabited the body of Pandora. He was shocked. He was exultant. That was the real attraction, the true compulsion for his absolute need for Pandora.

The girl was dizzy with fear. She was wet with desire.

'Do you have a boyfriend?' Wildman asked.

'Sort of.' The girl's voice was a whisper.

'Have you slept with him?'

'No.'

She couldn't speak any more. The sweat pouring off her was indistinguishable from the dripping pool water. She was running with liquid, inside and out. She could hardly stay upright.

Wildman leaned towards her face and kissed her gently on the lips. Slowly, in a dream, the girl responded. He put his arms around her, held her close.

Laura watched as the girl's arms raised themselves like robotic limbs and clasped his back. Laura had no idea what to do. The girl was hugging Wildman like a lover. She had changed from a little *voyeuse* caught in her act into someone who appeared suddenly to know the stranger she had been spying on.

Laura looked up and around the apartment building. There were no lighted windows. No faces that she could see. It was three in the morning. She could almost feel the dawn coming. She looked back at Wildman and the girl, who was now buttoning up his pants.

'I'm going to bed,' she announced.

'I'll call you tomorrow,' said Wildman. He smoothed his hand through his hair.

'What are you talking about?' Laura looked with desperation at the girl. What the hell was going on? Wildman looked at the girl.

'Go upstairs, get some clothes on. I'll wait here.'

The girl turned and walked away, obeying Wildman's command. After a few steps she broke into a long-legged barefoot stride. She didn't look back at Laura.

'Are you crazy? That kid's probably under age.'

'I thought you were going to bed.'

'I am. And you're not coming?'

'Not tonight.'

'What's happened to you?'

Wildman didn't answer her. He couldn't. He didn't know. All he knew for sure was what he was going to do for the rest of the night, and probably part of tomorrow.

Laura walked away from him. When she turned at the mesh

gate to look back, Wildman was sitting in a chair looking at the pool, waiting.

She didn't know whether to be angry or cool as the girl passed her coming down the cold echoing stairs. The girl was now wearing jeans and a sweater. She had no purse with her. Nothing. She was still barefoot. Neither woman said a word. One was smiling. One wasn't.

3

Wildman could see himself as a magician or warlock, bearing away the beautiful fair-haired maiden. The girl in the car beside him was a princess. No, a shepherdess. He was taking her to his castle or perhaps his cave. The night was dark but starry. The ride was a scene from a fairy tale.

Except that this was fiction made fact. The unwilling, frightened creature of fairyland was in this case happy to be abducted, seemingly pleased to be taken from the security of her home in the forest glade, thrilled to be whisked away into the unknown. She was traveling, not on horseback, but in an antique English car at high speed on a Los Angeles freeway.

Heading downtown the freeway lights streamed past the car like comets. Wildman looked at the girl as the lights flickered across her. She was curled up in her seat like a baby. But not a sleeping baby. This kid was wide awake, alert, on a different time clock, taking everything in. Being curled up was merely a protective pose.

The girl was aware that Wildman was looking at her, studying her, guessing at her. She did not look at him, and she did not look back or in the rear-view mirror above her. Her heart was thumping in her ears. Who was this man? Where was he taking her? She remembered having seen Laura around the apartment building. In a distant way she admired her cool appearance, her self-possession. Laura embodied the adolescent's longing for sophistication. Now, tonight, this man had taken the girl in preference to the woman. The thought that a forty year old man had chosen her gave her a feeling of ferocious excitement. She was aware of a violence in herself she had hardly experienced before except in some masturbation fantasies. She never imagined being raped. In her fantasy the girl herself was the aggressor. In her real life encounters with boys she was timid and evasive, never going too far. She had never been possessed.

In her imagination the girl had always wanted to be a siren, although she didn't know the word. She saw in herself a woman capable of luring a man to his death. While she had no experience of men, no technique of seduction, she felt she had some kind of obscure power over this man. He was going to be the first to make love to her properly. She knew that. For all her life he would remain the first. The fact that he was a complete stranger, that she didn't know his name or anything about him, made it right. This night would go way beyond her friends' fumbling affairs with boys, pointlessly swapping affections back and forth. This was the real thing. He would possess her and would in turn be possessed by her, she hoped.

Now the girl uncurled in her seat and stretched her legs. She uttered a sound, not speech but an animal noise. It sounded like a yawn. In fact, it was a deep growl. Wildman heard it and shivered involuntarily. Her movement and sound reminded him of his sister Florence, the way she woke in the morning in bed beside him. Florence and he had tempted fate. They had crossed the boundary of taboo to the land of passion where transgression was the natural order and desire the emperor and law-giver. It was Florence who had initiated in him a perpetual state of desire.

Since she had left America when she was fifteen he had held his memory of Florence inviolate. Their father, Charles Wildman Senior, was an army man. He had split up with his mother and they were divorced twenty years ago. His mother married a French dress designer and went to live in Paris, taking Florence with her. On Wildman's occasional visits to France he saw them both. But after Florence had herself gotten married and started a family, he stopped seeing her. She had betrayed him.

Wildman swung off the freeway at Alvarado. The girl realized this man lived downtown, actually lived there; the place where she thought no one lived, no one she knew. She had been downtown just a few times in her life, to Chinatown and a couple of Mexican restaurants on Olvera Street. As a small kid she had once been with her father inside the Bonaventure Hotel. She had ridden the outside elevator a few times and drunk a Shirley Temple in the lobby bar. She had never once been downtown after dark.

So it was a thrill. Wildman drove down the deserted streets. Traffic signals at intersections blinked a warning orange at night, no daytime switching from red to green. By day the traffic dominated the streets. By night the streets themselves ran things. The girl was suddenly nervous of getting out of the car when Wildman parked in an empty lot.

'We're there,' he said, and smiled reassuringly.

They walked across an empty street towards what looked to her like a factory. The girl's bare feet slipped on a slimy pool of automobile oil. Sounding close, but from a distance came the wail of police sirens. The thought of murder came into her head.

Wildman took out his keys to tackle a steel door in the wall of the building. There was a man lying on the sidewalk propped up against the wall. He was dead drunk. He wore a skirt that was hitched up high around his waist exposing his genitals. The girl stared, incredulous and scared, at the man, at his long dark hair and smeared lipstick. She clutched Wildman's arm. The man stared silently back at her. Wildman made a mental note of the way the man looked. It was an interesting image. He could use it somewhere in the screenplay he was writing.

Inside the building the girl's fear increased. They got into the ancient iron and steel elevator. There was a smell of rust and stale oil. Wildman switched on the naked light overhead. The open cabin climbed upwards past two, three, four floors. It shook and clanked. How could anyone live in a place like this? She wondered, was this guy some kind of weirdo? It reminded her of a scene from a horror movie with Mickey Rourke. Don't be scared, she told herself, you wanted this. The man's silence was getting to her. Please don't be a monster.

Two Doberman dogs were waiting as the elevator stopped on the fifth floor. Wildman pulled the squeaking doors open. He led her into his world. The dogs growled faintly. She backed up.

'This is Romulus and this is Remus.' He introduced her to the dogs. Their names struck her as peculiar, but no more so than what now confronted her.

The loft was the largest living room she had ever seen. The raw space had scarcely been converted. Wildman switched on some lights. Five lamps around the loft lit up giving the impression of a movie studio. On one wall there was a long mirror with a ballet exercise bar in front of it. There was an old broken statue of a woman. She thought it was in need of repair. There was a picture of a naked woman sitting on an unmade bed with one leg raised. It made her feel uneasy, a dirty picture. This was Wildman's favorite possession, a copy of an Egon Schiele drawing. On a trestle table there were model planes and cars. There were hundreds of books on free-standing shelves and lying around in piles. The isolated pieces of furniture were old-fashioned and decrepit. The few rugs were worn. She couldn't decide if the man was poor or just peculiar.

'Is this your home?'

'Some of the time.'

She looked at the four-poster bed that looked as if it had come out of an old costume picture.

'It's very unusual.' She didn't know what to say. She wondered what kind of work he did. She couldn't figure it out. 'Are you a collector?'

'No. I'm a stunt man.'

'In the movies? Or TV?'

'Movies mainly.'

Wildman bent down suddenly. He placed his hands on the floor, palms downwards, and threw his legs backwards and upwards. Standing on his hands he looked at her upside down. She laughed. He began to walk towards her. He was crazy.

'You try,' he said.

'I need something to steady me to start.' She didn't know whether to be amused or scared.

'Show me.' Wildman did not sound in the least threatening.

The girl walked over to a large wooden box, about six feet high. She couldn't imagine what it was for. She got down onto the floor and stood on her hands like him, using the side of the box to get her feet above her head. She gave herself a little push and was clear of the box. She took two uncertain steps towards him.

Her loose-fitting sweater fell away from her body and partially covered her face. Wildman looked at her white exposed breasts and pale stomach. Looking at her upside down, her breasts seemed magically to be drawn upwards, a reverse gravity. She was embarrassed.

'That's very good,' he said. He walked towards her. Four steps and he was looking right into her eyes. They were green in the artificial light. He put out his tongue. She giggled. He wiggled his tongue a few inches from her face. She put out her tongue in reply. She laughed.

'You make me laugh, I'll fall over.' She wobbled.

He leaned forward and touched her tongue with his tongue. He tickled and stroked the living thing inside her mouth. She stopped giggling. A dart of desire entered her body by the door of her throat. She couldn't hold her balance. Her legs parted a few inches. They had to. She toppled. He moved his legs decisively to trap hers. He held her steady, edged his lips to hers. Through her legs she was aware of his strength. She was secure. Wildman might have been holding her in his arms. He started to suck her tongue. Her arms quivered and lost their tension. When her breasts brushed his shirt the muscles in her shoulders simply gave way. Her hair touched the dusty floor.

Without her help he could no longer hold her properly. The scissors of his legs let her down gently. He eased himself backwards. He had the control of a gymnast. She fell with him, but softly onto his body, her fall comfortably broken by his chest and thighs. He put his arms around her back as they lay together facing each other on the floor. She lost control of her breath as he kissed her. He caressed her spine.

He stood up and pulled her to her feet. The sweater fell back, covering her body again. He looked at her. She shut her eyes and raised her arms above her head. He took the thick material of her sweater in his hands and lifted it upwards. When he began to pull her arms free she lowered them to make it simple. She seemed very tall. Pressing his face between her breasts he whispered to her: 'Why don't you undress me.'

This gentle command scared her. She had somehow expected him to do everything. She had no idea where to start. In a Richard Gere movie she has seen a woman unbuttoning a man's shirt. Now she tried cautiously to do the same thing with her right hand alone. It became a fumble. With both hands it was easy. When she got to his waist where the white shirt was tucked firmly into the pants and held by a black leather belt she had a decision to make. Either tug the shirt out or undo the belt. She dared not look up at him. She decided to unfasten the black metal belt buckle. She would have to move closer to him for this and needed the physical strength of her hands. She made the decision. Take his clothes off as she would take off her own, with definite movements.

Summoning all her courage she began unbuttoning his pants. Trying not to look at his white underpants she drew the pants right down to his boots. Shit. How was she going to get them over the boots? Wildman helped her by lifting first one leg, then the other, so she could pull his boots off in turn.

He'd taken the girl to revenge himself on Laura as he had taken Laura by the pool to avenge himself on Pandora. And behind Pandora there had been a thousand other women. And behind them, Florence. Behind Florence, his mother probably who had left him for another man. Wildman lived in a sea of women. But there was only one mermaid. Pandora.

The girl had undressed him. She now removed her own jeans. He was reminded of an inaccessible fish but with the sex and thighs of an available woman.

He knew this girl was a virgin, and it was a novelty for Wildman. Florence had been a virgin. But then so had he. He had never consciously tried to seduce virgins. They had no symbolic significance for him as they had for other men. Wildman preferred women with histories. He liked to imagine their previous experiences with men. He enjoyed the thought that they had slept with many men before him. He liked the idea that within hours or days of being with him they would be lying with others. He had no jealousy in him, not since Florence, not until Pandora.

Laura's fidelity irritated him sometimes. Her complete devotion suggested that there was something missing in her character. In a way she too was like a virgin, keeping herself for something. Her single-mindedness troubled him. Was it female or unnatural? He was sometimes touched by it. And sometimes he wanted to get rid of her because of it. In the end he didn't know why he was bound to Laura. Was it because he needed her loyalty as a kind of home base, an Ithaca from which he could wander like Odysseus? Or was her sexual steadfastness simply too strong for him? Like Penelope's perpetual desire, Laura's slave-love seemed an invisible but endless rope tying him to her forever. In that case, which of them was the slave? Thinking of mythology, he wondered about this girl's name.

'Betty May,' she said.

4

At dawn when Betty May woke she turned fearfully towards Wildman. Somehow irrationally, she didn't expect him to be there. He might have gone away, left her, abandoned her. But then, why would he? It was his place for Christ's sake. She was confused to see him lying beside her asleep. His eyes were shut. His body was unmoving. He was breathing. What was he dreaming? She was scared. He was alive. The loft stretched away from her like an empty stage.

The silence was unbearable. She faced away from him, took deep breaths, made a plan, devised an escape. Run. She started to get out of bed, gently, not to wake him. Don't disturb the beast. The sleeping dog. Then she saw the stains.

There were several. There was dried blood on her dark pubic hair and on her thighs. She was scared. There was no pain, but when she felt inside herself the blood started again. In a panic Betty May got into the tub holding her groin. She turned the faucet and sat in the tub as the water gathered around her body. Betty May knew what the blood meant. She was dizzy with apprehension. How could she stop it? He would wake and see the mess.

Wildman saw the stains when he woke. He looked round for her. He heard the bath water splashing. He was relieved. He tugged the sheet off the four poster bed. It looked like the aftermath of a murder. Betty May had not cried out when he had taken her. He had been neither gentle nor brutal. He had treated her as he would any woman. But Betty May wasn't any woman. She was a virgin who had given herself to him. He had

130

the strangest feeling that it had been a sacrifice. But for what exactly? And to whom?

He found her crying in the tub. Wildman took her head in his hands and kissed her tears away. He put his arms around her, hugged her until she finished sobbing. He saw the blood in the water.

'It'll stop soon,' he said.

'I hope so. It looks horrible doesn't it?' She smiled up at him weakly. A brave face, he thought.

When he kissed her she threw her arms around his neck. She pushed her tongue deep into his mouth. She wouldn't let him go. She wanted him violently, with more passion than she had known. She stood up with difficulty. He steadied her as he had when she stood on her hands.

Betty May reached down for his penis. She held him, not rubbing but pressing his hardening flesh between her hands. She sucked his nipples and rubbed her forehead against the hair on his chest. Her desire touched him. She was grateful. That embarrassed him. He eased her back into the bath. She looked up at him, smiling. She took his penis into her mouth. He wanted to resist. He tried to pull away.

Betty May moved her mouth forward as he moved back. She put her left hand under his balls, resting them for a moment in the palm of her hand. She felt completely different, released from some form of bondage. Now she wanted to eat him up, all of him.

Wildman was nervous she might squeeze his balls out of inexperience or in her passion. He had had that same fear with Pandora. He knew it came from a lack of trust. Betty May didn't sense that. How could she? What she wanted now was to see this man come. To watch what happened. Last night everything had been too dark, too remote, too fearful.

'Don't go away from me,' she said. 'I want to see. Please. It's all new to me.'

Wildman thought of Pandora. When he came, it was into her hands. The web of his sperm stretched between Pandora's fingers. He was hers.

Wildman heard the sound of the clanking elevator. He bent and kissed Betty May on the lips as she lay in the tub. Her skin was steaming.

'What is it? Is someone coming?' she asked. She was scared.

'Yes, but just stay where you are. Relax. Take your time.'

Fearfully, Betty May eased herself up. The bleeding had stopped now. The bath water was cloudy with redness. She wanted to get out of the water, dry herself, get dressed, leave this place. She felt trapped. It had been all right while there were the two of them. Now someone was coming, perhaps the woman who had been with him. Her clothes were several yards away on the floor. She didn't have the courage to ask him to get them for her. She sank back into the tub. Just don't cry, she told herself.

Wildman pulled on his pants and patted the waking dogs while he waited for Laura to appear.

'You really ought to oil the elevator,' she said, closing the open metal door.

'I wouldn't know where to start.'

Laura looked across the room to the box.

'She's not in there is she?'

'Of course not.'

Laura looked towards the screen which hid the tub from her view.

'I thought you might like me to take her back.'

'Now?'

'You're not thinking of keeping her here, are you?' She picked up Betty May's jeans and sweater and walked to the bath behind the screen. She didn't glance back at Wildman.

Laura was startled to see the color of the water. She didn't show it. She picked up a towel and held it out for Betty May. She watched the water pour down the girl's skin as she stood up.

'Thank you.' Betty May couldn't think of anything else to say as she stepped awkwardly out of the tub onto the wooden duck board that served as a mat.

Laura draped the towel around the girl's shoulders and held

132

up her clothes with a smile. Betty May took the jeans and sweater. She let the towel drop and started to get into the pants. Her legs were too wet to slide in. The skin immediately stuck to the material. She almost fell trying to get the jeans on.

Laura stepped forward. 'Let me dry you.' She began to towel Betty May's body. She was quite vigorous, deliberately avoiding any softness of touch.

Wildman watched Laura rub the girl's back and hair. She was like his mother drying Florence at bathtime. When Laura put the towel between Betty May's legs he turned away. Seeing the two women together stirred him. But this sensuality was weakened by a nervous feeling. Laura seemed to be clearing up after his mess, rubbing away the evidence of his crime.

By the time he'd called his agent and then Dave Pierce, the production manager of the movie he was just about to start, Laura had gotten Betty May ready to leave, as if for school.

'We're on our way,' Laura said.

Wildman went up to Betty May. She stood helplessly in front of him, clean and almost dry.

'I'll pick you up later.' He put his hands under her loose sweater and held her breasts as he kissed her. Betty May closed her eyes and shook her head, as if to say no.

'We'll see,' Laura said. She put her arm around the girl and led her to the elevator. Betty May finally smiled at Wildman as the cabin started its descent to street level. He knew he'd see her again.

'Be careful,' Laura said as the elevator went down. Wildman didn't know if she was addressing him or Betty May.

On the drive back to the Valley Betty May was silent and apprehensive.

'Did he come?' Laura asked as they hit a jam.

'What?'

'Did he have an orgasm with you?'

Betty May was dumb with embarrassment.

'It's a simple question.'

'I don't know.' She was stuttering. 'I guess so. I don't know.'

Betty May turned away, closed her eyes, sank into the car

seat, and hid her face in her jersey. No one had ever asked her a question like that, point blank. And a woman, too.

The question was important to Laura. She wasn't thinking about Betty May. She could see the other woman, Pandora, in the red dress, inside Wildman's mind, between them, a living ghost. She knew that all Wildman's behavior from now on would be controlled by that fleshy specter. She had a flash that he was becoming impotent.

In the afternoon Wildman went to a meeting with Dave Pierce. He had prepared a schedule of requirements for the scenes in *Ghost Town* requiring stunts. He had written out a rough costing.

'It's way too high, Charles.'

'How much too high?'

'Forty per cent.'

'Forty? Ten, twenty even, I could live with, but I don't see how I can lose that much.'

'You'll have to. This is not a big picture. The fat just isn't there.'

Wildman wondered if he should take the job at all. He hated this kind of cost-cutting.

'Use cheaper people,' Dave said.

Wildman thought about this. There were a couple of stunts involving the second lead actress that weren't too difficult. The stunt girl he was thinking of using was expensive. Good, but expensive. In the back of his mind was the wild idea of using Betty May. It would be difficult because she hadn't the experience, plus she wasn't in the union. But then the picture was a non-union production. He might be able to swing it. He wanted her with him. His feelings were ambiguous. The sight of Betty May's blood on the sheets had aroused a protective feeling. There was something destructive in it too.

He looked hard at his figures. Even with that possible saving on a stunt woman it wasn't close to what Dave Pierce was asking in cost reduction. He would have to take a big cut in his own fee. Maybe he should just throw in the towel on this one. He didn't want to do shoddy work. All Wildman's stunts looked good. That was his industry reputation. And his personal pride.

While Dave took a call Wildman thought hard about the whole thing. He looked at the location pictures on the wall of Dave's office. He looked at the photographs of the artists appearing in the movie. He glanced through the crew list of people working on the picture. He didn't recognize any of the names. Then he saw the name of the Production Designer: Alec Hammond.

The name Hammond caused him to take a deep breath. Now there's an odd coincidence. The name Hammond, as in Pandora Hammond. Then he saw the home address beside the name. It was Pandora's address. This Alec Hammond was her husband. She was this man's wife. He remembered the dull man beside the pool at night.

When Dave got off the phone he turned to Wildman.

'What do you think? Can you cut it?' he asked.

'I think maybe I can.'

5

Is knowing what you want the origin of criminal behavior? Is it the starting gate for wickedness? I knew when I began to plot the getting of Pandora, which is the only way I can truthfully describe it, that I was on a complicated and dangerous trip. Like writing a screenplay. You made notes on character, you scribbled down images that appealed to you, you imagined what your people would say, their dialog, what they might do, their actions, and you devised the plot, above all, the plot, the train of cause and the effect. It was tricky and confusing, but if you stayed true to your original aim, to what you wanted to achieve, the mistakes would be small ones.

I knew what I wanted. Now I had to consider what the other characters wanted. Betty May wanted me. She was awash in the sensuality I had aroused in her. For the time being anyway she couldn't live without me. The shooting period of the movie coincided with her summer vacation. She lied to her father and told him she was going with a friend to visit other friends in Arizona. I had the impression from her that her father was a domineering man. Maybe he was possessive because Betty May was all he had. His wife, her mother, had run off with a guy five or six years before. Neither of them had heard from her since. Lefevre had not re-married. He was a cosmetics salesman and was away from L.A. from time to time. This gave Betty May the chance to escape to Arizona. As long as she called him every two or three days his fears were allayed.

Betty May was instrumental to my plot line. She would do anything I asked. She wasn't a long way from Laura in her enjoyment of carrying out instructions. I couldn't say that all the women I had known were like that, they weren't, but the women who were most attracted to me were. What you wanted drove you.

I tried to guess what Hammond wanted. He seemed satisfied by Pandora. Who wouldn't be? He was smug. But everyone is capable of being seduced if only for a while. I was sure Hammond's middle-class attitudes, hearth and home and loving wife and daughter, could be jolted. He would have a tough time resisting Betty May. Especially since his wife would never know. A young girl has enormous sensual power if she decides to use it. I decided that Betty May would use it when they were both far from home in the desert.

So what had to happen in the story was this. Hammond would encounter Betty May on location. She would seduce him. When the shooting was over she wouldn't see him again. Then, when everything had gone quiet, Pandora would discover Hammond's infidelity. A letter from a 'friend' or an interesting photograph would arrive in the mail. Pandora would be shocked. It wouldn't matter whether he denied it or not. The effect on her would surely be traumatic. That was what I wanted. At that point when she found out I would meet her again. By chance, of course. The essence of a well-constructed screenplay was to make your careful design seem like chance. You had to beware of coincidence.

It worked brilliantly, the first part. Hammond went for Betty May. She visited him in his cabin on a nightly basis. He couldn't get enough of her. During the shooting I came and went, traveling between Flagstaff and Los Angeles. She carried out my instructions to the letter. At least, she said she did. I became curious though about Hammond. When I imagined him with Pandora I wondered how he made love, what he looked like, the things he said. The thought of him in bed with Pandora sickened me. I would never know what happened there. But I could find out how it was when he was with Betty May.

INT. WILDMAN'S MOTEL CABIN. NIGHT

Betty May comes silently into the room. She is surprised to see Wildman on the floor doing push-ups, first with his right hand, then with his left. She gets down on the floor and tries to crawl under his chest.

Wildman continues his exercises as if she wasn't there. His naked chest presses against her shirt front, up and then down. She giggles.

Wildman: Was I right?
Betty May: About what?
Wildman: About the slapping. Did it drive him wild?
Betty May: I guess so. Yes.
Wildman: And you? How did it feel?
Betty May: Not like you.
Wildman: Of course not.

He rolls over pulling Betty May on top of him.

Wildman: Show me what you did.
Betty May: Let me up then.

They get up and cross to the bed. Betty May pulls off her shirt and unzips her jeans. She climbs onto the bedcover and lies face down, her head buried in the pillow. Wildman gets onto the bed beside her. He slides his right hand into her panties.

Wildman: You're still wet.

He pulls her panties down her thighs to her calves. He leaves them there. She raises her bottom to him. He sees small red marks on her flesh. He kisses them. He puts his left hand under her and draws his fingers slowly from her navel to her pubic hair. Betty May twitches and lifts her back higher.

Wildman: What's his cock like? Thick or narrow?
Betty May: Kind of medium. I don't know. I haven't seen that many.
Wildman: Compared with me.
Betty May: A bit shorter.

She gasps as he slaps her bottom. Not with the pain, just with the suddenness. He climbs over her, pulls her to him.

Wildman: You're shaking.
Betty May: I can't help it.

He moves into her. Betty May's hands reach forward to the pillow. They grip it. She tenses.

Wildman: I want you to come like this.

Betty: I don't know if I can.
Wildman: You will. If I want you to, you will.

He moves her body back and forth like a device.

FADE OUT:

It wasn't Betty May now. It was Pandora. I was re-living
that moment in the bungalow when I entered Pandora's bowels
touching the depths of her. I remembered her acceptance of
me. It had been a moment of complete surrender, of physical
understanding. I remembered my remorse. I had to hold her
again. I belonged with her, we belonged together, inside each
other.

Betty May uttered a stifled cry. The knot of her body came
apart, unraveled rope. The tight resistance turned to a soft
hunger. She pushed backwards towards me. We moved
together. Betty May shuddered. She could no longer manage the
ritual movements. She went blind. She was deaf. She couldn't
remember her name or where she was or with whom. She had
no existence. She was annihilated. In silence. Through Betty
May's contact with Hammond, I reached Pandora. There was
no world. There was no devil. There was only our flesh. And
flesh is sad.

Then suddenly it went wrong. My screenplay fell apart in
front of me. Betty May's death shook me. It was my fault.
Technically, she may have died because of that pole on Hammond's set, but I had disregarded her inexperience in the field. I
was never going to openly admit it, but I was guilty. Overcoming
feelings of guilt could be the work of a lifetime. I couldn't let
that happen to me. I wouldn't let it happen.

My desire for Pandora had now lost a human life. Betty May
had paid for it. There was wickedness in that. But it wouldn't
stop me. In the end it was an accident. For days and nights
afterwards I clung to that notion. It was an accident. Accidents
happen. I've risked my life many times in stunts. But then it
was my life to risk. Stunting brought me near to death. It made
me feel alive. My life moved between sex and stunts. I named

my one-man company Cunning Stunts Limited. I had to admit I didn't much like the word Limited.

I could ignore my feelings of guilt during the day on the set. But at night the forces of dreams took charge and I was helpless, buffeted by nightmares. In my sleep, I returned again and again to my loft. The place became my own private echoing torture chamber. In my dreams I murdered Betty May, stabbed her, fucked her, to death. The blood, sticky patches on the bed sheets, swirling darkly in the soapy water of the tub, the blood of a virgin sacrifice was my doing. But the sacrifice failed to satisfy the gods. They were not impressed. When I woke, morning after morning, I felt as if I had come back from the dead.

The nightmares continued after the shoot had finished. I slept as little as possible with Laura. I didn't want her to see me wake up yelling my innocence, drenched with sweat. I thought incessantly of Pandora. I recalled every moment we spent together in the Bel Air bungalow. I re-ran my glimpses of her by the pool at night. I invented scenes between us. But they were day-dreams. When I received the phonecall from Hammond challenging me to a duel, only then did I begin to sleep easily, without fear.

My prayers had been unexpectedly answered. The gods were with me after all. Betty May's sacrifice had not been in vain. That phonecall was like the beginning of a slow cure for the sour sickness I felt in my liverish soul. I was on the mend.

Preparing for the duel became my therapy. I felt better, fitter, stronger than I had been for months, since my encounter with Pandora. I was back in action, feeling good, feeling free, and amused by the irony that I had to thank Hammond for that. I still had nothing but contempt for the man. Hammond was the archetypal foolish husband, the dummy who didn't know what he had, the ignoramus who couldn't understand the true beauty of his wife. He deserved to lose her. And he would.

Hammond's challenge to a duel with cars modified my opinion of him. It was an unexpected gesture, the chutzpah was crazy. It was absurd, a civilian challenging a top stunt man to a fight he couldn't hope to win. I had smashed more cars in my life than Hammond had even driven. Yet in his absurdity there was an undeniable courage. Where had that kind of bravery come from? Had Betty May meant more to him that I had guessed? Had she affected him in some way as intensely as Pandora had affected me? Maybe Betty May had opened more than her legs. She had opened a locked and secret door in the man's psyche.

There was also the question mark of Pandora herself. I had seen nothing in her relationship with Hammond to suggest her dissatisfaction with him. But I knew she must be dissatisfied. And she would not forget what had happened between us. Pandora had wanted me then. She must want me now.

It took me a full day to rig the Bentley. I fitted a new type of harness I'd been working on. It allowed several degrees of rigidity. It could be loosened and tightened before and after impact. This would enable me to adopt different body positions following the impact, positions that would look more convincing for the camera, than simply a man sitting up stiffly behind the wheel. I could fall sideways across the passenger seat or slump down almost to the floor with my head pointing at any angle. It could look very effective, as if I'd broken my neck. My aim as always was maximum realism.

I had to tell Laura something of what I was doing because I might need her help. She would be my second in the duel. You needed a second. Hammond was too stupid to think of that. Besides, who could he go to? How could he tell anyone what he was planning to do? I could imagine the reactions of Hammond's poolside friends in their designer clothes, their morals stitched in like labels, wearing initials that weren't even theirs.

'This is not a hit,' I told Laura.

'What do you mean?'

'It's not a woman.'

'Then what?'

'It's a man.'

'You're going to fuck a man?'

'Cute.'

Laura was prepared to do what she was ordered. But I could see she was uneasy. She knew it was connected with Betty May, with her death. She knew about the accident. I told her. She was very distressed, by the death of the girl, but more by the existence of Pandora. I wasn't playing by the rules any more. Laura could see that. I found that when I made love to her now it was always from behind. I didn't want to see her face. I was seeing another face. In my head I was with Pandora.

Perhaps I should have told Laura that the guy I was going to fight was Pandora's husband. I came close to it. In a way she had a right to know the truth. I didn't like lying to her. But I didn't tell her.

Hammond had aroused strange feelings in me. I had no sympathy for the man, but I found myself thinking about him at times when I should have been thinking only about Pandora. As the day of the duel approached I practically forgot her. My obsession was Hammond.

In my heart I knew I had made a mess of the duel. I wasn't sure if I had really wanted to kill him at the end but I had counted on crushing him with defeat. There was nothing psychological in the confrontation between me as Achilles and Hammond as Hector as we faced each other on the great plain before the walls of Troy, San Bernardino. In the classical world solutions were physical and outright. When Paris desired Helen he took her. They stayed together to the end of the Trojan war, in desire. Paris had no guilt in leaving his wife Oenone. And for Helen, Oenone didn't exist. Who now even remembers the name Oenone? So Hammond and his name would disappear from the story.

But I did not kill Hector. The best I had been able to do was let him think he had won. It meant we'd have to fight again. When he walked away from my blazing car satisfied with his victory, I thought hard about my next moves. Once again, I would have to re-write my screenplay. I extricated myself and immediately called Laura on the radio phone.

'He's alive, goddammit. He'll reach the highway in about

twenty minutes, maybe half an hour. Make sure you pick him up. I'll call you again in an hour.'

I then called a motor mechanic friend locally in San Bernardino. The guy came over to the flats with his tow truck. For five hundred dollars he did the business. There were no questions and no answers. I called Laura. Reliable as always, she had picked Hammond up on the highway. Now she was taking him back to Pandora. My Pandora. Your face, your body, your soul. You are what all this is for.

6

He returned to his downtown loft to wait for Laura. He fed the dogs. He needed to clear his mind. He started to work on a new model aircraft. He couldn't concentrate. A piece of balsa wood snapped in his hand. A half-hour's work wasted.

He looked through his mail. There was a letter from his agent with a photocopy of a rejection note from a guy at Paramount. His screenplay *The Box* had been turned down again. He knew why. It had been the same with previous rejections. Everybody found the story 'too dark'. They were scared, those people, by the way it told them what they already knew and feared. The world was dark. Only money, or the promise of money could brighten it for them. And brightness was what people paid money for. It mustn't be confused with illumination.

Wildman had always been attracted by darkness. That was one reason why he had constructed the box in the loft. He had read a book on the techniques of sensory deprivation. He was not particularly interested in brainwashing in war situations but he discovered some compelling facts about the effects of deprivation torture on its victims. Some people were able to resist longer than others. Not because they were physically stronger but because they possessed greater powers of concentration. They could control their minds by focusing their thoughts on specific subjects, things quite unrelated to their predicament. For example, one man who was a fine chess player set problems for himself in the blackness. While most people's minds under stress tended to drift, opening their imaginations to irrational fears, he was able consciously to focus on a problem to the exclusion of everything else. This man had been placed in a black, soundproofed box, for hours, and had remained unaffected by the experience.

Wildman saw that concentration, and obsession in its most extreme state, could be an insulation against the unsettling or destructive effects of unforeseen events. You didn't have to give in to the sensation that things, life itself, were outside your control. Since early childhood Wildman had felt he had been prey to the vagaries of other people's behavior. In his mind he felt his life was a constant losing battle.

His father, Charles Wildman Sr was a harsh, even sadistic disciplinarian. He ran the home on principles he had embraced in military academy. Wildman's mother had lived in fear of her husband. The early lives of the two children, Charles Jr and Florence, were governed by strict rules from waking to bedtime. Meals were always at fixed times. One period of the day was devoted solely to reading, another to play, another to a kind of question and answer session about their opinions and feelings. Private boarding school was like free time next to the discipline of home life. Their father's ruthlessness eventually drove their mother away and pushed the two children into each other's arms. Charles and Florence developed a kind of pact, and an increasingly sensual complicity in a world of their own.

The black box attracted Wildman as a form of discipline that came from inside himself. The device had originally been developed in an authoritarian technique for torture and mind-bending, but Wildman saw the positive side of its potential, a means of contemplation and mind-clearing. He built his own box perhaps unconsciously as a rebellion against the authority of his father. He saw it as a means of repairing the damage done to him.

Now, when he found himself distracted or confused, Wildman would enter the darkness of the box. There he could attain clear vision and self-control. The absolute darkness, the complete silence, the absence of any sense of time or the outside world, gradually freed his mind from uncertainty. He now entered the box to discover how to deal with Hammond. In the blackness he focused totaly on his opponent. He banished Pandora from his consciousness. He had no worries about her. She belonged to him. She was a given, a certainty, like breathing. She belonged to him. In the box, he became Wildmond.

Laura had been back an hour when Wildman emerged from the box. In the light of the loft he was faintly surprised to see her. He had forgotten he was waiting for her. In the dense blackness his mind had emptied itself of everything except the existence of Hammond. He watched Laura for a few moments as she worked at the ballet bar. She seemed an abstraction, a creature engaged in a ritual, a pure form moving without purpose, without sensuality. Wildman's mind was beyond sex. He now had a laser-like sense of purpose. He possessed a sudden and extraordinary feeling of health, of wellbeing. When he looked at himself, beyond Laura, naked in the ballet mirror, he saw a different man, fresh, stripped for action. It was as if he had been re-born, or created whole by a god who needed him.

Laura had seen Wildman in this state before; the relaxed muscles, the hypnotic eyes, a man with the steadiness of a statue. When he smiled at her in recognition, she knew it was all right to speak.

'I dropped him in Glendale.'

'How did he seem?'

'Pretty shattered.'

'Scared?'

'I guess so,' she said.

There was a question she had to ask. It had been on her mind for weeks. And while it was perhaps against their rules to voice it, she couldn't help herself.

'You didn't kill that girl did you? Deliberately, I mean.' She was half-expecting his anger. But Wildman was calm. He answered as if she had asked him if he'd like some tea.

'No. I don't kill people.'

'But you want to kill this guy.'

'I want to destroy him. Not physically, but from the inside out.'

Wildman turned away from her. He went to the table and

picked up a model plane. He held it aloft. His mind was clear. The plan was simple.

'*Iacta alea est*,' he said.

Seeing Hammond naked in his pool with Pandora would, weeks earlier, have pushed Wildman towards jealousy, the emotion he most despised. But now in his calm state it amused him. Make hay while the moon shines, he thought. From his concealed position behind the shrubbery he aimed to splash the plane down to interrupt the climax of their watery sex. That would be a beginning.

Wildman wondered if Hammond would ever read the message on the plane. If he did, would he be capable of translating it? Would he even know it was Latin? Probably not. A reasonable knowledge of Latin was one thing he could thank his father for. That, and the valuable ability to be content with his own company for extended periods. In different ways they heightened the physicality of his working life and the sensuality of the time he spent with women.

Seeing Pandora naked again as she climbed out of the dark pool she was unfamiliar. The paleness of the shining skin of her long back, her wet hair, seemingly dark now, not blonde, the remoteness of her thighs, her sex, small like a mole from where he watched, she was anywoman, not his, a generic creature, an example of a species. He preferred his memory of her, her existence in his imagination, to this distant projection. It was strange. Wildman found himself watching Hammond in the semi-darkness, in preference to Pandora. Hammond was his quarry. He felt close to him. Pandora was slightly disappointing. Laura would be pleased if she knew that, he thought.

The next step was to take the plane back. Let him examine it, worry about it, then before he can reach a conclusion, take it away. That would spook Hammond even more than finding the Bentley gone. Wildman knew Hammond would drive out to the flats, revisit the scene of the duel, just to make sure it had happened. He knew that because he himself would've done it.

The next evening Wildman tracked the family car to The Imperial Gardens. Laura made the call to Hammond from the payphone in the bar one floor below the main restaurant. An unnerving touch, that. The kind of thing you put into a suspense movie. Wildman had used it in his script of *The Box*. Even if *The Box* never reached the screen it would get made in real life. He'd see to that.

The next-day Wildman saw Pandora leaving the house for the weekend. He saw the daughter going to stay with friends. They both had overnight bags. He knew then that Hammond was his. Things were working out almost magically. Perhaps the duel had been meant to end inconclusively, just as poor Betty May's accident was meant. Wildman began to feel that there was another underlying pattern to it all. Beneath his plan there was an obscure strategy at work. The feeling re-inforced his certainty, his confidence.

Breaking into the house was simple. The lock on the kitchen door was easy to pick. The half-empty bottle of vodka told Wildman that Hammond had sought refuge from his fears. The dog was sleeping, drunk. Retrieving the model plane from the studio Wildman was again aware how strangely his concentration on Hammond had driven Pandora out of his consciousness. Even to consider kidnapping her was crazy. This was the obvious way to go. Take out the opposition. Being in the house at night gave Wildman a *frisson*, a taste of the real excitement to come the next day. At noon. On his way out he drank some vodka from the bottle.

On Saturday he parked his pick-up down the street from the house. He wore a poolman's clothes over his wet suit. He carried some pool equipment over his shoulder and casually went to the house to check it out. Hammond was there. There was an irony in the fact that he seemed unconsciously to be waiting for Wildman on the patio, reading *The Box*.

Wildman went back down the street and brought the pick-up right into the drive. He checked his equipment, took off his shoes, and went into the kitchen. He could see Hammond by the pool as he took off his top layer of clothing. He had the hypodermic in his waterproof belt bag. He was ready. This was the moment he had been waiting for since he emerged, clear-headed, from the box. In silence, Wildman moved out onto the sunlit patio.

He held the struggling body in his arms, in a swirling and erratic embrace. For a moment it seemed to Wildman as if it was Pandora in his grasp, struggling against her own desire, yearning violently for a release to re-state the primacy of instinct. When Hammond stopped struggling, when he gave in, gave up, surrendered his consciousness to peace, it was as if Pandora herself had relinquished her confusions. There was silence.

Wildman hauled Hammond's drenched clothed body out of the pool. He paused for a few moments to recover his own breathing. He looked round suddenly conscious of being watched. But the pool and patio were completely masked from the view of other houses. The sun was hot in yellow-gray sky, but to Wildman the scene had the chilly seclusion of night.

He carried Hammond into the kitchen. He placed his dripping body carefully on the tiled floor. He bent over him and began to take off his wet clothes. The fabric of his white pants clung to the man's body like a second skin. Wildman tugged and wrenched the clothes away until Hammond was lying naked face down on the floor. Hammond's skin was deathly pale. The pool water seemed to have washed away any color. Wildman examined him. There were small patches of hair on Hammond's shoulders and on his back above the soft buttocks. Wildman could see that he seldom exercised. Ten years from now he'd be flabby. Ten years from now the man would be a dim memory. Wildman turned the body over on its back.

Hammond's circumcised penis was thin like an artist's pencil. Wildman imagined it erect. He could see the penis moving towards Pandora's body. He could see her holding it, taking it to her lips, her hand under the testicles. He felt a wave of revulsion and looked away. He took Hammond's wet clothes and rolled them into a bundle. He wrapped them in two drying-up cloths. He found a roll of plastic clingfilm. He tore off two yards and sealed the bundle inside.

Hammond began to stir. He was coming around. Wildman unzipped the black rubber purse which was belted to his wet suit. He took out a plastic hypodermic syringe and fitted a fresh needle into it. The syringe was full of anaesthetic. Hammond was just starting to open his eyes and choke back to life. The needle punctured his vein inside his left elbow. Hammond gave a soft gasp. Wildman withdrew the needle and held him down firmly for ten seconds while the injection took effect. Hammond lay still again.

Now Wildman stripped off his wet suit. He folded it and put it in his pack. He pulled on his poolman's clothing over his naked body. Now he had to look for something to put Hammond in. Having come into the house in the guise of the poolman he needed something that looked like part of a poolman's equipment to take him away, some wrapping. He left Hammond on the kitchen floor and started to search.

Wildman went upstairs. He was only half-looking for a container or a wrap for the body. He couldn't resist going up to the bedroom. This was the first time he had seen the interior of her house in daylight. The contrast of afternoon light and shadow gave the place a somber charm. He glanced into the daughter's room. Paulette. Her name was on a flowered enamel plate screwed to the door. The shuttered light was instantly nostalgic to Wildman. Florence's room had looked very similar years ago. The bars of light thick with sparkling dust. The adolescent smell of flowers, the presence of furry animals, clothes from early childhood kept long after they were outgrown, framed photographs of parents and pets, equally important. Wildman moved on, up to the next floor.

He wanted to find Pandora asleep as she dreamed of him. He wanted to wake her with a kiss and make her dream reality. He wanted to pick her up, carry her downstairs naked in his arms, still warm with sleep, stop on the landing, kiss her breasts until her nipples changed shape, lick the mascara from her eyelashes until she giggled, lift her thighs to his lowered face and smell her like a flower. There would be dark pollen on his lips and nose as he inhaled her like cocaine, but slowly. He would wait for the rest until he had driven her back to the loft and, having risen in the inhospitable elevator, with her still in his arms, he would lower her onto his bed and she would complete her sleep there as he sank into her like a sun-warmed stone dropping through clear salt water.

Now, watched by Paulette looking quite serious in a shiny black and white framed photograph beside the bed, Wildman selected a few of Pandora's clothes from the hanging closet and dressing table drawers. He was tempted to take the red dress he had given her. He decided it was too dangerous. She would miss it and her suspicions might be aroused. Besides he had another red dress. He took a salmon colored nightgown, a pale green cashmere sweater, a pleated white linen skirt, the bra she had worn with him, and two pairs of white panties, one with lavender lace. From the bathroom he took a fresh cake of Guerlain soap, *Fleurs des Alpes*. When he smelled it he smelled her.

In the garage Wildman found a yellow oilskin sheet. He brought it into the kitchen and wrapped Hammond in it. In two trips he carried his victim, some pool cleaning equipment, the plastic-wrapped bundle of wet clothes, his wet suit, and Pandora's almost weightless garments. The soap was in his pocket.

Wildman backed his pick-up out of the drive, turned in the street, and drove away. He wondered if anyone had seen him. He thought not, hoped not. He got onto the freeway heading downtown. He smiled to himself again at the irony of Hammond reading his screenplay by the pool. When the man woke up he would be in the box, in the screenplay. Funny.

One thing stuck in Wildman's mind, and he didn't know why. The serious face of Pandora's little girl beside the bed watching him as he took her mother's clothes.

Part Four

1

I slept on the plane. The sleep of the dead. I was exhausted. My body felt slack and I ached. I woke when the cabin attendant brought a meal.

The seat next to me was empty. I had put my *People* magazine and a paperback Ludlum on it. I was hungry for new words to read. After lunch I went back to the book. But I couldn't concentrate, not on another conspiracy story. Why were we so obsessed with tales of bad men's conspiracies to conquer the world? We all knew our lives were more or less out of our control, twitching in the laps of the gods. So we stopped believing in the gods. Or God. Now we believe in the stars. Astrology has replaced mythology. Popular progress.

The effect of reading was always to make me want to write. I used to keep a diary. And for years, until my marriage, I was an insatiable letter-writer. Letters were my downfall. Maybe downfall is too strong a word. On one occasion my passion for writing had cost me dearly. I wrote letters to prove I existed. They alleviated my unhappiness, expressed my joy. If you write something down that you feel you seem to control the feeling. Like pain. When you hold the bit that hurts, it helps.

At fifteen, I had an affair with a friend of my father. Or rather, Luke Wright had an affair with me. He used to visit my father on our farm. That was about the time it stopped being a working farm. It had been a family business, but my father never had any real interest in it. He leased the land to a neighbor and concentrated on the only thing that really interested him, Latin poetry. He compiled a book of translations of Horace. He took a dozen of the odes and arranged various translations side by side. There were five or six versions of each poem culled from centuries of Horace enthusiasts. He then added a modern American translation of his own.

My father was fascinated by the idea of an original work which was capable of wide and diverse interpretations. He didn't believe objective truth existed. About anything. He believed we made up our own truths from where we stood. I used to think that was dry, academic stuff and I had no time for it. Recently, I've begun to think that the old man was right. Truth is utterly subjective.

Luke worked as an editor at the Princeton University Press who had published my father's book 'Versions of Horace'. My father took a shine to him and invited him to stay at weekends. In the mornings they would discuss Horace and in the afternoons, while my father took a nap, Luke would come to my room.

I suppose I must have flirted with him. He was about thirty and my father was over fifty. I was flattered that he took an interest in me. The afternoons began habitually with a discussion about my schoolwork. Then it moved on to questions about friends and of course boyfriends. At that time I had never actually gone to bed with a boy. The idea still scared me.

What Luke seemed to want was for me to take my clothes off and change into something else. He told me he wanted me to look more grown-up. Whether I looked more grown-up in a bikini or not I have no idea. But the whole performance gave me a taste for amateur striptease. A taste I've never lost.

Luke drew the line at intercourse. He would hold me, stroke me and suck different parts of my body. He never asked me to do anything to him. I didn't like to take the initiative. I longed to hold his cock which he did not take out of his trousers. I had to imagine it.

It was this desire that started me off writing letters to Luke at his office during the week. To begin with I didn't know whether he received them or not, because he didn't mention anything about them when he saw me. I didn't ask, being too shy, but after several letters in which I begged him to let me touch him, take him in my mouth, come inside me and so on, I panicked. I began to imagine that someone else had opened the letters, a girlfriend, or someone in the office.

One cloudy Sunday afternoon when he was about to leave, I burst into tears of desire and frustration. I had to know if he'd gotten them. I stopped him just as he was driving away. I remember, I leant into the car and asked him point blank. He said yes, he had received them. I said, I don't get it. Then, without expression, he drove off.

I went back into the house, more tears. My father called me into his den.

'I'm ashamed of you,' he said.

'Why? What have I done?'

'Do you understand the meaning of the word trust?'

'Yes.' I understood that word very well.

'Then what are these? What do they mean?'

My father held up a sheaf of papers. I could see immediately what they were. My letters to Luke.

'How did you get them?' I shouted. 'They're none of your business.'

'Luke is a friend of mine, Pandora. You wrote this, this filth to him.'

'And he gave them to you. He gave them to you!' I burst into tears. I was close to being crazy with hate. Luke had given my private letters to my father. It was inconceivable. But it had happened. I wanted to kill Luke.

'Perhaps it all went wrong when your mother died, I don't know.' My father sat down.

'Give them back to me. They're mine!' I tried to grab them from him. He held the letters out of my reach.

'I hate him. I despise you. I want to leave home. I want to get away from here.'

'You've dishonored me.'

'They're private. Private letters.'

'Pandora, you have no sense of honor. Just like your mother.'

That was one of his favorite themes. Honor. I guess it came

from the so-called classical world, where women had no sense of honor. That apparently was a male province. Women had to make do with love.

I couldn't understand why Luke had shown the letters to my father. I was too young to understand that men, given the chance, respected each other more than they respected women. Men had honor. Luke's betrayal was the bitterest of my life. Still is. It was a matter of honor.

Some years later I figured Luke and my father had had some kind of homosexual affair. I didn't like the idea. It seemed like a betrayal. But of what I wasn't sure. It was just that my father had never had a good word for women. Not even for my mother. He didn't try to replace her. I don't remember him inviting a woman home. Only men. Young men.

My father had found this nice young man at Princeton. They liked each other. Luke had never talked to me of his women friends. I assumed that that was discretion. But why would he enjoy coming so often to see an old man for the weekend? Why wasn't Luke out there punching beaver, as it used to be called. I had imagined that Luke secretly came to the house to see me. Whereas, all the time, he and my father . . . It was incredible. Luke never returned to our farm. I got over him, but I never forgave him.

There was a driver waiting for me at the airport in Portland, Maine. The guy held up a small blackboard with the name chalked on it. MRS HARTEN HAMMOND. My father liked to include his own name like that. He wanted to remind me of his power. The driver's blackboard was mine, from my nursery at home, given to me by my father when I was six to write Latin words on. He loved rubbing out my mistakes.

The journey from Portland to Rochester, New Hampshire, took about an hour and a half. As always for me it was a trip back into the past. There had been so many occasions for it. From school. From New York. From trips to Europe. Sometimes I arrived in Boston, Mass. For some reason New Hampshire could never be reached directly. You always had to go to another state first. New Hampshire was a place that didn't quite exist. It was a geographical image for the past. Eventually I started calling it Old Hampshire. I sometimes called our white wood house my Tara, sometimes my Manderley. One day I would inherit it. But I'd never live there again.

For the first time my father didn't come out to greet me as we drove up. I was immediately worried. He had not been well last time I came back. His eyes had gotten worse and he had started to use two sticks instead of one to help him walk. I could see my childhood crumbling in front of me.

Matilda, his housekeeper, greeted me. She was pleased to see me, I thought. I didn't like Matilda. She was looking forward to his death and her legacy.

'Your father hasn't been too well. I'm glad you came, Miss Pandora.'

Father struggled to his feet as I came into the drawing room. He slipped against the shiny brown leather chair, his dry hand squeaking on it as he fell back. He was unhurt, but he looked as if he'd been struck by lightning. I noticed he had two shaving cuts. I apologized as if it had been my fault.

'He's been very excited. He knew you were coming.' A woman's voice. But not Matilda's.

I saw her standing on the far side of the drawing room in shadow. She was about twenty-five, looked like a librarian with her owl glasses. She actually held a book in her hand.

'I'm Elaine French,' she said with a Boston accent. 'I was just reading to Mr Harten.'

'Hello. I'm Pandora.'

I could now understand how I had missed Miss French as I came into the drawing room. I'd been worried about my father and had thought of nothing else.

'Miss French comes to read to me,' my father said with some pride, as if she had asked to do it.

'Don't let me interrupt you,' I said.

'It's almost time for me to be gone,' said Miss French. I thought she sounded relieved, but I could have been mistaken.

I watched her cycling away from the bay window. I turned to my father.

'It's nice you've got someone to read to you,' I said.

He was asleep. I didn't wake him. I examined the book Miss French had had in her hand. *The Woman Of Andros* by Thornton Wilder. I'd never heard of it. I checked the publication date. It was an early work, written before *The Bridge on the San Luis Rey*. I wondered if it was also about destiny.

My father was a dying man. It was an inescapable fact. I saw that during dinner. He hardly spoke. He was pleased to have my company, but he was alone behind his eyes. His brandy was his real friend. I was really depressed.

'Do you ever think about your mother?' He suddenly asked me as Matilda poured the coffee.

'Not often.' I had to admit it. Maybe that wasn't the right answer, but I didn't care. I had no real picture of her other than the portrait on the stairs.

'I guess not,' he said. 'She was here last night. But I was asleep. So I didn't get to see her.'

My father got to his feet, wobbling inside and out, and started to blow out the candles. Matilda took over.

'That book I'm reading reminds me a lot of your mother.'

That was the last thing my father said before going slowly, painfully and hopelessly up the stairs to bed. To dream again of my mother, perhaps. And then find a way to deny it. I let Matilda go to bed as well. It was only nine o'clock. I went into the downstairs toilet and burst into tears.

I couldn't find *The Woman Of Andros* in the library. I tracked it down in his den. I read a few pages. It was the story of a prostitute on a Greek island B.C. Was that how he saw my mother?

I looked around his den. I was looking for clues. I wanted to find out what had killed him. A detective in the library. Who or what killed my father? The change in him seemed so dramatic from the last time. It didn't occur to me for a moment that he was actually much the same as the last time, and that it was I who had in fact changed. Subjectivity is a hard discipline.

I opened a book I remembered my father had given to me when I was at Sarah Lawrence. *A Smaller Classical Dictionary* by William Smith LLD. 'To Pandora, my one daughter, affectionately, Father.' That was the inscription. This edition was printed in 1910. Originally, it had been published in the nineteenth century. There wasn't a date. The flyleaf merely said 'The first edition of this book (100,000 copies) being already exhausted, a second edition is hereby issued.' Is that comparatively more than Robert Ludlum sells today in hardback?

I opened the *Classical Dictionary* and turned, as I did when I first received it, to page 377 and the entry, PANDORA, the name of the first woman on earth.

'When Prometheus had stolen the fire from heaven, Zeus in revenge caused Hephaestus to make a woman out of earth, who by her charms and beauty should bring misery upon the human race. Aphrodite adorned her with beauty; Hermes bestowed upon her boldness and cunning; and the gods called her Pandora, or "All-gifted", as each of the gods had given her some power by which she was to work the ruin of man.

'Hermes took her to Epimetheus, who made her his wife, forgetting the advice of his brother, Prometheus, not to receive any gifts from the gods. Pandora brought with her from heaven a box containing every human ill, upon opening which they all escaped and spread over the earth, Hope alone remaining.

'At a still later period the box is said to have contained all the blessings of the gods, which would have been preserved for the human race, had not Pandora opened the vessel, so that the winged blessings escaped.'

I closed the book. I had long since ceased to care about the first woman on earth, and all the classical references to her evil. Bull. I liked my name, with its two parts. I preferred it to Eve, who was also bad from the word go. During the course of this evening my father hadn't once called me Pan, as he usually did. But neither had he called me Pandora. Tonight it had just been 'you'.

I looked at his recent writing, a translation of Ovid's *The Art Of Love*. I knew he would never finish it now. I started opening his desk drawers out of boredom as much as nosiness. I found piles of letters in envelopes. One old pile was wrapped in silver ribbon. I couldn't resist looking at it. I knew they had to be treasured love letters, maybe from my mother.

As I read them I shivered. My skin prickled. They were my letters to Luke Wright. My father had kept them all these years. He had probably read them over. I was dizzy. I didn't know what to think. I read bits and pieces of them.

Why had he kept them? I couldn't let him keep them. I put them away in my handbag. Fuck him. Talk about betrayal. I could have left the house then and there.

On my way upstairs to bed a thought struck me. I stopped climbing. I saw what had happened. My father had instructed Luke to come to my room while he took his naps. He told him to undress me. Then later Luke had told my father what had happened. All the details of how I looked. No, that was going too far. My father wasn't that sick. He just wasn't. No. NO. But Luke had given him the letters. And he had kept them.

I finally fell asleep in my old room with the small ceramic plaque on the door which said 'Pandora'. I slept in my old hand-painted bed, surrounded by ducks and lupins and rabbits, all pale green and yellow, chipped now. This was where I had undressed for Luke. And for my father.

I went angrily to sleep. I started to dream, stopped, awoke, then began again, a different dream, another story, alternative characters. Dream is pure fiction, of course, and resists realistic interpretation. He came into me again. The man with the scar.

Now I was living with him. Paulette was there too but she was grown-up, only a few years younger than I. I was some sort of writer and lived by the ocean. He had a job but I don't know what it was. He came and went during the day, sometimes in the middle of the night. In my dream I would wake, frightened to find him beside me in bed. The silence came and went. Somehow, I had become used to it, like a small cold that wouldn't clear up. There was sex but it was all written down, not acted out. It was perfectly satisfying. We wrote and sometimes spoke sex to each other, a kind of pornography. The crisis that woke me was when I found him fucking Paulette. I watched them on several occasions without getting angry. God knows why. Then I confronted Paulette. We fought. I strangled her. When she was dead I realized that he had left. I was alone. It was horrible. I woke shaking, terrified.

The sense of being alone, left alone, abandoned, stayed with me as I showered and got dressed. I had the feeling it would never go away. Then it occurred to me that something was missing from my dream, as far as I could remember. Alec hadn't been there. It was as if he was forgotten or dead or never existed. Scared, I called home. He wasn't there. I panicked. Where was he? The machine wasn't on. I called again, thinking I might have dialed a wrong number. This time I got the machine. I listened to his voice. 'We're both out at the moment, but please leave a message and we'll get back to you as soon as possible.' I left a message telling him how I loved him and missed him. I was pathetically relieved. The dream was pure fiction. Pure nonsense.

When I got downstairs breakfast was set out on the dining room table. Matilda was hovering. My father had not yet appeared.

'Your car's been ordered for eleven o'clock,' she said.

'Thank you.' I wished it was there now.

Last night I had planned to confront my father with what I'd discovered. I wanted to tell him he was an asshole. When I thought about all his strictures and moralizing to me about my loose behavior, and the constant classical references designed to make me feel shitty and corrupt, I felt physically sick. Now I couldn't eat the eggs. I longed for some frozen yoghurt. I ate the pineapple instead.

When he appeared a quarter of an hour later, he looked so frail, so helpless with his two canes and thick glasses, I felt sorry for him. I couldn't be contemptuous of his wasted life. His dreams of bringing Ovid and *The Art Of Love* within the reach of the modern American reader of Robert Ludlum seemed not just fanciful but downright ridiculous.

He thanked me for coming to see him. He asked how Alec was doing.

'I never go to the movies,' he said, 'but I sometimes watch things on TV.'

After breakfast we went into the library and said nothing to each other. He read yesterday's *Boston Examiner* with the aid of a heavy rectangular magnifying glass. He had not only grown much older since I last saw him, he now smelt too, that dandruffy smell of old age. I couldn't wait to leave.

My father didn't come to the door to see me off. I hadn't really expected him to. My last memory of him was this crumpled old man, half-asleep in his chair with last night's cognac, probably waiting for the girl to come on her bike and read him some more to keep him alive.

On the flight west I re-read my love letters to Luke Wright. I had forgotten almost everything I had written. They were sex letters really, wildly explicit and very clumsy. I was struck by how my handwriting hadn't changed at all over the years.

2

The sun was way down when my taxi from LAX exited the freeway at Century City. I was looking forward to getting home, achingly wanting to be with Alec and Paulette. The Sunday evening traffic was heavy. I was impatient. It was one of those commonplace gold and mauve California sunsets that makes everything seem symbolic. To me at that moment it represented a solid and warm security, the equivalent of a burning log fire in New Hampshire.

I overtipped the driver and hurried to the front door. Our three cars were parked, two in the garage, one outside the house. So they were home. Great. I don't know how long it took to grasp the fact that the house was empty, and the truth that something awful had happened. When there was no answer to my calls for Alec and Paulette, I ran, stumbled from room to room, upstairs and down, terrified suddenly that I would find their dead or mutilated bodies. All those news reports of family massacres, those stalk-and-slash movies, those headlines and pictures of other people's deaths, filled my vision like a hideous spread in a Sunday magazine.

When I ended my panicked search on the patio, I began to relax in a breathless way. There were no dead bodies. I thanked God. They were out somewhere having dinner. That was it. It had to be. But then it was odd that Alec hadn't left me a note. He usually did. And how had they gone to dinner without taking a car? No. They must have gone with someone else, someone who had come by and picked them up. Who could I call to check, to find out? I felt sick, nauseous. I sat heavily in a chair beside the pool. On the table was a screenplay called *The Box* and some notes Alec must have made in his usual way, with a couple of rough sketches.

At the precise moment I decided to call Clarisse Balfour and make sure Paulette had been picked up, the phone beside the pool rang. I rushed over to grab it, knocking the chair sideways. It was a woman's voice.

'Mrs Hammond? We've been so worried.'

'Who is this?'

'This is Clarisse Balfour.'

'Oh. Is Paulette there?'

'Yes she is. We were getting worried. She thought your husband was going to pick her up after lunch.'

'I'm so sorry. I don't know what happened. Alec's not here. I'll come over right away. Tell Paulette I'm coming. I'm so sorry.'

I drove fast and badly to Bel Air. The sunset was over. It was now a smoky dusk. For no good reason I hated it. I was relieved that Paulette was there, but where was Alec? Perhaps Paulette knew. She must know something.

But she didn't. I could see she was shaken.

'Maybe Dad just forgot.'

'That's not likely, is it?' Mrs Balfour said.

'He didn't get my UFO book.'

'He must have been held up somewhere,' I said desperately. Then I thought, shit I didn't check the machine. Alec would have called from wherever he was. Why didn't I think of that?

I gulped the gin and tonic Clarisse had given me, thanked her and got to my car with Paulette as fast as I could. In the car I was the nervous child, Paulette the consoling mom.

'I'm sure Dad's fine. He just forgot.'

'No, he wouldn't forget.' How could he, knowing I was away?

'Slow down, Mom.'

I tried to but I couldn't. It was darker now, outside and in my mind too. I wanted to cry. Calm down, Pandora.

'Mom, just don't worry. Dad can look after himself.'

There was nothing from Alec on the machine. I listened like

an idiot to my own message to Alec. In the kitchen the vodka bottle was half empty. I stared at it. He'd gotten drunk, gotten into a fight, was lying hurt somewhere. Call the police. No, it's too soon. Maybe not. When did he leave the house? Why didn't he take the car? I poured a drink, didn't bother with the ice. Think carefully and clearly. He didn't take the car because he was too drunk to drive. Good. So he went somewhere in a taxi. Yes, that's what happened. Of course, Alec took a taxi. But where? And why, why the fuck didn't he call?

Paulette was in the tub in our bathroom. I put a towel around her as she got out and hugged her tightly, steadying myself, not drying her.

'Are you hungry, Mom?'

'No darling. Are you? I'll fix you some supper.'

'I'm stuffed.'

'So you enjoyed yourself.'

'It was great. I loved spending the night away. It was like a hotel.'

When Paulette was in bed I called the police. They took down all the details.

'Has this ever happened before?'

'No. Of course not. Never.'

I could hear in the sergeant's tone of voice that he thought I was worrying unnecessarily. Well, maybe I was, but how could I help it?

Having thought I would never get to sleep I went out like a light. Paulette woke me the next morning, Monday, to take her to school. I was still in my clothes. In the car I burst into tears. It was stupid in front of Paulette, but I couldn't stop myself. It was pathetic. In the space of a few hours she had seen her stable, confident mother collapse into a shaking creature. It hadn't taken much, had it Pandora? I could see the extent to which I depended on Alec. His disappearance threatened me. Even though Paulette was safe. Yet in a way it wasn't just Alec. I was sure he would re-appear. I knew the mystery would be cleared up. It was my home, my life at home, the stability of it all, all of that was under threat. It was somehow connected to the discovery about my father. That betrayal, so long ago, had affected me as if it were now, in the present. Everything seemed so insecure, so fragile.

It was all impossible. I felt nauseous again. I was in a jigsaw. I struggled, tortured by the shapes that wouldn't fit. There was no border, no frame to it, no guide in the design. There was no box for the pieces. Crazy connections came into my mind. My dirty letters to Luke all those years ago, which I now had stuffed in my purse, they suddenly belonged to the present, to all of this. They could easily represent my feelings for the man in the Bel Air bungalow. The letters were fantasies, things I had only wanted to do with Luke. But I had actually done those things with the man just a few weeks ago. Had that been some obscure wish-fulfilment realized only after twenty years? Crazy. Crazy.

The next day an unsmiling detective came by to get more details of Alec's disappearance. I felt stupid. I couldn't add anything to what I'd already told the sergeant on the phone.

'How old is your husband?'

'Thirty-eight. He'll be thirty-nine in December.'

'How long have you been married?'

'Thirteen years.'

I looked at the man. There was something distracted, bored even, in his voice and manner. This was not his favorite work.

'What's the most common reason for people . . . people who disappear?' I was looking for reassurance. How I expected to get it from this guy I didn't know.

'There's no one reason. I guess most people who disappear do it deliberately.'

'Deliberately?'

'They're running away from something.'

'What things?' Did he mean their partners?

'Debts mostly.'

'Alec doesn't owe money.'

It wasn't boredom I had detected in his manner. It was contempt. He didn't like me.

'You're the person most likely to know the reason, Mrs Hammond.'

'I don't know.'

He made some notes, glancing around the living room. What had he seen? A clue? Or was he just checking me out, the way I lived?

'Had you had a quarrel?'

'No. Never.'

'Never? That's remarkable. Now, I have to ask you some personal questions.'

'Go ahead.' How personal?

'Has your husband ever attempted suicide?'

I was shocked. 'No. Never.'

'Never. As far as you know.'

'Well, yes. But I would know, wouldn't I?'

'You say he has no debts. But did he ever speculate or gamble?'

'Alec hates gambling.' It was true, Alec had an aversion to gambling. He'd hated our one trip to Vegas. A senseless waste of money.

'Has he made a will?'

'A will?' These were questions I hadn't even thought of asking. What did they mean? 'Yes, I think he has.'

'Do you know who the beneficiary is?'

I felt cold. The implication of this question was clear.

'I am. At least, I assume I am.'

'That's natural.'

I went on the defensive. 'But in fact I have money of my own. Private money.'

Now his distaste was clear. He nodded as if to say 'I thought so'.

'I understand you were out of town when your husband disappeared.'

'I was in New Hampshire visiting my father. I can prove that if you're suggesting –'

'I'm not suggesting anything, Mrs Hammond. I'm trying to help you. That's all.'

'Yes.' I despised this man. Why was murder always the first thought? Was money always the primary motive?

'Do you know if your husband was having an affair?'

'No I don't know.' I was mad now. 'Of course he wasn't having an affair.'

'I have to ask.'

Yes, and you love it, don't you? I couldn't wait to get rid of the guy. He gave me the creeps.

'Look, I know as much about my husband as it's possible to know. We're happily married. It's as simple as that.'

'These aren't accusations, Mrs Hammond. Just questions. You want your husband back, don't you? It may be that he had an accident. It could be as simple as that. But there's no report of his being found so we have to consider other possibilities.'

'I've told you what I know. There's just no more I can tell you.'

'One last question. And please try not to be aggressive, Mrs Hammond.'

'I'm not aggressive. I'm horribly worried, that's all.'

'Is there anything you can think of that you might have done that could've caused your husband to leave?'

'What sort of thing?'

'Were you, are you, having an affair?'

'No. No. And what would that have to do with anything?'

'I'm looking for a motive for his leaving home.'

'No. No affair. Nothing.'

'Good.'

He left, leaving the smell of his aftershave with me. I went upstairs. I sat down on my bed. I was drowning in fears. I suddenly saw from the outside that Alec's disappearance could be interpreted in a dozen ways. And they all seemed to lead back to me. I was implicated.

I had to talk to someone. Beverly came over. I told her what had happened. I could see in her face that she thought it was a woman, another woman. Alec had run off with a woman. It had to be on her mind after her discovery of Jimbo's infidelity.

'I don't believe it's a woman,' I said suddenly.

'I didn't say that.' Beverly's tone wasn't convincing.

'That's what you thought.'

'It's a possibility. You may have to face it.'

'I won't. I can't. A thing like that I'd know.'

'That's what I thought. But I didn't know. Some men are hard to read.'

I had never had a moment of sexual jealousy in my life with Alec. Not once. But what about that man at the Bel Air? That had never happened to me before. Beverly was right. Everything was possible. Supposing Alec had met a woman. A sudden thing, just like that. Except that he hadn't come home. He'd gone on. Gone away. With her.

3

Hammond felt he had come back from the dead. In the blackness of the box he recovered a sort of consciousness. His fractured memory didn't feel like a collection of pictures from an exhibition of his past. It was more like a shopping list, a plan for things to do. There were faces. Dora, asking how it went. How what went, he didn't know. Paulette, angry with him for having forgotten something. Forgotten what? Her birthday perhaps. There was a memory of his mother, just a burning photograph, his father drunk, holding a flaming Zippo. Things gone, things undone and, most worrying, a sense of purpose that he couldn't identify.

He moved his arms and felt the sides of the box. There came an agonising twist of pain in his right calf. A breathtaking cramp. He thrashed from side to side. The pain in his leg stretched to snapping. He banged his hands against the interior of the box, trying to create new pain to rid himself of the other. He was a hopeless knot unable to stretch and untie itself. There was no imagining in him, no help inside or out. He was all tension, an insect trapped and wounded. After a while, minutes or hours, he relapsed again into unconsciousness.

Wildman had bought two pairs of swimming goggles. He had carefully painted their lenses black. In movies you always made two of everything in case something went wrong. They were called repeats. He'd followed the details of his screenplay closely. He put one pair of goggles around Hammond's head, then tied his hands behind his back and bound his ankles together. He used the strongest mountain climber's rope. It was bright orange and a half inch thick. He folded Hammond's naked body ready to ease into the open box. Looking down at the man's genitals he suddenly felt it looked wrong. He didn't want to see Hammond's penis flopping about. Or perhaps he didn't want Laura to see it like that. Not yet anyway.

Laura knew nothing of the kidnap. Wildman wasn't sure how she'd react. He hoped she would just accept it. He needed her later. There hadn't been a woman in his screenplay, not until about half-way through. It was essentially a story of men. Maybe one day he would re-write the script, the way Pandora was re-writing his life. The thought made him momentarily uneasy. It implied that she had some control over these events whereas she was totaly innocent of them. This was his story.

Wildman dressed Hammond in a pair of his own undershorts before putting him into the box and locking it. While the anaesthetic wore off he fed the dogs. He gave Hammond six hours before doing anything more. He bathed and re-read his screenplay. Then it was night.

INTERIOR. LOFT. NIGHT

Hammond, bound hand and foot, wearing black painted goggles, is dragged by Wildman across the floor. Wildman sits in an old leather chair. He prods his victim with a pole he uses to adjust the ventilator. They are alone.

Hammond: (*gasps*) What do you want from me?

Wildman: We want you to understand.

Hammond: (*confused*) Understand? Understand what?

Wildman: That your life is about to change.

Hammond: (*nervously*) What do you mean?

Wildman: We want you to adjust to new circumstances. You will no longer be living the way you have.

Hammond: (*angry*) You're crazy. What has this got to do with Betty May?

Wildman: Very little. We have a different situation now. There are, however, certain things you will be allowed to keep.

Hammond: (*hopefully*) Is it money you want?

Wildman: That's your first thought, isn't it? Money. The root of everything. This has nothing to do with money. You can keep your precious money. You can keep your house too. We won't want it.

Hammond: (*uneasy*) We? Who's we? Is there someone with you?

Wildman: Yes. There is. Her name is Pandora.

Hammond: (*scared*) Pandora? What are you talking about?

Wildman: Your wife. Former wife.

Hammond: (*hysterical*) My wife! You fuck. You're lying.

Silence. Wildman says nothing.

Hammond: (*controlled*) My wife's away. Out of town.

Wildman: She's back.

Hammond: (*defiant*) She won't be back till Monday.

Wildman: This is Wednesday. You've been out of touch.

Hammond: (*shaky*) What do you want with my wife? I don't believe any of this.

Wildman: It's very simple. I've taken your wife away from you. She's mine now. You'll have to find someone else.

Wildman prods Hammond in the crotch with his pole. Hammond reacts, wriggling away.

Hammond: Where is she?

Wildman: She's asleep in our bed.

Hammond: Our bed! Where is she?

Wildman: Rancho Park Drive.

Hammond: That's my house.

Wildman: Technically perhaps. But I'm staying there for the time being. Until Pandora and I find a more suitable place. We're thinking of moving to the beach. As a matter of fact that was her idea. I like it.

Hammond: You're crazy. You're fucking nuts.

Wildman: On the subject of nuts, that's part of the problem. It's my nuts she wants. Not yours.

Hammond: OK, OK. Now just tell me what it is you want. Let's cut out the crap.

Wildman: You're the crap. And that's exactly what I intend to do. Cut you out. I know you pretty well now. You won't want Pandora after I've finished with you. Remember Betty May? What you did to her I'm doing to your wife. They like the same things. Pandora's found out she likes rough treatment. She comes lying face down. She's never known anything like it.

Hammond: You cunt. You fucking cunt.

Wildman: Just listen. You know what she likes best? When I take it out of her ass she begs to suck it clean. That's her favorite thing. So far. You didn't know you were married to a whore, did you?

Hammond: Shut up. Shut up. You're lying, you fucking shit.

Wildman: Don't shout. I can hear you. I know this must have come as something of a shock. But in time you'll come to accept it. I know you will. Then you can start a new life.

Hammond: I'm not listening to this shit. I know what you're trying to do. It's not going to work. You want to fight, I'll fight anywhere, any time.

Wildman: You've got a short memory. We did that. You lost. You had your time with her. Now it's over. It's history. That's what you are, Hammond. History.

Wildman stands up and pushes the pole firmly into the victim's groin. The victim's mouth screams.

CUT:

Something was moving across his skin. Things were digging into his chest. They were soft. Unidentifiable. Then they became sharp.

The things dug into his skin, his chest muscles, around his nipples. He opened his eyes as his consciousness increased. The blackness remained. Open-eyed, he was blind. He struggled to remember. Nothing came to mind. His breathing was erratic. The only part of him that he could move freely was the tongue in his mouth.

The things scraped down towards his navel, through the hair on his stomach. He tried to move his hands. They were roped together behind his back. As he twisted them he inadvertently freed his memory. Some of it. The tightness of the ropes prompted his memory of the tight blindfold. He had forgotten why he couldn't see.

The things probed his abdomen. They pinched his softer flesh. Fingers. The things were fingers. The sharp parts were fingernails. Too sharp for a man's hand. Too delicate. The muscles in his chest became tense with the promise of pain. It was Betty May. Betty May had returned from the dead. She was crawling over him. As the fingers reached his groin he panicked. This was her revenge. Now her fingers terrorised him. The nails scraped his penis. He cried out in imagined anguish. He knew what was going to happen. She was going to tear him to pieces.

Violently, he twisted and turned. He tried to thrash himself free. He wanted to hit her, to kick her away. But the torture was relentless, inescapable. He could imagine nothing except what was happening now and what was going to happen next. Strangely, Wildman didn't figure in it. Her fingernails touched his balls. He screamed. He could feel the vengeful hands tearing his genitals from his abdomen. Then something penetrated his sick fear.

A smell entered his consciousness. He sniffed. The scent was pervasive, increased by his sightlessness. It was an acute perfume. He tried desperately to place it. That scent. It was familiar. He knew it. A flowery freshness. Where did it come from? The struggle to remember gave him some respite from his terror. He fought fear with memory. The nails scratched circles on the flesh on the inside of his quivering thigh. Then he knew. Something in that movement prompted his memory. Dora. It was Dora's scent. Her bath soap. That's what it was. His mind seized up. It wasn't Betty May. It was Dora. He could no longer struggle against the fingers. He was lost.

As Wildman had hoped Laura accepted what he called his house guest. How could she do otherwise? But inwardly it scared her. She had no direct fear of Wildman. She knew him so well. She began to fear the incursion of the outside world. Kidnapping was a federal offence. Wildman's obsession with the woman was one thing. This was something else. The police would see her as an accessory, an accomplice. It was all going way beyond the

176

rules of the game. It was scary. Laura was only partly reassured by Wildman's calm certainty in what he was doing.

His instructions to her had been 'Take him to the edge, but don't let him come.' He had told her to wash herself first, using the cake of *Fleurs des Alpes*. He had not told her it was Pandora's soap. He gave her the underwear he had taken from Pandora's bedroom. The panties fit perfectly. The bra was loose. Laura felt awkward. In all their previous games and rituals Wildman had never asked her to touch another man. Since meeting him she had not had sex with anyone else. She hadn't wanted to. Her one irrepressible desire was to please him. If this was what he wanted she would perform without question.

She felt as she imagined a prostitute must feel, except that the reward here was not money. The payment was pleasure. Not hers. His. It was a sharp sensation, half making love to another man, someone she didn't want or even know. Feeling the flesh of a man who was blindfolded and with his hands tied was like performing an operation. She tried to remember him dressed as he had been on the highway when she picked him up. But this was a different man.

Hammond helplessly responded to her caresses. His legs twitched, his cock hardened, his back stiffened, his breathing became irregular. He wet his dry mouth. Laura watched him beside her, under her, as she moved around him. She suddenly felt the power she had over him. Surprisingly, she herself became aroused. Aware of being watched by Wildman she didn't know whether this was permitted. Was it what he secretly wanted? Should she show her feeling? She wondered if her growing excitement was the result of being observed. It was voyeurism in reverse, not watching but being watched.

Hammond's face was contorted in imagined pain. Laura took it as pleasure. As her hands twisted around his penis the torture of desire took hold of him. The woman's covered breasts touched his forehead, his cheeks, his lips. He opened his mouth, not to speak but to grasp the warm material pressed into it. He tried to suck, but the breasts moved away. He groaned in his dizziness. A hand gently squeezed his balls. A tongue licked his

177

cock. He was close to exploding as a mouth enfolded the head.

Wildman took Laura by the shoulders and firmly pulled her away. Kneeling beside Hammond's body she turned to him. Wildman was standing naked behind her. She took his hard penis into her mouth.

Hammond ached with frustration. Where was the mouth? He could hear the sucking sounds close by. He could hear a man's groaning. He could smell Pandora's soapy scent. Pandora.

'Leave her alone,' he gasped. 'You cunt. Leave her alone!'

As Wildman came he whispered one word: 'Pandora.'

Hammond thrashed about on the floor of the loft. He was in a fury. Wildman had fucked his wife. He knew it. It wasn't some crazy invention of a madman. It was fact. When he got out of this he'd kill him. He'd kill the cunt. This time for sure.

He was raving, shouting, open-mouthed like a madman. He felt Dora's hands on his chest. She was bending over him. He whispered her name. Her lips touched his. Then he felt the sticky substance on her mouth. She pushed some of it into his mouth with her tongue and breathed the rest into him. Hammond spat violently. But it was too late. He couldn't get it out of his mouth. He screamed, Dora, and as he screamed he choked. And as he choked Wildman went down his throat. And on slowly into his body.

4

Alec had found out. That was it. Pandora knew it. He had found out about her and the man at the Bel Air. Shocked, disgusted, betrayed, he'd walked out on her. Pandora tried to imagine his state of mind. He would be desperate, speechless, vengeful. That's why he hadn't called. Maybe he had gone on a bender. Maybe he was with another woman. He had a reason. Her. He had found out that his devoted wife Dora was really promiscuous Pan, her dark and pagan other self. Her divided nature was responsible for his leaving. Pandora had no one to blame but herself.

How Alec had found out wasn't important now. Perhaps he'd somehow traced the red dress. Perhaps he had spoken to a waiter at the Bel Air. Perhaps Beverly had found out, and, in her own jealousy and misery over Jimbo, she had told him. It simply didn't matter how Alec had come to know. He knew. That was enough.

Pandora had never been self-pitying. It was her strength. As a child she never cried, except in physical pain. Now even in her extreme unhappiness tears wouldn't come. She was guilty but she accepted the responsibility for her actions. She might have wished it had been different, that she hadn't done it. But she had, and it couldn't be undone. In moments of cold reason she told herself that Alec would have to accept it too. It wasn't the end of the world. There were times in the days after his disappearance when she felt anger towards him. She told herself that his running away was cowardly. Alec ought to be able to take it, to face it. Remembering his drinking days, she could see the weakness in him, his desire to escape reality. She didn't like these feelings. She knew she was blaming the victim for a crime, an easy escape from guilt. She understood the psychological twist of it. She recognized the perversity of the feeling. She was aware of the lie it contained. But it was there in her mind and undeniable. There were times when she despised Alec for what she had done.

Pandora had no one to talk to, so she addressed herself. She became her own mirror. For a week after Alec's departure her only companion was her daughter. If Paulette had been a bit older she might have talked it out with her. Paulette was super-intelligent and a good friend, but she was twelve years old. Under no circumstances would Pandora ever undermine Paulette's love for her father. Alec was a good father, a good husband, a good man.

They both missed him. Mealtimes were sad affairs with just the two of them. Bedtime became distressing. Pandora found ways to compensate, she thought, for Alec's absence. She spent time in the kitchen cooking special meals. Of course, Paulette noticed it. There was way too much food on the table and it was made more evident because Pandora herself hardly ate anything. She drank much more wine now but it had less effect than before.

Pandora washed Paulette's clothes before it was necessary. Even the maid remarked on the piles of ironing. There was more work for her with just two people in the house than there had been when Mr Hammond was at home. Pandora started taking Paulette to school earlier than was necessary. Then she would be waiting outside the yard fifteen minutes before the children were released.

Paulette was embarrassed by her mother's attentions but she stifled it. She saw her role now as her mother's best friend. There were times when she longed to get away from school, from home, to be with David Wing. She missed her father less when she was thinking of David, imagining them together. She longed to go and stay with him but she knew that was impossible now with her dad away. Deep down Paulette believed her dad was dead, that he'd had some kind of accident and had been killed. She wondered if Pandora thought that too. But she kept silent. David suggested that she consult a Chinese psychic, who was a family friend, to find out for sure. Paulette wanted to suggest this to Pandora but she didn't dare. Not even when her mother bought her the book on UFO's her dad had promised but never gotten around to. There were increasingly long periods of silence between mother and daughter. They were running out of things to say.

Every day Pandora called the police. After a week it became an empty ritual. She asked for news when what she really wanted was to tell everything she knew or guessed. When she passed the local church which looked, as Alec had told her, like a bank, she considered going inside. Occasionally, she felt a compulsion to confess. She came close to telling Beverly everything. But she was vaguely suspicious of Beverly. She cried off tennis. In her mind Beverly was associated with the Bel Air.

Pandora couldn't concentrate on her reading. She dipped into novels but every time there was a scene of love-making she stopped. She had no sexual desire. It had all drained away. Just like the fat in her body. In the first week she lost five pounds. And it showed. In her face, her upper arms, her thighs and most noticeably in her breasts. Her bras became uncomfortable. She couldn't bring herself to buy any new ones. She wore less make-up. She dressed severely. She swept her hair back. She aged a couple of years. She consciously suffered. She began to think of herself as a widow.

Instead of tennis she went to her gun club. Shooting was something she could do alone. The trip to Sherman Oaks gave her a target. She spoke to no one at the club. She stayed an hour or more, firing, firing, firing at the enigmatic colored circles. Wearing her black ear muffs to baffle the sound of her weapon, brought back memories of her bouts of deafness. She waited for the moments of silence, but for some reason they didn't come.

They would be useful now that she wanted to block things out.

One morning Pandora woke up feeling suddenly fresh, much less depressed. Not having eaten anything to speak of for several days she suddenly felt like food. Not the little comfort of frozen yoghurt but a proper meal, three courses and a whole bottle of wine. She decided on The Ritz, a cajun style place west of Beverly Hills. She made a reservation for lunch, just for herself. She stopped off and bought a book on the way, a nice, fresh print-smelling novel: *Wildlife* by Richard Ford.

Pandora mopped up the remains of her gumbo appetiser. She was eight pages into the novel. She was struck by a coincidence. Here she was eating at a cajun place and the story she was reading was set in New Orleans. Odd. She looked up, sensing the presence of a waiter. The man stood there smiling pleasantly at her.

Pandora's heart missed a beat. Her hair prickled. It wasn't possible. Until he spoke she held on to the idea she was imagining him.

'Hello,' he said. 'I didn't mean to startle you.'

Pandora feared for her voice, that she wouldn't be able to control it. Her conscious mind blacked out. It was jammed with memory, obscenities. Take hold of yourself, for Christ's sake. She spoke but couldn't hear what she said. She was engulfed in silence. She was staring at his face like an idiot trying to read his lips. He was speaking but she heard nothing. He was looking at her, a question on his face. What was the question? She hadn't heard it. So she couldn't answer. Now she was dumb as well as deaf. It was a nightmare. Pandora prayed for sound. She screamed for noise. It came with his voice.

'Are you all right?'

'Yes. Yes. I'm fine.'

'Were you expecting someone?'

'No. I'm alone.'

'Do you mind if I sit down?'

She shook her head, tried to smile. Wildman eased himself gracefully into the booth, sitting opposite her.

'How have you been? Still playing tennis at the Bel Air?'

She had to find ways to answer his questions. She felt now

like an embarrassed, scared little girl. Say anything. Just speak, for God's sake. Anything.

'You were right about the dress. It does suit me.'

'Good. I thought it would.' He paused, wondering whether to risk the next step. He'd have to face it some time. Why not now?

'Look, my name's Charles. Charles Wildman.'

Pandora suddenly realized she'd never tried to give him a name before. She hadn't even guessed at it, or tried to invent one. She just thought of him anonymously, as the man. The man with the scar.

'I'm Pandora. Pandora Harten.'

Why had she said that? She wasn't trying to conceal her married name. It had just slipped out quite naturally. Yet it wasn't natural. She never used her unmarried name. Did it mean she didn't want to be married, not with him? Was she ashamed of Alec? Did it have something to do with her trip home?

Wildman was surprised. Why had she invented a name for herself? He saw she was fingering her wedding ring. Who was Harten? Had she been married before? Maybe it was her maiden name. He hadn't thought about her as anything other than Hammond's wife. Whatever it was, it was a good sign. He had been truthful. She had been evasive. He had the advantage.

'Pandora's an unusual name.'

'My father was, is a classical scholar. He chose it.'

'Pandora was the first woman. In Greek mythology. It's like the Judaic Eve.'

Pandora remembered the books on the classical world in the bungalow. A curious thing to have in common.

'I like this place too,' he said. 'I got to appreciate Cajun food when I was working in Louisiana.'

'I've never been to Louisiana.' She didn't have the nerve to ask him what he did.

He could see she wanted to know about him. So he gave her something to think about.

'I was in New Orleans and in Baton Rouge taking photographs for a magazine article.'

'Was it about Cajun food?'

'No. It was about old cathouses.'

'How interesting.' She shifted in her seat. The sexual implication unnerved her. He knew it would.

'What did you order?'

'The blackened salmon.'

'Good idea.' Wildman flagged the waiter and ordered the salmon. 'It's interesting the way blackened fish has become fashionable. A few years ago we would all have sent it back to the kitchen. We would have thought it was burnt.'

'Would you like a glass of this wine?' she asked tentatively.

'Thank you.' He asked the waiter for a second glass, and went on. 'You know, it's very funny meeting you like this. I thought about you the other day.'

'You did?' She was dreading this. She should never have let him sit down.

'I saw someone who reminded me of you. In Sherman Oaks.'

'Oh yes. Well, it might have been me. Was it on Friday?'

'Could have been.'

'I went to my gun club on Friday. It's in Sherman Oaks.'

'Gun club? Are you a crack shot?' He laughed.

'I don't know about that.'

'We all need targets,' he said.

'I guess so.' What did that mean?

'It's useful for self-protection. Especially for a woman living alone.'

'I don't live alone.' What was he getting at? He must know she was married from her ring. Maybe he thought she was divorced. Although in a way she was right now. She was alone.

The blackened salmon arrived. Wildman didn't pursue the subject of living alone. Enough of that, he thought, and tried something else.

'I almost didn't recognize you just now.'

'With my clothes on, you mean,' was what she half-wanted to say.

'With your hair back like that. You look different. More serious.'

'It's a question of mood.' She wondered how that sounded.

'You seemed so happy before.'

'Look, I'd rather not talk about before.'

'I understand. I'm sorry.' He lowered his eyes.

She hadn't meant to rebuff him like that. His manner was so pleasant and open. She didn't want to appear pinched or up-tight. After all, half of what happened was her.

'I was going to say . . .' he paused, waiting to see if she wanted to hear a secret.

'What?'

'Well, that woman, you remember the woman who came into the dining room.'

'Yes.'

'She shot herself.'

'God. I'm sorry.' Pandora felt a wave of guilt. Had it been because of her?

'She'd tried it before. Things had been over between us for months. But I guess she just couldn't accept it. It's very sad.'

'When did it happen? I mean, how long after . . . after us?'

'The next day. But look, it had nothing to do with that. You mustn't feel guilty. Life goes on.'

'Not for her. Poor woman.' Pandora was touched by the fact of telling her. It wasn't exactly a confession but it did denote an unexpected trust. Wildman wasn't smiling any more. He stopped eating. He drank some wine.

'Anyway,' he said, 'it's all over now.'

Pandora had never in her life considered suicide. But Alec, he might. She thought about Alec, trying to imagine where he might be, what he was doing. But nothing came to mind. There was a blank.

'It's strange,' she said. 'Since we met my life has changed quite a bit.'

'For the better, I hope.'

'Not really.' She hesitated. Should she get into something she might not be able to get out of? She wanted to talk to someone. She had never imagined talking to this man. He was the very last person she would turn to. And yet if he were the cause of Alec's leaving, maybe it wouldn't be so wrong. Tell him. A little of it, anyway. When he appeared her thoughts had been sexual. But now he seemed more of a friend. No, an acquaintance. Not even that really. Just a man she would never see again. Ever. It would be talking to a stranger.

Wildman could feel she was about to open up. Should he go further with his story? It had worked well so far. He decided Pandora needed a prompt, something to give her confidence.

'I miss her in a way,' he said. 'Now she's gone.'

That did it. It was such a sympathetic thing to say.

'My husband has disappeared.' She had confessed it. The coincidence that he had also lost someone seemed an irresistible connection between them.

'Disappeared? You mean, he left you?'

'I'm not sure. I came back ten days ago from visiting my father and he'd gone.'

'You don't know why?'

She shook her head. 'I called the police. You know. They still haven't found him. I don't know what to think.'

'That's terrible.'

'It's just that I don't know why. There was no reason.'

'Perhaps he had an accident.'

'Perhaps. I don't know why I'm telling you this.'

Wildman watched her face closely. She didn't seem all that distraught. She wasn't about to cry. That was good. He would be her friend. She could confide in him. It was perfect. The sensuality would always be there under the surface.

'I'm sure he'll turn up. Hopefully he's not hurt.'

'The thing is I have a feeling he won't. I have this thing in my head that he's gone for good.'

'Have you thought of hiring a private investigator?'

'No, I hadn't thought of that.'

186

'It might be an idea. The police don't always treat these cases very thoroughly.'

'Don't they?'

'There's so much crime in this city, they don't give priority to missing persons.'

'No, I guess not.' He was probably right. It was an idea. 'I don't know any private detectives. Maybe I should look in the yellow pages.'

'You want a reliable agency. There's no way of telling from the yellow pages which is the best.'

'I could ask some friends, I suppose. But it's not something I want to broadcast.'

'Obviously not. Look, it's none of my business, but if you like I could ask some people I know for advice.'

'That's very kind of you.'

'I know a couple of people on the *L.A. Times* and maybe they could help.'

'I'll think about it. I'm still so confused.'

'Let me give you my number here and if you decide to, I'll see what I can find out.'

Wildman took out his pocket notebook and wrote his name carefully, giving the number of the loft. He put the page down on the table beside her wine glass. She smiled at him. A smile of gratitude and confidence.

Wildman didn't want to leave her. To be close to her again after so long raised his spirits. He was sure that within weeks, if not days, she would be his. He wanted to take her in his arms now and keep her there. It was hard for him to look at his watch and say: 'I ought to be thinking of going.'

She wanted him to stay. He offered to pay for lunch. She wouldn't hear of it. She had his number. He was there if she wanted him. He hadn't asked for her number. When he shook her hand Pandora felt a rush of warmth. She remembered their handshake in the bungalow after they had made love. Now suddenly she wanted him again. Are you crazy?

She watched him go. He waved at her through the street door of the restaurant and disappeared. She poured herself more wine. For the first time in days she imagined a man other than Alec. She looked at the note he had written. The man had a name. He was real. Pandora felt lifted. She couldn't return to her book, but she finished the wine and the rest of the blackened salmon. Thank God for coincidence, she thought.

5

Pandora felt queasy when she returned home. Having felt healthily hungry earlier in the day she was now nauseous. Tidying Paulette's bedroom, bending over the bed to pull the sheets taut, she suddenly needed to vomit. She dashed into the adjoining bathroom, her throat burning. She retched but nothing would come. She knelt with her head over the toilet bowl. What was the cause? Food poisoning? Despair over Alec? She had enjoyed the food at lunch. Alec's absence was now more a fact than a fear. He simply wasn't there. Dead or alive, he wasn't with her. Unable to vomit, after a few minutes Pandora left the bathroom and flopped down on Paulette's half-made bed.

Why had that man reappeared? To torment her? As if there wasn't enough wrong in her life already. She looked at Paulette's clock. Three fifteen. Shit. She was going to be late picking her up. No, wait. Was it Wednesday? Yes. Thank God. Wednesday was Paulette's piano lesson. She had until five. Pandora closed her eyes:

He had been really very pleasant, relaxed, and quite forthcoming about his life. He was open. Charles Wildman. She could remember his name easily. She even had his number. If she needed it. His idea to hire a private detective wasn't stupid. The police were useless. Why then, she asked herself, don't I start making enquiries right now? Get on with it. Find Alec.

Consciously diverting herself for a moment, Pandora looked at the small, tidy pile of books on the table beside Paulette's bed. School books. Texts. One title caught her eye. *Delta of Venus*. She pulled it away from the others. The author was Anaïs

189

Nin. She'd heard the name, but hadn't read anything by her. Pandora turned the pages. She saw and now remembered that Anaïs Nin had been a friend of Henry Miller. The book was a collection of pornographic stories. How had Paulette gotten hold of it?

Leafing through the pages, Pandora arbitrarily selected one story to read.

It was about a woman who went to a fancy dress party in the Bois de Boulogne in Paris. All the masked men began seducing the masked women. It was a free for all. No names, no faces even, just random screwing. The woman, who had arrived alone, was taken by a man she didn't know. She got an incredible and unexpected thrill out of the encounter. She found him irresistible. He took her away in a carriage out of the wood. They went to a cheap hotel in Paris and fucked their brains out. Then in the morning he told her he hadn't been a guest at the party at all. He was a common laborer who happened across the scene, stole a mask and picked a woman, any woman, her.

The reaction of the woman in the story disturbed Pandora. The woman didn't mind that the man had gate-crashed the party and wasn't from her class. She'd had such a great time with him. But why had she gone to the party in the first place? And why hadn't she tried to resist him? The implication was that they would never meet again.

The relevance of the story troubled Pandora. Why had she chosen that particular one? It struck her that her life now was a kind of sequel to it. Unlike the woman, she had met her mystery man again. She now knew something about him. He knew things about her. They were no longer nameless. It wasn't abstract, masked pornography. They were on the brink of becoming real people.

Pandora put the book back in the pile, third from the top, exactly as she had found it. She got off the bed and straightened the covers. The nausea of an hour ago had gone. She left the house and drove to pick up Paulette, wondering how, if you just read the story, would you know that it had been written by a woman.

*

Two days later when the phone rang Pandora didn't bother to pick up immediately. She would leave it to the machine. In the days following Hammond's disappearance she would have grabbed it, praying that it was he.

Now she listened to Alec's voice repeating the instruction to leave a message. It didn't sound like Alec any more. It was just a man's voice, impersonal, characterless. After the beep came a female voice. It was Rosie, Alec's assistant. She wanted to talk to him. Clearly, Rosie didn't know of his disappearance. The calls for Alec had dwindled recently to one every couple of days. Pandora had given up returning them, stopped lying to his friends saying he was out of town. But they were invariably men friends or acquaintances. This was a woman.

Pandora invited Rosie over. She had met her several times but they weren't close. From Pandora's tone of voice Rosie could tell something was wrong. She was not prepared for Pandora's story.

'I'm going crazy, Rosie. I don't know what to think. I don't know how to start looking for him.'

'What about the police?'

'Nothing. A guy came over. He just made me feel awful. As if it was my fault.'

'I don't know how to tell you this . . .'

'What?' Pandora shivered. Rosie knew something

'. . . or even if I should. It happened while we were on location in Arizona.'

Now the die was cast. Pandora waited, scared. Rosie was scared as well. Her first loyalty was to Hammond, who was a friend and had given her a couple of good breaks professionally. But Rosie sympathized with Pandora. Men could be assholes.

'There was a girl working on the movie,' Rosie said, as calmly as she could. 'This girl was a stunt woman. Alec had an affair with her.'

'Oh God.' Pandora's mind went numb. 'Who is she?'

'It doesn't matter.'

'It does to me!' Pandora heard herself shout.

'It sometimes happens on movies.'

'He's with her now. What's her name? Where does she live?'

'Hold on, Pandora. He's not with her.'

'How do you know? Of course he's with her.'

'She's dead.'

'Dead?'

'She died during the shoot. There was an accident during a stunt. She was killed.'

Pandora shook with panic. 'Who killed her?' Was Alec a murderer?

'The point is he blamed himself for the accident. He felt the construction of the set, his set, was responsible. You see, Betty May was injured by an upright.'

'An upright? What's that?' Pandora gasped in a maze of confusion.

Rosie explained the stunt. She described what happened. Pandora listened without properly comprehending the detail.

'If she's dead . . . where's Alec? I mean, what's the connection?'

'I don't know if there is one. Truly, I don't know. But afterwards Alec pretty much went to pieces. He's a calm man as you know, but the whole thing got to him.'

'Was he in love with her?' Pandora struggled to remember the girl's name. Pandora hadn't taken it in.

'No. I don't think so. It was just a casual thing. But her death turned it into something else. Alec was shattered.'

Pandora thought back to when Alec returned from Arizona. How had he seemed? Maybe he had been a bit distracted. Then she remembered the day he came back cut and bruised. He'd never explained that. She remembered thinking he'd gotten into a fight. But if the girl was dead then none of that made sense.

'What do I do?'

'I don't know. Nothing, I guess.'

'I must find out where the girl lived. Someone must know something.' That fucking cop was right. Beverly was right. There was a woman in it.

'I checked the cast and crew list before I came,' Rosie said. 'There's no address or phone number for her on it.'

'What was her name?'

'Betty May.'

'Betty May what?'

'I don't know. I never knew.'

'How can I find out?'

Rosie began to regret all this. She shouldn't have told Pandora. But Hammond had to be found.

'I'll see what I can find out,' Rosie said. 'But I honestly don't think that's important. Look, Pandora, there's probably no connection. Perhaps I shouldn't have told you.'

'You had to tell me.'

Pandora became silent. Rosie wanted to leave. She called her service for messages. There were none.

'I have to go,' she said. 'I've got to make some calls.'

Rosie left, feeling lousy. She regretted coming to see Pandora. She should've let sleeping dogs lie. She had thought of giving her the number of the production manager. Or even the stunt co-ordinator, Wildman. They would probably know where Betty May had lived. But Rosie was guilty now. She'd gone far enough. Too far. The destroyed look on Pandora's face as she left the house frightened Rosie. She could see that part of Pandora's world had caved in. For Christ's sake Hammond, wherever you are, come back to her.

That night Pandora had fallen asleep in the living room watching TV. The sound of gunfire from a late night action movie woke her. Blearily, she turned the television off by remote. Now she was aware of the sound of a wind outside. She struggled out of her chair, looked at her watch. It was two thirty. She picked up her shoes. As she stretched and prepared to go upstairs to bed, she heard a sound. She stopped and listened. The noise, a closing door perhaps, seemed to come from the direction of the kitchen. Had she left the patio door open? No, she remembered locking it. It came again, the noise, a softly knocking door.

Pandora came into the kitchen, switched on the light. The

door was banging in the wind. She crossed the room to close it. She almost slipped on the floor. Pandora gasped with surprise. The tiles were wet. She looked down. There was water over the floor. Three or four small pools. She checked the dishwasher to see if it was leaking. It wasn't. Examining the wet floor she saw that the water was in a line to the banging door.

Now she was scared. Someone had come into the kitchen with wet feet from the pool.

'Paulette?' Pandora called out. It had to be Paulette. She must have taken a midnight dip. She now heard, or imagined she heard, a splash from outside. Paulette was in the pool. She opened the door and looked outside. She saw no one. The wind rippled the surface of the water. Pandora thought, Paulette never swims at night. She hardly used the pool at all. She had no interest in sports. It hadn't been Paulette. It had been someone else.

Pandora was afraid to turn on the patio lights. She shivered. Turn on the lights. You have to find out. Now. Do it! Trembling, she pressed the switch. The pool area was deserted. Suddenly, Pandora knew who it was. It had to be Alec. He'd come back.

6

In the morning, after a night of broken dreams and unfulfilled desires, Pandora made a decision. She would give Paulette her wish to let her stay with David Wing's family. Out of her own selfish misery she would make her daughter happy.

If Alec had indeed come back in the night it had been to scare and not to stay or resume his life with her. If Alec had not been the intruder the event was still connected with Alec's disappearance. Perhaps someone come to look for him. Rosie's story of the dead girl puzzled and scared Pandora. For the first time, she felt there had to be a criminal aspect to the whole mystery. Perhaps the suspicious cop had been right, after all. Alec had had an affair so there were other parts of his life that she knew nothing about. Was it possible she didn't know Alec at all? You read all the time about people's strange private lives which emerge with a crisis, lives that had been hidden, often for years.

Pandora didn't truly want to be alone in the house but neither did she want her daughter to be caught up in what seemed an increasingly sinister affair. In reaching her decision to let Paulette go to the Wings' she felt immediately freer. She felt a surge of love for her daughter. If Alec was involved in something unpleasant or dangerous she wanted to protect her from it.

The atmosphere of Pandora's social life had been affected by Alec's disappearance. Her friends, apart from Beverly, had begun to implant doubts in her mind. He was working for the

CIA. He was involved with the Mafia. He was in debt. He was into drugs. He had decided to escape from it all, start a new life in another place. The organization he had been working for had found it necessary to move him, to give him another name. While Pandora dismissed all conspiracy theories as absurd and groundless, the fact remained that his unexplained disappearance must have a background. Unless he had been killed or died in an accident there had to be a history behind what happened. Had to be. Pandora knew only that her peace of mind was now destroyed. It would not return until Alec returned or was found. And even then damage had been done.

Paulette was over the moon when her mother told her she was to stay with the Wings for a few days. She packed her clothes for the second time in a month. She quivered with excitement on the drive to Alpine Road at the west end of Beverly Hills where David lived.

The disappearance of her father would, Paulette knew, be always connected with visiting friends, being away from home. It was during her stay at the Balfours' house that he went missing. Now she was on her way to the Wings' and he seemed further away than ever. The night before, Paulette had seen a CNN interview with the family of a hostage who had been held in Beirut for over five years. His children had grown up without him, the wife had said. Three weeks was not five years, she knew, but if her dad was dead then she too would grow old without him. It had to be faced.

Both David's parents were Chinese. Mr Wing had originally been a businessman in Hong Kong. He had come to America and married his wife in San Francisco eighteen years ago. Mrs Wing was a Chinese scholar at Berkeley. They had three children. David was the one in the middle, between two girls. In her fantasy Paulette had imagined the Wings' house on Alpine to be a pagoda. In fact it was a single storey, ranch style house with a rectangular front lawn, a three-car garage, an oval pool in back, and a satellite dish on the roof. The only noticeably Chinese element was inside the house. Several objects around the living room, vases, watercolor pictures, and cushion covers, were identifiably oriental. Paulette had somehow expected an interior like a Chinese restaurant. She had imagined the scent of dried eastern herbs. Instead, she was engulfed by the smell of old cigar smoke. Mr Wing was a heavy smoker. Paulette was disappointed.

David carried her bags to the bedroom which had been prepared by evicting the youngest daughter Karen, who now doubled with her older sister Nancy. The room was a nursery. The sight of the toys and soft animals made Paulette feel grown up. David asked her if she wanted to unpack. He showed her two drawers in the closet which had been cleared ready for her things. He smiled at her. They both knew they had achieved something. They would be living together for a while.

Pandora drank the hot jasmine tea, prepared by Mrs Wing's maid, as quickly as she could. She wanted to avoid too much talk about Alec's disappearance. She was embarrassed. She was a failure as a wife. She felt now like an outsider in this family home, as if she was a poor cousin dependent on charity, unable to look after her own daughter.

'Paulette can stay as long as she likes,' Mrs Wing told her.

'Just a few days. I'm still making enquiries about my husband.'

'If there's anything we can do to help, just tell us. It must be very upsetting for you both.'

But Pandora wasn't thinking of Alec, even though she was talking about him. She was wondering if she had the courage to call Wildman. She thought of his lips as she kissed Paulette goodbye.

'Don't worry too much Mom.' Paulette was secretly relieved to see her mother go. 'I'll be fine.'

As she kissed her mother she kissed David. Her skin tingled with anticipation. Now I've got someone of my own, she thought. She could see herself eating breakfast with David, both of them wearing their night clothes. She could see David sitting at the end of the bed. She would be able to hold him.

Pandora's hand shook as she dialed the number Wildman had given her. She sat on her bed looking at her reflection in the tall mirror. What are you doing? She addressed the other. Hearing the phone ringing somewhere far away Pan, or was it Dora, moved her head to avoid her image. There were three rings before he picked up.

'Yes.'

Pandora was terrified by the curtness of his voice. Hang up. Hang up!

'This is Pandora.'

'How are you? Are you all right?' The tone of his voice was soft, caring, welcoming.

Pandora relaxed. 'I was wondering . . . if we could meet.'

'Of course. When?'

She could hear he was glad she rang. Their voices touched.

'I was thinking maybe tonight, if you're free.' She was hesitant.

He wasn't. 'I'll come over. Or do you want to meet outside?'

'No. Here's fine. About eight.' Was that a horrible mistake? Maybe she should have suggested dinner somewhere. But she wanted him to herself, not with people around.

'I'll be there.'

She felt he was about to hang up.

'Wait. You don't know the address. It's 12570 Rancho Park Drive.'

'Don't worry too much,' he sounded like Paulette trying to reassure her. Had he written the address down? Would he remember it?

'I'll see you then.' She started to shake again. Well, she could always call back and cancel, couldn't she?

There was a pause as if they were both waiting for the other to say something else. Then he was gone. She replaced the receiver feeling like a teenager making a secret date. The photograph of Alec smiled at her from the bedside table. What was he smiling about? Her, or that girl? But if he had had one girl he must have had others. Had he been screwing around for years? Who was she really married to? But then, who was Alec married to? What kind of a wife was she? A whore. She decided then and there sitting on the bed she would talk to the man and nothing more.

Wildman turned from the phone to look at Hammond. He was sitting slumped in an armchair. His eyes were dull. His face was unshaven. His hands were hanging limply over the arms of the chair. Wildman looked at Laura. He saw a dancer he used to want.

Laura was standing beside the open door of the box, drinking tea in a glass. She wondered about the phonecall. Who had called? Had it been her? Laura was scared. Hammond was a zombie. They had broken him. Why had she gone along with it all? They were animals. It was grotesque. She was his accomplice in a crime from which she had nothing to gain. She was contributing to her own destruction. Was this what happened when you loved someone more than you loved yourself?

'When are you going to let him go?'

'Not yet,' Wildman said.

'You can't just keep him here.'

'He's all right.'

'He doesn't remember his own name.'

'Maybe we should give him a new name. Any suggestions?'

'Don't joke about it.'

'It's not a joke. If I hadn't done this he'd be trying to kill me. All I've done is neutralize him.'

Wildman knelt down in front of Hammond.

'Do you realize you tried to kill yourself?'

Hammond stared blankly at Wildman.

'Yes.'

'You crashed your car. You're lucky to be alive, you know that?'

'Yes.' Hammond stared helplessly into Wildman's eyes.

'Do you know how long you've been here?'

'Yes.'

'How long?'

'Yes.'

'You've been here since page five.' Wildman smiled to himself as he thought about his screenplay. If Hammond were an actor in the movie he couldn't be giving a more convincing performance.

'I have to go,' Laura said. Had she the courage to leave now and never come back?

'Drive carefully.' Wildman seemed to be reading her mind. He made it sound like a threat.

David Wing was sitting on Paulette's bed. He wore a black bathrobe. Paulette was listening to his voice, which was just beginning to break. He was telling her a bedtime story.

'Once upon a time, a very long time ago, in the middle of the world in a country we now call China there were eight days in the week. There were eight weeks to the month and eight months to the year. This eighth day was known as the day of desire. It was the one day of the week when every man and woman could do exactly what they wanted, but just for one day.'

'That must have been wonderful,' Paulette said, tucking her legs under her as she sat in bed, the covers pulled up around her.

'Yes. It was everybody's favorite day. But eventually they stopped having it. The Emperor issued a decree that the eighth day would no longer exist. From then on they would have only seven, like us today.'

'Why?'

'Because people started to do things they wanted on other days. They couldn't resist. They cheated and spoilt the whole thing. And so the day of desire disappeared.'

'What a shame.' Paulette wanted David to stay with her in the room. She couldn't help wondering if this day was actually one of those long-forgotten special eighth days. Even at twelve years of age David Wing knew the power of restraint. He kissed Paulette on her forehead and went to his own bedroom. Paulette lay awake for a long while after that. He hadn't closed her door.

7

The front door bell rang. I was on the stairs, on the way down.
I stopped. I didn't want to answer it. I don't know how long I
stood there. The bell rang again. I didn't want to open the door.

I shouldn't have called him. Did I really want to see him?
What would we talk about? What would I say? What would he
do? Would we make love? Was that what I wanted? I felt like
an adolescent, confused, waiting to be led.

I physically shook as I opened the door. Be brave, you must
want to see him. His face was a shock. He was smiling. His
smile faded when he saw my face.

'What's the matter?'

'I'm very frightened.'

He touched my arm. 'I don't blame you after what you've
been through.'

I pulled away. The need to be held was very strong. I closed
the front door and went into the living room. He followed me.
I could feel him watching my back, my legs. He was remembering.

'Would you like a drink?'

'I don't think so, thank you. But you go ahead.'

Shaking, I poured myself a glass of something, anything.
When I tasted it I realized it was sherry. I detested sherry. I
blurted out the story of the water in the kitchen.

'I believe it was my husband who came back.'

'Why would he do that? And not show himself, I mean?'

'I've given up theorising.'

'You really should have a private detective.'

'Yes, you're right.'

'Unless . . . unless you don't want to find him.'

'Of course I want to find him.' What did he mean? He came towards me. I wanted to run, head for the door, for the window, out.

'You don't want to drink this. Why don't I get some ice and fix you a proper drink?'

I said, 'Do you mind if I sit down?' Why would he mind, it was my house. I was dizzy. I felt myself losing control. As I sank into a chair he bent down in front of me. Don't take my hand. Don't touch me. I didn't say the words. Could he read my thoughts?

'Why did you call me?'

'I don't know. I really don't know.'

'Of course you know. You wanted to see me. I wanted to see you.'

'I'm ashamed.'

'I don't believe that.'

He took the glass from my hand. As he did his finger stroked my wrist.

'I have so many problems,' I said. 'You don't need that.'

Everything that had happened to me seemed suddenly to have come from this man. I looked at him. You are my problem, whoever, whatever you are.

He leant forward and kissed me on the forehead. I didn't respond. He kissed my eyes. I closed my lids. His fingers touched the back of my neck. I had a sensation of falling. His lips caressed my nose before reaching my mouth. He waited for me to open my lips. I needed the warmth. His tongue found mine. Then it curled upwards running slowly along the inside of my teeth. I knew we would make love. He put his hand inside my dress. I started to fall to pieces.

As he took my left breast into his mouth, I had a sensation of unremitting madness. My nipple grew between his lips. His tongue painted it larger. I put my arm around his head, grasped his hair with my fingers. He wasn't just a lover, making me feel wonderful, he was an opponent challenging me to a sensual duel.

His moves required a response. I put my free hand between his legs. He moved back leaving my breast exposed, wet with his saliva, instantly cooling.

'Do you want me to take my clothes off?'

'Put on your red dress.'

'Now?'

'Now.'

'Do you want me to change my underwear?'

'Change everything.'

'Do you want me to wash?'

'I'll do that for you. Later.'

'I'll take that drink.' I pulled my dress closed over my skin. I turned away from him and headed for the kitchen. At the open door he caught me, his arms around my waist. His face was in my neck at the back. His tongue was in my hair. I inclined my head towards him. I shook in his arms. He took a thick strand of my hair in his mouth, between his teeth. He pulled. It could have hurt but it didn't. Without moving his hands his arms tightened around me. I became breathless. He whispered something in my ear. It was indistinct.

'What?' I was afraid of speaking more in case my voice cracked.

'I said, the die is cast.'

What a strange thing to say. It reminded me of something. I couldn't think what. He picked me up in his arms. All thought vanished. I weighed nothing. He carried me up the stairs, climbing two steps at a time. He was all strength, not carrying me at all, but transporting me.

In the bedroom he watched me undress. Then he turned away as I went to the closet to put on the red dress. Having felt clumsy I now felt nimble, a dancer. The dress was cool and loose against my body like a veil. He turned to look at me. I waited. Without taking his eyes from me he took off his black leather jacket and pulled his black cotton shirt over his head. It seemed a female gesture. Looking at his muscled torso I saw a different body from the one I remembered. Only the scar was the same. He held out his left hand. I grasped it lightly and moved close. His grip suddenly tightened. I felt my knuckles crack. Felt them, but I heard nothing. I realized my silence was back. My deafness. I wasn't afraid this time. Nor was I unnerved. The silence seemed natural. Perhaps this was what it was for. I slid down to my knees and pressed my lips to the scar. I licked the long-healed wound. It was hard, a thin plaster of taut skin. I pushed the point of my tongue into it. I had an irrational desire to open it, dissolve the stitches with my saliva, enter his body.

He put his hands down beneath my chin. He began to undo the buttons of his pants. He unbuckled his belt as I licked the hair below his navel. I felt the leather of the belt move under my chin. I was liquid. I closed my eyes. Now I was blind as well as deaf.

In the dark silence I pulled his pants downwards. His undershorts must have come with them. His penis grew in my hand. Then everything was speeding up. My mouth was open and full. He was inside my head.

We were on the rug. His hands moved across my body, taking the veil away. I opened my eyes. I saw red, like bright sunlight through closed eyelids. The dress covered my face. He didn't remove it. He held my hand in his, outstretched on a carpeted rack. I was stripped. Not undressed, stripped bare, Not simply naked but exposed. He pushed my legs apart with his knees. I could imagine myself spread, wide open. I was being prepared.

Leaving my hands stretched east and west his fingers parted the lips of my vagina. He came inside me slowly. There was no aggression. He was waiting for me to draw him in deeper. Through the wetness I felt the suck of my womb. I was a fissure of soft rock on the shore. As the wave broke the warm salt water ran into me filling up instantly, overflowing foam, lingering for a while, then drawn out with the tide, drawn away in the thirst of the moon. I was alive and waiting for the next wave, the inevitable return.

My passion was repetition, an erratic pendulum. He removed the dress from my face. As I felt the material move I opened my eyes. His face was hanging over mine, a smiling mask. His lips moved. I could hear nothing. It didn't matter. The smile of his joy was enough to make me cry. I sobbed in silence. He kissed the tears from my cheeks and lifted me onto the bed like a child.

Was that what I was becoming in his arms, a child? It was an astounding feeling, completely unexpected. Before, our sex had produced the sensation of a knot being tied tightly, hardening into a cramp of desire. This time, it felt like a disentanglement, an uncoiling. He spoke again. I shook my head. I couldn't hear what he was saying.

He turned me over onto my front. My head was pressed into a pillow that smelled of soap. I felt him get off the bed. There was a dart of fear. I twitched. He was leaving me. Don't go, I wanted to shout. I resisted looking to where he went. I waited like a patient in the hospital. I trusted him.

In my deafness I lost a sense of time. He could have been gone for an instant or an hour. Hearing nothing, I gasped when the bed moved again. There was a sensation of warm wetness on the soles of my feet. What was it? It tickled slightly. Then the spongy feeling stroked wetly upwards to my calves. He was washing me.

As his hands and the sponge moved gently upwards to my thighs the lower parts of my legs began to cool with the warm water. Knowing this, he began to dry my skin with a soft towel. He moved my thighs apart with his hands. He washed and stroked my skin. I was aware face down that my breathing was becoming irregular. He massaged my buttocks. I clenched my muscles. It was involuntary. Did it seem like rejection? The warm water now reached my pubic hair. The evenness of his movements began to torture me. I desperately wanted to turn over, to watch him. When I moved a little he applied pressure to keep me still. He dried my hair but did not try to open my vulva. Instead he parted my buttocks. I was panicked. I moved my knees and tried to lift myself upwards. I was expecting him to press me down again. But he allowed me to raise my bottom a few inches. He squeezed the sponge and water ran down the crack. I was sick with desire.

He cleaned me slowly and carefully like a gun. I trembled. I felt his breath as he blew between my legs. Now he pulled me up and put his lips to my bottom. He parted the cheeks with his hands. There was a pause before I felt his tongue. My mind was giving way. I had no thoughts, no fears, everything was liquid anticipation. The point of his tongue found the knot. I cried out. His hands held my flesh open. His tongue massaged and probed me. My thighs started to twist and move from side to side. His grip increased. I felt the walls of my bowels collapsing inside. I started to come. The rocks melted. He opened me and I toppled, weightless and ecstatic. I no longer felt the grip of his hands. I floated and plunged inside myself. I was alone in a vast space. Deaf and blind, I was free. I needed nothing. There was nothing. Nothing to hold on to. Nothing to support me. Nothing to save me. I simply died.

Later, when I regained consciousness, I found him beside me. His eyes were closed. I took his face in my hands and kissed him. His cheeks were vaguely rough. His beard had grown while I slept. I wanted to devour him now. I was hungry for his flesh. He lay alongside me like a warm statue. I stroked him, molded him to my shape, played with him like a great doll. He was mine. He belonged to me. I took his penis in my mouth. I wanted only to make him come. Everything begins and ends with the body. My nose pressed into his soft hair. He was touching the back of my throat. I could not hear myself suck. When his mouth opened the cries of his orgasm were silent. I pulled my lips along the length of his penis which glistened with his come. I licked his testicles. He shivered. His penis quivered against my face. He had not been in my womb, yet I felt he was alive inside me. He spoke, but I heard nothing. It might have been a secret, a revelation. I nodded, smiled and fell on to him. We were together within each other.

I woke when the radio alarm came on, rupturing the silence. I was damp with sweat, at the back of my head, under my arms, between my breasts, damp and chilled. He was gone. I sat up. Why had he left without saying anything? I had no illusion that it had been a dream. I got out of bed and went into the bath-room, not to wash or pee, but simply to look at my body. I don't know what I expected to see. Some kind of change, I suppose. There were no marks, no bruises. No evidence. The insides of my thighs ached. The muscles, unused in tennis or swimming, had been stretched when he opened them, like a compass, wider than ever before. I put my hand between my legs, trying to recall or recreate how I had felt with him. I touched myself between my buttocks, but it wasn't his tongue. I put on Alec's bathrobe without thinking about him. His absence now seemed horribly insignifant. It was the absence of the man with the scar that controlled my thoughts.

That scar. I could see it. I could feel its artificial tautness on my tongue. It was an emblem of the man. Why didn't I use his name? I knew it. Charles Wildman. I had his phone number. Call him. Call him now. But what would I say? Thank you very much for last night. How pathetic. No. What I wanted to say was, come back, come back quickly and bring your scar with you. I want to touch it. Why? Because it's like a light at your center. It shines and warms me.

I went downstairs. I felt soft, boneless, without purpose. What was I going to do today? I had no plan, no schedule. I went into Alec's studio. I wanted to see him there. Be there. Appear. Not Alec. The other. Pandora, you're sick. A bit of illicit sex and it's gone to your head. You've got big problems and all you're thinking about is getting laid. But that wasn't it. It was the ecstasy I was remembering.

I stood in the studio, looking around, out of the window. Was it possible I would never see Alec again? Was this stranger some form of replacement in my life? Something touched my face. I jumped and struck out at it. It felt like the wings of an insect. There were two loose wires hanging from the ceiling. I was puzzled, then I remembered that Alec had hung the model plane from them. The plane that had mysteriously splashed down into our pool at night while we were half-making love in the water. I looked for the plane. It was gone. He must have put it away.

On my way down to the kitchen I remembered the strange

Latin inscription on it. *Ilea Iacta Est.* The die is cast. Wait. The die is cast was what he had whispered in my ear. I felt a new surge of desire. I went to the phone in the living room to call him. I looked in my purse for his number. I started to dial, but my nerve failed me. I replaced the receiver and instead called the Wings' to talk to Paulette.

'Has Dad come back?' was her first, immediate question.

'Darling no, he hasn't.'

Paulette's silence that followed seemed to imply my guilt. It was Mom's fault that Dad left. You've ruined all our lives.

The brief, hesitant conversation that followed about are you comfortable and David's very nice isn't he, and is there anything you need, was the sub-text of accusation. Why aren't you doing more to find Dad was what Paulette was really thinking and wanted to say. When I hung up with a kiss I felt wretched.

In the kitchen, waiting for the coffee machine, I burst into tears. I sobbed. I howled. I sank to the floor and shook. I let it all come out as I almost never did. I felt myself changing, physically changing. Like Dr Jekyll after drinking the potion that would turn him into Mr Hyde. I was scared at the center of my own horror. But somewhere in that sticky fear washed by my tears there was a flying dart of elation.

8

Pandora was reading the screenplay *The Box*, which she had found by the pool the evening Hammond had disappeared. She imagined that it was the last thing he had read before he went. She thumbed through the pages, reading bits without concentration. It seemed a bizarre kind of movie.

INT. LOFT. DAY

He carefully, delicately unlocks the door of the box. He bends down, reaches inside. From the semi-darkness of the interior he pulls the folded legs of the Woman. He eases her out, grasping her waist. The Woman's eyes are open, but she seems unconscious, a dead weight. When she is completely out he lifts her bodily and carries her towards the bath tub on the far side of the loft.

The bath tub is full of water. The Man lowers the Woman into the water. She begins to stir. He props her up and starts to wash her with a sponge.

The shrill ringing of the phone interrupted Pandora's reading.

'Miss Pandora, this is Alice. I have bad news . . .'

Pandora's heart burned, a spear of flame punctured her stomach.

'Your father has had a stroke. Last night. He's been taken to hospital.'

'Oh God. I'll come and see him.' She was breathless.

'He's unconscious. We don't know if he'll recover.'

'How did it happen?'

Pandora hardly heard Alice any more. The details didn't

matter. She was paralyzed. After Alice, she called the Wings. Paulette was in school. She told Mrs Wing she was going to New Hampshire. She fumbled in her memory for the number. It didn't come. Only tears of frustration. She had to look in her address book to find her childhood.

'I'm so sorry,' said Mrs Wing. 'Everything seems to be happening to you.'

The necessary cab ride, the crowded airport, the interminable waiting, the slowness of the flight, the drive through the familiar landscape to the unfamiliar destination, the bright labyrinth of the hospital, the questions to the bearded doctor whose name she couldn't remember, the opening door of the white room, the sight of her father's head unmoving, the inexpressive face, an unshaven yellowing ivory mask, a final, deathly image. Pandora kissed the dry cool forehead, her eyes shut tight. She knew he would never speak again. The pale silence of the man and the room was overwhelming.

Pandora was terrified. She stayed in the hospital for an hour, talked to Alice about things other than her father, lied about Alec, omitted everything important that had happened since her last visit. There were moments when she couldn't hear the words she spoke. She listened only to her thoughts. Please die quickly, quietly, without last words for me to remember. There's nothing I want to know. There's nothing I want to say. I have nothing to confess. I'm completely alone. I dread the next minute, the next hour. I hate my life. The future is a blank, a white hole. I can't imagine anything. I have no feeling. I don't want to drink or eat or sleep. I have no desire.

As Pandora slept in a hotel room near the hospital, her father died. At three in the morning, west coast time, David Wing came quietly into his little sister's bedroom and climbed into bed with Paulette.

'You know, there is a way to find your dad,' he said quietly. He put his arm under her neck.

Paulette felt prickly. 'How?'

'We know an astrologer. She's a kind of clairvoyant.' He

moved his hand from under her neck to stroke her shoulder. He had never touched a girl before like that.

'What does she do?' Paulette wanted to respond to his caress, but she was scared. She didn't know what to do. That sex book was no help.

'She sometimes finds missing people.' He stroked her arm down to her hand.

'How?' Paulette took David's hand in hers. Their fingers locked. Her hand was larger than his. But his hand was stronger.

'She takes something they own. A piece of clothing, or some object they're very attached to, like jewelry. She holds it and begins to imagine their lives.'

'Just by holding it.' Paulette felt a great warm surge of courage. She slowly brought their clenched hands together and pressed them against her nightgown above her breast. She had made the first important move. She wasn't afraid of him.

David suddenly imagined Paulette naked. Even at twelve years of age her body was much fuller than his older sister's. He wondered about her pubic hair. He felt a tightening in his groin.

'I could ask my mother to talk to her.'

Paulette inclined her head into David's shoulder. It was bony. He was so skinny.

'She'd need something belonging to my dad.'

Tentatively, David stroked Paulette's hair. He heard her breathing, sighing. He looked at her. She had closed her eyes. He felt her small breast which seemed to grow. He unlocked their hands and carefully placed his palm onto the material of her nightgown. He didn't dare squeeze. He had read that a woman's nipple becomes hard when she is aroused. This wasn't happening with Paulette.

She put her hand over his and pressed. Kiss him, a voice said. You're braver than he is. You do it. She shifted her whole body sideways. Her lips brushed his. Neither of them opened their mouths. This was enough for now. It was wonderful.

They stopped talking and lay together, their arms around each other. There was no possibility of sleep, not like this. They loved each other's warmth. They both knew there was so much more to come. But not this time. At around five in the morning David climbed out of the bed. He tucked Paulette in tightly. He kissed her. She pushed her fingers through his hair.

'I must go,' he said.

'Yes, I know.'

'Tomorrow I'll get in touch with the lady.'

'OK.'

Paulette watched him leave the room. He turned at the door. Neither of them spoke. David closed the door. Paulette turned out the bedside light, hugged herself and went straight to heaven.

By the time Pandora got to the hospital Alice had already made the provisional arrangements for the funeral. Alice had waited until eight before calling Pandora. She felt proprietorial about the death.

Pandora stared at her father. His appearance was unchanged from the day before. It seemed to her that he had been dead since then. She didn't kiss him. Her earlier panic left her body like an exorcized demon and flew away somewhere. Pandora cried with relief, not grief.

She drove at midday to the house. She expected to be engulfed again by memories. Surprisingly, she felt distanced from the past. Her memories belonged to another person. Walking from room to room, feeling her legs move, aware of her fingers turning door handles, hearing her own footfall, this other person became unexpectedly practical. She began to think of what could be done to the house, a new bathroom, roofing the conservatory in glass, an easy-to-clean floor in the kitchen. She was looking at the house like a potential purchaser. No, not a purchaser, a vendor. Pandora realized she was thinking about selling the place. She smiled at herself in a mirror, opened her handbag and applied make-up. She wanted to look beautiful.

Alice watched her, caught her in this irreverent act.

'Will Alec be coming to the funeral?'

'No. He's away at the moment.'

'You told me he was at home.'

'Did I?'

Pandora called the Wings' and got the number of the school. Paulette was allowed out of the class to take her mother's phonecall. She wasn't frightened. She'd guessed what it was about. She hardly knew her grandfather. She wasn't shocked or tearful. She knew Pandora hadn't been close to him. Her mother's voice was calmer than it had been for a long time. Paulette thought it's her father who's dead, not mine. She had stopped thinking Hammond was dead. Perhaps the Chinese astrologer lady would find him. She went back to the classroom. She smiled at David. The teacher asked her if she wanted to go home. Paulette wanted to say, I haven't got one, I've got a lover now instead.

The funeral was dismal. Pandora prayed alongside her father's elderly friends, not for his departed soul but just to be on the plane to Los Angeles. Alice had been wanting to say something to her for the past three days. As they kissed perfunctorily beside Pandora's waiting car outside the cemetery, she came out with it.

'I think I loved him more than you,' she said.

Pandora couldn't argue. She knew she was callous.

On the plane she began to think about Wildman. During the week in New Hampshire she had told herself she wouldn't see him again. The death of her father was a symbolic end to that. Wherever Alec was it didn't matter. She fantasized about selling the house in Rancho Park together with her father's house, sell the lot and start again. Buy a new place and live with Paulette. Begin a new life. Why not? But Wildman stepped into her mind and wouldn't leave. He was again a living presence. Pandora's thighs tightened in the stirring memory of those ecstatic moments. Her loins throbbed. She shifted in her seat and upset the glass of wine on the lunch tray in front of her. The cabin attendant leant over and spoke to her, but Pandora couldn't hear a word the woman said.

*

Home again. Again it was seven in the evening when Pandora got out of the taxi in front of her house. For her this was always the dullest time of the day. There was nothing to do at seven o'clock except drink or get ready for dinner. But what dinner? With whom dinner? A meaningless sunset, an everyday symbol of nothing, a Californian loop, the pale mauve and orange light recalled her last return from New Hampshire. One thing was different. Alec couldn't be gone again. That was certain.

The two brass coach lamps, which Alec had taken from a movie set two or three years ago, burned an empty welcome either side of the front door. Why were they burning? She must have switched them on before she left in the pretense that some-one, everyone, was home. Home. Whatever happened to that concept?

The hall and living room were dead silent. Pandora's feet ached. She kicked off her high-heeled shoes. Wasn't it a broken heel trapped in a wooden bridge that had started everything? Call him. There's nothing else to do. All her other choices had been used up. Do you want to call him more than you want to call Paulette? You're a bad mother and a faithless wife. First, a vodka.

Pandora went into the kitchen, her stockinged feet chilled by the tiles. The blinds were drawn. In the gloom she reached for the light. She gasped. The fluorescent lamps flickered on. The momentary strobing effect accompanied the staggering arrest of her heart.

Sitting at the kitchen table was a bearded man, wearing dark glasses and a raincoat with the collar turned up. He was looking straight at her though she couldn't see his eyes.

'Alec!'

Pandora ran over to him and put her arms around him. When she touched him Hammond didn't move. He felt damp, his clothes, his skin, as if he'd been out in the rain. Pandora was unnerved.

'What happened to you? Are you all right?'

The damp, stiff figure did not reply.

'Where have you been?'

Had he somehow lost his memory? The shock of seeing him declined, but a greater fear grew. Hammond's sudden presence scared Pandora more violently than his absence.

'Please darling, tell me . . . where have you been? Why did you leave?'

Then she saw the gun. Her gun. It was lying on the kitchen table in front of him. Pandora was confronted by a hyper-realist painting, a man in dark glasses in a raincoat sat at a wooden table with a gun before him. His silence, his immobility was completely threatening. Pandora saw a portrait of a man who had just shot someone. Or was he a man who was thinking of shooting someone. Himself? His wife? The gun belonged to his wife.

'Alec. What did happen?'

She asked the question knowing he wouldn't answer. She went to him again, kissed him, put her arms around him. Nothing came back. She waited, inwardly shivering. She wanted that vodka. She went to the fridge and took out the bottle. Cold air fanned her face. She trembled as she poured two glasses, looking at Alec.

'What happened . . . to you? Where have you been? Tell me please. I don't care. I just want to know. Please.'

She put one icy glass in front of him. She ought to take the gun away. She couldn't. She wanted to take his glasses off and look into his eyes. She couldn't. She imagined his blind gaze. That was scary enough.

The phone rang. She dropped her glass in fright. She was aware that Hammond did not react to the sound. She looked at the phone on the wall by the door. Answer it. It could be Paulette. Don't answer it. It could be him. Why the hell wasn't the machine picking up? The phone rang many times. Pandora left it and bent down to pick up the pieces of broken glass. The shards sparkled around her feet like jewels. She picked them up with her right hand and carefully put them into the thick, intact base of the vodka glass.

The phone stopped ringing. Hammond slowly stood up. She felt him looking down at her. She had to look up at him. He came forward, putting the gun into the pocket of his raincoat. The raincoat wasn't his. She had never seen it before. Where had he gotten it? She stared at the buttons. It was a woman's coat.

She was trying to stand when he moved again. He was going to hit her, kick her. Irrational, but she felt it. Alec, what's happened? But Hammond didn't touch her. He passed her. The tail of the black coat brushed her shoulder. She now realized that his legs were naked. He was wearing shoes without socks. The soles trod, deliberately, she thought, on the broken glass. The crunching echoed in her ears and the sound stayed after he had gone from the kitchen.

Pandora mechanically cleared up the broken glass. She remained in the kitchen for several minutes alone. She drank his glass of vodka at a gulp. Her heart burned seconds after her throat was seared.

When she came back into the hall she looked around for him. He must be upstairs. Oh God, what shall I do? She put her feet back into her shoes. She slowly climbed the stairs, wobbling. The studio door was shut. She could see the light was on. She was too scared to go in. Helplessly, she stayed outside for several moments. Then she climbed up to the safety of her bedroom. Was anywhere safe?

Pandora undressed in a sick daze. She brushed her hair. She kept her bra and panties on under her night-gown. She pulled the bed cover down. It was eight o'clock. It seemed like midnight. Pinned to the pillow she saw a piece of torn paper. Two words were written on it in thick green felt-tipped pen. Pandora cried out as she saw them, scrawled in a child-like hand, block letters and small letters mixed, seven in all.

FUck yOu

9

When Pandora woke in the morning Hammond was not beside her in the bed. Where had he slept? She went nervously to look for him He wasn't in the house. Had he gone again? She saw that the bedcovers in Paulette's room were rumpled. So he had slept in his daughter's bed. She wouldn't try to call Paulette now. She'd go over to the school to pick her up in the afternoon. She wouldn't, couldn't bring her home, not to this domestic madness. Pandora was near to tears.

Hammond hadn't left the house exactly. At nine o'clock Pandora found him sitting in the passenger seat of his car listening to music. He was still wearing his dark glasses. He hadn't shaved, but he had changed his clothes. He was wearing black jeans and a gray denim shirt. No socks or shoes. She looked at him through the windshield. He didn't acknowledge her presence.

She left him there and called the police. Pandora simply told them that her husband had come back so they needn't look any further. And yes, he was fine. They could close the case. When the cleaning lady arrived she told her the same story. She couldn't imagine what the woman would think when she saw him. Pandora didn't want to imagine any more. She was exhausted by the nightmare.

At some point during the morning Hammond returned to his studio and closed the door. At lunchtime Pandora knocked. There was no answer. She summoned what was left of her courage and went in. Why was she really so afraid? He hadn't actually done anything. It was his silence that most unnerved her. Hammond was sitting at his desk drawing. The studio floor was littered with sketches, all drawings of what looked like a packing case, or a box. He was working on designs for that strange film script. Well, it was good that he was doing something. She could see there was no point in asking any more questions. He didn't even reply to her enquiry about what he wanted for lunch.

Pandora thought of calling Beverly. But she didn't. She called Rosie instead and told her Alec was back. She didn't describe his behavior. She was too embarrassed. Yet she knew she had to talk to someone. Dr Fleming perhaps. What would she say? Come and see Alec. There's something wrong with him. He's acting strangely. No, I have no idea where he's been. He doesn't speak to me. No, doctor, we don't need a marriage counselor. We need a psychiatrist. God, I need someone to talk to. There's only one person I want to see. No, I can't do that. Can't.

Wildman was waiting for Pandora's call. He watched Laura exercising at the ballet bar. She had the best body of any girl he ever had. He used to tell her that. By comparison, Pandora's figure was unstructured, a little loose. Her flesh was healthy but it could use toning. It was ripe, a few pounds overweight. Pandora's body was old-fashioned, Laura's was contemporary. He could be objective about Pandora's body, but not about Pandora. She filled him with desire every time he thought of her.

She was a creature of passion. Laura had become an object, someone to look at, admire, but no longer challenging. He saw her now with the eye of a camera. As she danced she appeared as a set of contacts, beautiful movements, eloquent moments, some to be preferred to others, aesthetically speaking. Pandora aroused Wildman in what he would call a mythological way. She was the essence of woman, related to the gods themselves. There was immortality in her. When he thought of her she flowed through him. There were moments when she made him shudder. She existed now in his blood. He wanted nothing other.

Laura glanced occasionally at Wildman in the mirror. She

had learned to recognize when he was thinking of Pandora. He became very still. His natural athletic agitation left him. The tension, that quick danger that everyone felt in his presence, disappeared. In its place grew a decisive calm. His silence scared her. Laura knew that if she didn't act soon she would lose him. And without Wildman she would be cast adrift. But how could she act? She knew her own nature well enough to recognize her deep passivity. Outwardly, she was a sunny picture of mobility and physical purpose, a woman of action. Inwardly, she inhabited a dungeon of reliance. Chained and manacled in the darkness, she waited for her man, his instructions, his spoken requests, his physical needs. But she had waited too long for the sound of his footsteps, for the turning of the key to her cell, for the glorious stirring of her heart at his demands. Even here in his presence she sometimes felt like an abandoned child. Laura had no desire to break out of her cell. She had no dreams of escape. Her happiness lay in being visited. While she kept her body fit, her spirit sickened.

The effect on Laura of Hammond's collapse had been profound. The destruction of his psyche had appalled her. To uncover the needs of a human being and arrange for their fulfilment, even against their conscious will, was admirable. Wildman had done that for her. He had filled her shell with living tissue. But to syphon off that same life in someone, as he had with Hammond, was destructive, against nature. She felt she was witness, and accomplice, to Hammond's inner death. She felt something similar. His neglect of her had produced a sense of death-in-life.

Laura felt powerless. Yet she had to save her own existence. Look at him, waiting silently for her to call. She had never known him wait for a woman before. It was Pandora who had brought all this about. She was the virus. She had provoked this man, changed him, obsessed him. She had infected his life. And so, Laura reasoned, it was not Wildman who had to be stopped, but her.

Laura's body ached. She ceased to dance. She lay down on the floor, breathing deeply. Wildman sat silently in the chair

Hammond had sat in. Together, the sleeping dogs yawned dreamily. Romulus wandered lazily over to Laura and licked her feet, as if to say, wake up, it's time.

'Dad's come back. He's at home.' Pandora caught Paulette as she came out of school with David. The Wings' driver was waiting for them.

'That's wonderful.' Paulette laughed with relief. Then she saw something was wrong. Pandora's face, while smiling, was creased with anxiety.

'What's the matter, Mom? Is Dad all right?'

Pandora drew her daughter aside. 'Can you wait a minute, David?'

Paulette was frightened. She suddenly saw Hammond limping, wounded, a war victim.

'Darling, Dad's not really all right.'

'What happened to him?'

'I don't know. He's at home. He's not . . . not very well.'

'Is he sick?'

Yes, Pandora thought, he is. But she said 'He's not talking much. I don't really know where he's been, or anything.' How could she say out loud 'Your dad's a zombie.'?

'I want to see him.

'I'm not sure that's such a great idea.'

'Mom, what are you talking about? I have to see Dad.'

And Pandora had to agree. She would try and explain things in the car home. She made her excuses to David, who looked put out and uneasy. Paulette impulsively gripped his hand.

'I'll call you later,' Paulette said, taking the initiative, making it easy on her mother.

In the car she waited for more information from Pandora. Tell me, tell me, tell me. But Pandora's courage failed her and she said nothing the whole drive. When they stopped at some lights on the way Paulette kissed her mother as if to say, 'Don't talk Mom, it's all right.'

Pandora wondered whether to ring the bell when they arrived home. She was frightened by the effect Hammond's crazed

221

appearance might have on Paulette. Ring the bell she thought, not to have him come to the door, but somehow to warn him they were back. Warn him? Hammond didn't even know that Pandora had gone to pick up their daughter.

They both heard the music as they got out of the car. It was very loud. Pandora looked around to see if any neighbors were watching. The whole street could hear it.

'Isn't that Stravinsky?' Paulette said. She knew *The Rite Of Spring* was one of her dad's favorites. She had often heard it playing in the studio while he worked. Now she could see the fear the sound brought to her mother's face. Pandora unlocked the front door to be enveloped in the full dynamic range of the movement *The Game of Rape*. She instinctively took Paulette's hand as she pushed the door shut behind her. There was no sign of Hammond. She felt he was waiting in the kitchen, although the music was yelling its warning from the upstairs studio. It seemed to Pandora that her recent life of unease that had begun with her discovery of Hammond's disappearance, was a chain of musical movements in which she opened door after door and entered room after room in her own house increasingly terrified at what she would find. Was this moment the crescendo?

Hammond was not in the kitchen. Paulette didn't want the Coke or the milk Pandora offered her. She only wanted to see her father. She tried to imagine him. Pandora hated the music. She prayed for it to stop. The empty rooms were so full of dangerous sound that the house seemed jammed with crowds of people at a party that had gotten out of control. Paulette felt it too. The physical stillness of the kitchen full of sound conjured an irrational fear of violence. And Paulette knew nothing of her father's state of mind.

'I'll go look for Dad,' Pandora said. 'He's probably in the studio.' She wanted Paulette to stay in the kitchen while she would try to reason with Hammond, prevent him from scaring her. But Paulette didn't want to be left. She followed her mother closely, clinging like a small child, like a nervous puppy.

They came back into the hall. They looked up and saw Hammond descending the stairs. Paulette gasped. She wanted to turn away. She couldn't. She wanted to scream. She didn't. Pandora closed her eyes for a moment, and shook.

'Alec!'

Hammond was naked. He dripped with water as if he'd just gotten out of the shower. His dark hair clung to his white face. His penis was painted scarlet. It was raised without being fully erect. He spoke quietly, reasonably he thought.

'Paulette. Come and kiss your Dad.'

Paulette now let out a scream and yanked away from Pandora. She ran to the front door, tugged at it, wrenched it open, ran outside. Pandora could hear her cries, inarticulate, full of fear.

Hammond started down the stairs towards Pandora.

'Alec, how could you? Why are you doing this?' Pandora was limp, sickened. 'You're disgusting.' She didn't want to say that. It was no way to talk to someone obviously crazy, to her husband, the man she loved. He advanced on her. His red penis seemed to harden. The music became more strident. The chords were cries from slashing weapons, steel on flesh.

'Get away from me!' Pandora yelled, feeling herself losing control. She ran out of the house, slamming the door behind her. After a few moments, Hammond sat down on the stairs.

Pandora drove Paulette over to the Wings'. Through her sobs Paulette shouted at her mother.

'What's happened? What's the matter with Dad!'

'I don't know, darling. I don't know.'

Paulette seemed to be accusing her.

'Why did he do that to himself? He's horrible.'

'He's not well. I don't know what's wrong.'

'You can't go back there.' Paulette tried to grip her panic. She wanted to erase the image of her dad looking like that. 'Stay with me,' she pleaded.

'I'll stay for a bit. But I have to go back. I have to do something. I can't leave him like that.'

'Why did he do it?' Paulette knew she would never forget the red penis, the dripping hair and shiny white skin. She knew she was in for nightmares. Pandora felt something beyond the

223

horror, the madness of the scene. Beyond any pity she had for him was a revulsion which made her savagely angry. Maybe it was irrational, but Pandora now knew she wanted to get back at him. She didn't even want to know why he did it. Infected by his craziness she wanted revenge.

The music was over. Hammond unfolded the handwritten pages. He read them again. He had forgotten how many times he had read them. The shock was still fresh and still numbing.

'I want to take you in my arms. I want my breast in your mouth. I want to be wide open. I want you to enter me. I want to explode. I want to suck . . .'

Bitch! Alone in his studio, still naked, Hammond cursed Pandora. Fucking bitch. How long had she known him? The letters weren't new. So she had been seeing him for months, years maybe. For the first time since he returned home Hammond was aroused. He stroked his penis with the pages Pandora had written to Luke over twenty years ago. He felt his testicles tighten. He could see Pandora doing her striptease at the end of their bed. Whore.

Hammond couldn't make himself come. Wildman had taken his sperm. Well, it wasn't over. Hammond was back and ready for action. Now he would finish the job. Kill them both. He looked at his sketches of the box. They'd tried to brainwash him. Yes, they'd tried, the morons. But it hadn't worked. The treatment hadn't taken. It had been a master stroke appearing naked. Now Dora, his beloved wife, thought he was crazy. Stupid bitch, she believed it. He smiled. Now all he had to do was . . . was . . . what was that girl's name? The one Wildman had murdered in Arizona. She had a name, what was it? Fuck it. Was it Paulette? No. He'd remember in a bit. Of course he would. Hammond's mind was clear.

10

Pandora stayed with Paulette in the Wings' house for three hours. They sat together in the living room. David and his mother had left them alone. She calmed her daughter, although she knew that what had happened was only the beginning of a terrible period in their lives. It was incomprehensible but she would have to deal with it with cool logic. The vengeful sensation remained. A door to violence in her nature had been splintered with an axe. Hammond's raised red penis had been like a bloodied weapon, sticky and slimy from a killing, a murderous maleness.

'I'm scared, Mom,' Paulette whispered in Pandora's ear as they clasped each other tightly outside the house. What she meant was 'I'm scared for you, Mom.' Pandora knew that.

'Be brave, darling. I'll call you later.'

'I never want to go home. Never.'

This was Alec's real crime, Pandora thought. His words, come and kiss your dad, echoed in her head. Nothing could be more horrible.

She tried to figure out a plan as she drove home. Confront him. Call the doctor. Call the police. Talk to a friend. Beverly? Rosie? Her dead father? Now she was getting crazy. And nauseous. The closer to home she got the stronger became the bile of fear in her throat. She arrived home planless.

There were lights on. She had expected total darkness. There was silence. She had expected loud music. It was like her deafness. Her ears were numb. The cicadas alone told Pandora she could still hear. Her palms and armpits were damp with sweat,

225

telling her she could feel. Once again she opened the door to her nightmare.

The television was on in the living room. Hammond was sitting in an armchair. He was dressed in jeans, a white shirt and loafers. He was clean and dry-haired. There was a glass of milk in his hand. On the table beside him sat a tuna sandwich on a plate. He smiled and beckoned Pandora.

'Come and sit down, darling,' he said affably. 'I've fixed us a sandwich. Come and get it.' He laughed quietly at the comedy program on TV. 'This is quite amusing,' he said.

Pandora had no clue how to react. Was his madness over or was this pleasant old domestic manner another aspect of it.

'How are you feeling?' she said limply.

'Great. I had a bath. I took a nap. I feel great.'

'Good. I was really . . . worried.'

'I guess I was depressed.'

'Do you want to . . . talk about it?'

'Not really. Maybe tomorrow.'

'All right. I'm really tired.'

'You must be. Why don't you make it an early night. You sure you don't want a sandwich?'

'I think I'll take a bath and go to bed.'

'I won't be long coming up. I was thinking of taking a dip but it's chilly out there. See you in a bit.'

Hammond blew Pandora a kiss. Icy fingers caressed her face. She went upstairs. She quivered at each heavy step.

Pandora needed a bath. In fear she took off her clothes. She ran water into the tub. Suddenly she could see herself struggling in the water as he held her under until she lost consciousness. Half an hour passed and Hammond hadn't come to bed. She dried herself hurriedly listening all the time for his feet on the stairs, glancing often at the half-open door imagining him standing there his penis throbbing scarlet. She was damp from the bath as she called Paulette. It was ten thirty. She hoped it wouldn't wake the whole house.

'Dad's much better . . . he's watching TV . . . he seems fine . . .' What else could she say?

'Mom, are you sure?'

'Yes.'

'You're not lying to me?'

'Darling, no. I'm going to bed now myself. I'll call you in the morning early.'

Paulette wasn't reassured, Pandora knew that. She felt guilty. She ought not to have left her. But then maybe Alec had really snapped out of it. It was possible. Two days of craziness. Maybe he'd just come right out of it, whatever it was. Could she give him the benefit of the doubt?

Pandora curled up in bed. She left one light on. She couldn't bring herself to sleep in the dark. Like a child, fearing nightmares, she craved the comfort of a nightlight. It seemed hours before she dozed off. The last thing she remembered was the open bedroom door she so desperately longed to close. And lock. But her fear of the axe splintering the wood was greater than the fearful acceptance of her fate. So she left the door open.

Paulette kept the light on in her room. David saw it and came in. He sat on the bed and held her hand. She hadn't spoken a word of what had happened except to say that her father was back. But David could feel her fear and it troubled him. He tried not to pry.

'I'm glad you're still here.'

'It's just that Dad's not very well. Mom thinks it's better if I stay for a while.'

'At least we won't need the astrologer to find him,' David said. 'But she's good at other things too.'

'What do you mean? What other things.' Paulette tried to concentrate on what David was saying. Forget the horror. Hold hands. Let him take her mind away with his touch.

'It's called *fung shui* in Chinese. It means wind water. What this lady does is to help you get rid of the bad things.'

'What sort of bad things?'

'Bad luck. She can help you change your luck. Or bad spirits. She can advise you how to get rid of them. *Fung shui* means the balance of natural forces, wind and water.'

Paulette wondered if her dad had become a bad spirit. Maybe that's why he was behaving the way he was. Maybe he was possessed. Was that crazy? It was like some horror movie.

'What's her name, this lady?'

'Mrs Long. Would you like to meet her? She might be able to help you. Fix the trouble at home. You could tell her about it. If you wanted.'

'I don't know if I believe in this stuff. Maybe it only works if you're Chinese.'

'Isn't it worth a try?' David wanted to introduce Paulette to Mrs Long, not just to help his friend who was so unhappy but to create another bond between them. We are lovers, aren't we, he thought.

'She might be able to help my mom,' Paulette said. 'I'm really worried about her.'

David kissed her lightly on the lips. Hesitantly she moved her tongue in her mouth forwards past her teeth and touched his lips. David shivered as if he'd been given a twenty volt shock. He moved back and stroked her hair.

'I'll call Mrs Long tomorrow.'

'Thank you.' Paulette privately thought, it's too late, it's already happened.

After David left the bedroom Paulette closed her eyes but left the bedside lamp on. Her frightened memory drifted back to other less violent images of her father on those occasions when she had seen him naked. In the bath covered in soap, getting dressed in a hurry to take her to school and swimming in the pool at night with Mom. She had watched them from her bedroom window. It had seemed marvelously romantic. And when they had made love in the water it had seemed like a scene from her book, *Delta of Venus*. She remembered the night when that model aircraft landed in the pool like a UFO. It had interrupted the scene. Then he had climbed out of the pool all shiny and naked.

Even in her dreams Pandora was somehow aware that Hammond had not come to bed. She awoke with the morning light. She hadn't drawn the drapes the night before, unconsciously wanting to be surrounded as soon as possible by the available light. She turned off the lamp beside her bed. Her mouth was sticky. She went to the bathroom and brushed her teeth. She was putting off having to go downstairs and discover the state of mind he was in. She paused on the stairs outside the studio. Should she go in, return to the mood of the night before and ask if he'd like coffee and English muffins. The door opened very slowly. Perhaps it was her own fear that cast the event in slow motion.

Hammond was in his favorite pale blue pajamas, the ones she had bought for Paulette to give him last year on his birthday. She smiled, 'good morning'.

Hammond said: 'I want to suck your balls. I want to work my finger into you. I want to feel what it's like to be taken from behind. I want you to squash me into oblivion.'

'Stop it!' Pandora screamed at him. 'For fuck's sake stop it!'

She wanted to run downstairs, to get away, but she was paralysed, a frozen image of herself. In that instant she knew he wanted to attack her. She felt the force of the slap, but not the pain. It was so sudden. Incarnate violence. She fell sideways. She gasped, cried out but she heard nothing. She saw herself thrown out of the studio. She saw herself tumbling onto the stairs. There was no sound. Inexplicably, the film she was watching was running silent. The sound, like the pain, would come later.

He crashed on top of her as she lay on the stairs. His hands tore at the buttons of her long nightgown which was twisted around her legs. She struggled to be free. His face was contorted with anger. He was screaming 'Bitch! Bitch!' His right hand grabbed her between her legs. She tried to sit up. He shoved his fingers into her. They were like knives. Knives? She realized that the pain had arrived. Her forehead banged against his and increased his fury.

Gripping the flesh of her thighs he was trying to move her, pushing her face against the wooden uprights of the bannisters. She glimpsed his hard penis which was sticking out of the opening of his pajama pants. It was no longer red. She felt cool air

229

on her bottom as he threw the material of her nightgown up around her shoulder-blades. Struggling and crying, Dora felt the confused terror of the attack. With the strangest detachment, Pan knew that he was turning her round to sodomise her. There were two of her, one feeling, one regarding. Involvement and objectivity.

His hands wrenched her buttocks apart. Dora could feel it. Pan could see it. He started to push into her. The pain was stunning. Dora yelled 'Stop it! Stop it!' Pan screamed inside her head, 'Don't let this happen!' Pandora was being torn apart. He won't stop. You must stop him. She gave one giant violent heave thrusting her bottom upwards, towards him, at him. Her flesh was her only weapon. Her buttocks slapped at his groin. With terrific force she bent and crushed his hard penis. Her flesh became rock. If his penis had been a bone like a dog's it would have cracked. He gave out an animal cry of pain. His hands left her thighs and went too late to protect his throbbing, agonised penis.

This was the moment. Using the fulcrum of her elbows on the stair carpet, Pandora heaved herself upwards. The tense and hard-soft weapon of her buttocks struck at him again. Hammond fell back, clutching his pain to control it. She scrambled up onto her knees. He was growling in agony. She turned around, looked down at the creature. She ought to have felt disgust, revulsion and hatred. But those confusions fled. Instead she wanted nothing more than to squash him, emasculate him, eradicate him, to pulp him like a dangerous insect. It wouldn't be murder. It would be beyond self-defense. It would be natural. She wanted to stamp on his stupid penis. The hatred in his eyes stopped her. There was the force of evil in his look. Criminal evil. The compulsion to destroy. He suddenly reached up and grabbed her hanging right breast. He pulled it trying to tear it from her chest. Pandora yelped in pain. Something popped in her head. She raised her right foot and rammed the heel into his abdomen. She felt the heelbone sink in below his navel. Hammond gave a cry. His eyes rolled in their sockets. Air whistled out through his teeth. His hand dropped her breast. He fell back groaning, crumpled, twisting on the stairs. Grasping the bannister rail she hauled herself up. Don't kill him, a voice said, don't kill my dad.

Pandora left Hammond growling on the stairs, a maimed male animal, his wretched genitals quivering limply out of the slit in his pajama pants. She wanted desperately to wash her body, scrub her skin, be cleansed of the disease. But she was in a hurry to get out of the house. She chose fresh underwear, brushed her hair violently, went to the closet for clothes. All the time she glanced round at the door fearing the monster's re-entry.

She thought she heard a sound. She ran from the bathroom to the table beside her bed. She pulled open the drawer and fumbled for the gun that lay next to her packet of contraceptive pills. She removed the safety catch. The weapon was armed, ready to fire. Her stomach heaved. She continued quickly to dress, holding the gun in her hand all the time.

Pandora pulled a dark blue dress from the closet. Moving the gun from hand to hand she struggled awkwardly to get into it. The tight sleeves were difficult. When she finally checked her appearance in the mirror, she shrieked out loud at what she saw. The blue material had been cut in several places. They were razor cuts, not wild slashes but careful incisions. In her haste to be clothed she hadn't seen them. She fought the onslaught of tears.

Returning to the closet pulling her dress off again, gasping for air, she wondered if he'd cut all her clothes. Then she saw the red dress. She took it from the hanger and inspected it quickly. It was untouched. She put it on. There was less difficulty with this dress. The cut was looser, the sleeves wider. Even as she pulled the dress down around her body Pandora was aware that in that choice there was an implication. She experienced a frisson of memory. Charles Wildman had been far from her thoughts in the past few hours. Now he was back.

She grabbed a coat, took her black bag, slotted her feet into elegant but flat white shoes. She was vaguely worried about the matching, but there was no time, none at all. She wondered whether to hide the gun in her bag or keep it in her free hand as she left the bedroom. She was scared. She held the weapon ready.

Hammond was still lying on the stairs. He had moved to one side, covered himself, and was facing away from her. He lay quite still, curled, seemingly asleep like a dog. Pandora edged past. She expected him to whip around and grab her legs. It didn't happen. She sighed with relief as she reached the bottom of the stairs. She hurried across the hall and left the house.

Pandora parked her car and went into a coffee shop on San Vicente Boulevard. She had two urgent calls to make. The first was abortive.

'She went to school two hours ago,' Mrs Wing told her.

Of course. Pandora looked at her watch. It was ten o'clock. Her sense of time had collapsed. Mrs Wing must have thought she was crazy. Well, she was crazy.

Pandora made an excuse, tried to sound together and told Mrs Wing she'd call Paulette later in the afternoon. She took several deep breaths before making the second call. She opened her bag and took out the piece of paper with the number he'd given her. She dialed. Please, please be there. I need you.

Wildman answered the phone in the loft. Laura was in the tub. She wouldn't hear the conversation. None the less he made it brief. He had waited a long time for her call.

'Meet me at the Shangri-La Hotel in Santa Monica. I'll be there in two hours.'

Pandora sat down at a table in the coffee shop. She ordered tea. Her hand shook as she lifted the cup to her lips. She needed a friend. The sexual memories confused her. The last thing she wanted now was sex. She wanted only to be with someone who could stop the horrible pounding of her heart.

When Hammond heard the front door close he whispered 'Goodbye Dora', without opening his eyes. She was finally gone. The pain in his crotch was easing. He was pleased. So far so good. He'd gotten rid of the bitch. He knew she would go to Wildman. Perfect. Now he could get to work, put his plan into action. He had been thinking all night about writing to him. He had wanted to say something succinct, to the point. He had read through a dictionary of quotations. Since Wildman had written to him in Latin on that model plane, something in that language would be appropriate. He needed a phrase to top 'The Die Is Cast'.

Around four in the morning he had found it. Eureka. It was fucking brilliant. SI TU NON VENERIS AD ME, EGO VENIAM AD TE. He made no attempt to pronounce the Latin but he read the translation out aloud several times: 'If you do not come to me, I'll come to you.'

Part Five

1

Hammond tried to figure out how to get his message to Wildman. A simple phonecall, a message on the machine, a straightforward letter; they were direct but lacked import. Ideally, Wildman ought to find it. Maybe in the glove compartment of his car, or taped to the bathroom mirror. Stapled to that fucking box. His thoughts were interrupted by a ring at the front door. Hammond decided to ignore it. He was expecting no one. He wanted no one. He was enjoying being by himself. The bell sounded again. Fuck off, whoever you are. Maybe it was the mail man with a package, another script from his agent. Leave the thing on the doorstep. The ringing continued. Perhaps it was some kind of message, Wildman trying to reach him. Hammond left his studio and went downstairs.

He looked through the spyhole. There was a woman out there. A woman he didn't recognize. She was wearing dark glasses. Was she one of his ex-wife's friends? The bell rang again, for the fifth time. Hammond opened the door. The woman who stood there, dressed in black, jolted his memory. Behind her in the drive was an old white Mustang. Shit. This was the woman who picked him up on the highway in San Bernadino. She was the dancer woman in black who had driven him back to Los Angeles. How had she found him?

'I want to talk to you,' Laura said without emphasis. 'Can I come in?'

Hammond hesitated. He felt the chill of danger. What did she want? More than that, what did she know?

Laura realized that Hammond didn't properly recognize her.

He probably remembered that she was the woman who picked him up on the highway, but it was clear that he didn't realize that she was also the woman with Wildman in his loft. His memory was erratic. He didn't immediately connect her with the woman who had done things to him there. He had been blindfolded for much of the time. The brainwashing had crumpled most of his recollection.

'Come in.' His voice was hoarse. He was afraid of her, but intrigued as well. In his mind she was connected with Wildman.

Laura's plan depended on Hammond realizing that she was Wildman's friend, and that they had a common interest. He would want his wife back. She wanted Wildman back. Together they would work on that. She would have to explain her relationship to Wildman. She would have to tell him that she knew everything. Then what would he do? Throw her out?

Hammond looked dazed and Laura took the initiative. She sat down in the living room without being asked.

'Mr Hammond, I want to talk about Charles Wildman,' she said bluntly.

'You know him?' Hammond was again confused. 'How did you find me? How did you know my name?' This turn of events shook him. He wasn't in control of this. Don't ask questions. Don't appear weak.

'Want a vodka?' he asked, needing one himself.

'Thank you, no.'

Without another word Hammond left the room. In the kitchen he attacked the bottle from the fridge. Two quick shots. He felt his confidence return. He went back to the woman, carrying his glass, having returned the icy bottle to its home. Don't get drunk.

'Take off your shades. I want to see your eyes.'

Laura took them off.

'I know about his affair with your wife.'

'I'm going to kill him.'

It was a statement of fact. Laura replied in the same tone. 'You've tried that once.'

'This time I'll make it.'

'You won't.'

'You'll see.' Hammond smiled. He felt he was getting the better of her. She wasn't so unassailable.

'I won't let you.'

'You won't be able to stop me.'

Laura saw that her task of persuasion was going to be difficult. She softened her manner.

'All you really want is to get your wife back.'

'Not true.'

'You don't want her back?'

'Not now she's been with him.'

'Look Mr Hammond, he's fucked hundreds of women.'

'Now he's fucked the wrong one.' Hammond's hard look and aggressive tone worried her. And the fact that he wasn't interested in who she was or what she wanted.

'I just want him back, that's all.'

'You'll get him back. Don't worry. He'll be in a body bag.'

Pandora awoke not knowing where she was. To begin with she thought she was home. But the bed felt wrong. The tall mirror had gone. The outside street noises were unfamiliar. There was way too much traffic. She panicked, sat up abruptly. Where was Alec?

Wildman appeared in the bathroom doorway. She put the pieces together. It was a frightening jigsaw. He could see her fear. He sat on the bed beside her.

'What time is it?'

'About four.'

Pandora had slept the whole day. She reached out and took his hand. She put his fingers to her lips. She smelt him, a sensual, comforting scent. Why was he so good to her? Was he good for her? He hadn't tried to make love to her the night before. She had slept in his arms. Now he stroked her naked skin. She felt the breeze from the open window. She couldn't hear the ocean above the traffic but she knew it was there. He bent down and picked her up. That physical strength was devastating. She melted.

239

Wildman lowered her into the warm bath water he had prepared. She was a baby. Or an invalid. He soaped her. She dissolved.

Wildman identified his enemy. More than Hammond, who no longer counted as a man in her life, it was Pandora's despairing lostness that could get to them, undermine them. He knew she needed him, desperately needed him now, but that wouldn't be enough in the long run. She would need self-reliance, self-possession. They would have to live together, not just be together. She wasn't like Laura. They were partners, but had separate lives. He and Laura came and went and they liked it that way. Wildman was unsure how to hold and keep this woman. Desire had brought them together. It had to be sustained, renewed. The essence of desire was that it must never be satisfied. Otherwise it would cease to be desire.

As he dried Pandora who was wrapped in the Shangri-La bathrobe, he got a flash. She was thinking about her daughter.

'Do you want to call her?'

'Who?'

'Your daughter.'

'How did you know I was thinking about Paulette?'

'Because you were.'

The momentary telepathy produced a wave of reassurance in Pandora. This was an exceptional man. But that same moment produced in Wildman a stab of discomfort. Paulette was the person he most feared. If Pandora were to leave him for anyone it would be for her.

Hammond drained his drink, but didn't go for another. He'd been listening to this woman's pleading for half an hour. He was bored. Fuck her. He wanted to get on with his work.

'I love the man. It's that simple,' she said calmly.

'That's your problem.' A question entered his mind. 'If he's slept with hundreds of women as you say, if he's now with my wife, why the hell do you want him back?'

'I don't mind about the others. Your wife's different. He wants her. He wants to keep her. And . . .'

'And?'

'And she wants him.'

Hammond froze. 'How do you know that?'

Laura didn't answer. She had scored a point.

'Maybe she does. Maybe she doesn't. Either way, she's not having him.'

'But you don't want her back. That's what you said.'

'You can't stop me. No one can. Do you understand? No one can stop me.' He heard himself shouting. Laura sensed confusion. Good. They could move on to the next stage. Hers.

'Where are you, Mom?'

'I'm staying in a hotel.' Pandora was speaking from the phone in the lobby. She and Wildman were on their way out. He was waiting for her at the desk.

'How is Dad?'

'I can't live in the house with him. He needs help.'

'What are you going to do?'

'I honestly don't know, darling. Maybe I should get a doctor for him.'

'Or go to the police.'

Pandora shivered. 'I can't do that. I can't.' She felt herself close to breaking down.

'I'm all right Mom. I'll be fine.' Paulette reassured Pandora as best she could before she hung up. She knew that sometime soon she would have to look after her mother. David took her hand and squeezed it.

'I've spoken to Mrs Long.'

Paulette smiled. 'What would I do without this man?' she thought.

'I'm not going to leave your side,' Laura said. 'I'm going to follow you.'

'Everywhere?'

'I'll even come into the toilet while you're taking a shit.'

'You're crazy.'

'You're not going to kill him.'

'Does that mean you're planning to stay here with me?'

'Exactly.'

'I'll throw you out.'

'Physically?'

'Of course physically.'

'If you do I'll come back in.'

'And if I go out?'

'I'll come too.'

'You couldn't keep it up.'

'You'll see.'

'What happens when I go to bed?'

'I'll come too.'

'You're going to get into bed with me?'

'I'm not going to fuck you. I'll just be in bed with you.'

'What happens if I try to make love to you?'

'I don't think you will.'

'Why not?'

'Because you'll be thinking all the time about him. There'll be three of us in bed.'

'You're right. I wouldn't fuck you in my wife's bed.'

'I forgot her. That makes four of us in bed.'

'This isn't a game. I could go to the police. They'd remove you.'

'Not after what I'd tell them. You won't go to the cops. As long as you want to kill him, you're stuck with me.'

'If I promise I won't kill him?'

'I wouldn't believe you.'

'So there's no way you'll leave?'

'No way.'

'You think I wouldn't kill a woman.'

'Not this woman. I'm pretty tough, you know. I know a few tricks. Remember, I live with a stunt man.'

'I ought to have a key,' Pandora said.

'Why?' There was a sudden, and to Pandora unexpected tone of distrust in Wildman's reaction. They were standing together at the Concierge's desk of the Shangri-La on their way out to the ocean and the afternoon sun.

'Well . . . I'll want to come and go, won't I?'

Wildman turned to the Concierge with a winning smile. 'Let Ms Harten have a key of her own.'

Pandora's skin prickled. A key of her own! This was not the moment to discuss loose phrases. But she didn't like the sound of this one. Certainly she had turned to Wildman for help, but not to be taken care of. She popped the spare key into her purse. If she was now in a prison, and she prayed she was not, at least she had her own key. As they came out of the hotel, down the four freshly painted white cement steps, Pandora sensed that Wildman intended to take her arm.

She longed for a drink. There was no bar in the Shangri-La, just drinks in the refrigerator in the room.

'I'd like a martini,' she told Wildman, instructing him in retaliation for his growing possessiveness.

'Good. I know a place. We can walk.'

'Outdoors or in?'

'Whichever.' He took her arm. 'For Christ's sake don't be mad at me. It's too soon for that.'

He smiled, sort of. Truce. Pact. She smiled back. She kissed him, put aside their edginess. Why couldn't they be as they were in bed? Together, grasped in agreement, in a place, in a state, in a position between a man and a woman where you could do, if not say, anything you wanted. If you timed it right.

'Where does he live? We'll start there,' Hammond said.

'He doesn't really live anywhere,' Laura said. The last thing she wanted to do was take Hammond back to the loft. 'He stays in hotels a lot of the time.'

'Hotels? Why?'

'He likes hotels.'

'Where was I taken? Was it your place?'

Laura avoided Hammond's question. 'He met her in a hotel.'

'How? Dora never goes to hotels. She lives here.'

'She plays tennis, doesn't she, at the Bel Air Hotel with a friend.'

'Let's start there.'

'He wouldn't go back there.'

Not to the scene of the crime? Hammond knew that you always went back to the scene of the crime. It was as inescapable as childhood.

'I think you know where they are.'

'I'm telling you I don't.'

Hammond left Laura in the kitchen and went up to his studio. He took the yellow pages and began systematically to call every good hotel on the west side of Los Angeles. He couldn't imagine Wildman taking Pandora to anything other than a luxury setting. If you are on the run with a woman like her you don't go to sleazy hotels or cheap motels. You would, he reasoned, want an atmosphere of comfort. He'd soon put an end to that. 'If you won't come to me, I'll come to you.'

Despite her threat to remain at his side, Laura left him alone. In her mind she went through the places she'd been with Wildman. Attractive, up-market places to play the game, to make the hit. She knew now Hammond would find them however long it took. He was obsessed. He would never let up. She had a certain sympathy for him, for what he had endured. He was uninteresting as a man but there was an animal courage in him she found vaguely attractive. He was a victim. Like her.

Laura wondered if Wildman had taken Pandora out of town. She had gone with him to Santa Barbara a few times. They both liked Santa Barbara, the marina. Wildman enjoyed being near the ocean. Yes, he would want to go there. But she wouldn't. She was a mother. That was crucial. She wouldn't want to be too far from her daughter. So Santa Monica was a good bet. In the past they both liked the art deco style of the Shangri-La. Laura felt that she was now somehow looking not for Pandora but for herself.

2

'I need a change of clothes,' Pandora said. 'But I don't want to go home.'

'Let me buy you some. I'd enjoy that.'

'I can buy my own clothes.'

'What I meant was, let me choose them.'

That's odd, Pandora thought. No man has ever asked to do that before. Never in my life. Alec in happier times had occasionally bought her a scarf or a pair of tights but he had never gone with her to a store or boutique, never made a suggestion or said this is what I'd like you to wear. She ought not to be so touchy now. Be flattered. Remember the red dress. He'd been right about that. After all, she was wearing it.

They went to Eugenie in Santa Monica, a boutique specializing in imported designer clothes. Pandora had bought things there in the past, usually when there had been a sale. This time there was no sale. She would have to pay the exorbitant tab. The days of careful housekeeping were over. The days of careful everything were over.

Thinking about money little Pandora could see her father handing over pocket money on Saturday after breakfast, counting out the dollars with what she always felt was reluctance. Now he was dead and she would be quite rich. Rich. Was all that had happened, the chaos of her recent existence, to be compensated with an inheritance?

The salesgirl in Eugenie recognized Pandora.

'Hi Mrs Hammond. How are you today?'

Pandora flinched. She hadn't expected to be recognized.

Would this girl assume Wildman was her husband? Alec had never been in the shop. Was she worried about infidelity? Pandora had to smile. What the hell did that matter now?

Wildman left her side and began to look purposefully through the lines of dresses. Pandora joined him. He was holding up a silver dress in pleated metallic fabric. He looked at the label. It was Japanese.

'Isn't that too dressy?' Pandora didn't like it.

'You've just never worn silver before.' Wildman didn't care.

'Never.'

'Maybe it's time for a change.'

He removed the dress from its hanger and gave it to Pandora.

'The fitting room's right there.' The salesgirl pointed to the curtained cabin. 'It's a fabulous dress.'

Pandora still didn't like it. She didn't want to put it on. But neither did she want to get into a discussion. As she pulled the red dress over her head in the fitting room she looked at herself in the mirror. She was startled. There was an ugly bruise on her left breast. She found two more bruises, one on her upper right arm, the other on her left thigh. It looked as though she'd been beaten up. Well, she had. The memory of Alec's attack on the stairs sickened her. With trepidation she twisted around to examine her bottom. She winced as she saw the marks on her flesh. She touched them, pressed them, producing a dull ache.

'How does it look?'

Pandora jumped. Wildman had parted the curtain and was looking at her.

'Did he do that to you?'

'I don't want to talk about it.'

'You don't have to.' Wildman wondered how he could have missed those bruises the night before. Perhaps they'd taken this time to emerge. Or had he been so thrilled at her presence at the hotel he simply hadn't really looked at her.

'Here. Let me help you.' He picked up the silver dress, folded it, reached up and slipped it over her head and shoulders. He straightened the hem. He turned her around in front of the mirror.

'I'm not sure,' she said.

'It's perfect.'

'It doesn't go with my hair.'

'We'll change your hair.'

'Change it? How?'

'Dye it. Black.'

'I've never dyed my hair.'

'Until now.'

'What are you trying to do to me?'

Pandora knew what he was doing. He wanted her for himself, looking the way he wanted her to look. He wanted to alter her so that she no longer resembled Alec's wife.

'Do they sell lingerie here?'

'Yes, I think so.'

'What size are you? 36C?'

Pandora smiled. He was spot on. Did he know her so well, so intimately, or was it just women he knew?

'Black. A soft line. Nothing see-through.'

'Look, I'm not sure about this . . .'

'Pandora. I'm sure.'

That was the first time he'd used her name.

Hammond stayed in the Mustang, illegally parked on the ocean side of the street, while Laura went in to check the hotel register.

'Is Mr Wildman registered?'

'There is no one of that name in the hotel.'

The middle-aged clerk watched the computer screen. He shook his head.

'That's strange,' Laura said. 'I was supposed to meet him here. He's a tall man, six two, dark-haired, dressed usually in black. I think he said he was with a woman.'

Laura knew that Wildman often stayed in hotels using a false name. He had several credit cards in different names. She tried to remember them now.

'There is a gentleman staying here who fits your description but his name's not, what was it you said, Wildman?'

'Oh. I wonder if –'

'Are you a detective?' The clerk was suddenly suspicious. What he really meant was, are you this man's wife trying to catch him with another woman?

'No, no. Do they have women detectives? This is very difficult. If Mr Wildman's used another name, well that's not my affair. Look, I have another appointment soon. Could I just leave a message just in case he's the same man?'

'I guess so.' The clerk was still reluctant.

'I'll just go back to my car and write it. Can I take some notepaper?'

'Sure. But can't you write it here?'

Laura returned to Hammond. She wasn't sure what to write, if anything. She told Hammond she thought Wildman was there but registered under another name.

Hammond laughed. Dumb bastard.

'Give me the paper,' he said. What a wonderful stroke of luck, he thought, as he carefully copied out his Latin dictum. Laura had thought they would merely watch and wait for him to appear with Pandora.

Hammond sealed the Shangri-La envelope and gave it to Laura. She hadn't seen what he had written. She wondered if it was really for Pandora.

She handed the envelope to the desk clerk, who was now distracted with a couple of businessmen checking out. The clerk pushed the letter towards his assistant.

'Put this in Mr Hammond's box, will you?'

Laura was chilled. That was weird. Wildman had checked in under the name of his enemy. She couldn't tell Hammond. He was crazy enough.

Wildman insisted that Pandora wear the silver dress and the new lingerie. The old stuff was packed into a bag by the salesgirl. Pandora paid with her platinum Amex card. It matched her dress.

'Pandora!' It was a female voice surprised, uncertain. Against the evening light from the street stood a familiar woman. There was a man with her.

'Hi Beverly.' Pandora prickled with guilt. She hadn't called Beverly to tell her that Alec was back. She hadn't been in touch. And here she was buying clothes with a strange man. What would it look like?

'My, you look just great.' Beverly stared at Wildman. She knew she had seen the guy somewhere before. Where? Wildman smiled back at her pleasantly. He gave no sign that he remembered her from the dining room at the Bel Air. Pandora made no move to introduce Wildman.

'Hello Jimbo,' she said to the man with Beverly. So he had come back. They must have made it up. Jimbo awkwardly shook hands with Pandora. He was too nervous to kiss her. She must know the story. He nodded to Wildman. Beverly had told him about Hammond's disappearance just the other day. So Pandora had grabbed herself another guy. That was quick, Jimbo thought.

'Alec is back.' Now she had to tell Beverly. It was like a joke. Both our husbands are back. After tennis we can talk about it all. But Pandora wouldn't be playing tennis for a while.

'I'm so glad. I knew it would work out.'

Beverly curbed her inquisitiveness. The girl had ditched Jimbo. So he had come home. He had had nowhere else to go. They never really do. Now Beverly was back in the driver's seat and Jimbo was drowning in guilt and humiliation. On one level things were fine.

'I must get back,' Pandora announced. Among the ritual goodbyes Pandora heard Wildman, as he shook Jimbo's hand, say 'Good luck'. What did that mean? He couldn't know about Beverly's trouble. What an odd thing to say.

Outside they walked to the parked car. The flat white shoes weren't right with the new clothes. Wildman touched Pandora's arm.

'You look wonderful,' he said, meaning I feel wonderful with you at this moment.

On the short drive back to the hotel Pandora suffered a wave of nausea induced by connecting her experience to Beverly's. Two women, both with children, both with husbands who left home and returned. Two men, one of them chastened, the other crazed, each of them having attempted sodomy, anal rape. What did that mean? She remembered how appalled Beverly had been catching Jimbo in the act. The male frustration, the sexual violence, was that aggression provoked by us?

She glanced at Wildman. Was he the healer who washed away the sins of sodomy with a flannel and warm water? Did he protect the sphincter, or awaken it? She was having an affair, not of the heart, but of the bowels. She shifted in her seat. The shocked memory of the scene on the stairs came back into her mind. She put her hand on her bag lying beside her. She felt the hardness of the gun inside.

Wildman picked up the keys at the desk. Pandora went to the elevator. The clerk handed him the envelope addressed to 'Mr Hammond'. Wildman's hand twitched involuntarily. Who could possibly know he was here? And 'Mr Hammond', who would know he had checked in under that name? Or was the note for Hammond himself? That was crazy, unless Laura . . . While Pandora waited, he tore open the envelope. The Latin was simple. Clearly a quotation. But he couldn't identify it. He stared at the words. Out of the corner of his eye he saw Pandora coming over to him. Wildman stuffed the envelope and the page into his pocket, and joined her. They went up to the room.

Pandora could sense his unease. Wildman went into the bathroom and closed the door in two stages, leaving it ajar, then shutting it. The hesitancy seemed untypical. She looked at herself in the mirror. Not bad. Perhaps he was right about this silver dress, as he'd been right about the red dress. He was accurate about her, in bed, in clothes, in everything it seemed. She found it sensual but scary too. She ought to call Paulette. And say what? There was nothing to say.

Should she go to the police after all? But a wife testifying against her husband? She was paralysed. Just stay with this man, this sympathetic, dominating stranger, just for a while, and try to figure things out. Everything was twisted. There were no straight lines.

Si Tu Non Veneris ad me, Ego Veniam ad Te. The note had come from Hammond. Unless Hammond had listened in to Pandora's call to him. Laura must have gone to see him. So she was with him now. Why the fuck had she done that? The plan had been working so well. Now the die was cast again. There would have to be another confrontation, another fight, another duel. This time he would have to kill him. That much was certain.

Except that this time he would have Pandora with him. Should he tell her now about the Latin challenge? How much should he explain? Would it be enough to say that Hammond was threatening him, threatening them? That wouldn't surprise her. Of course she would never go back to him. Not now. On the other hand, would she stay with the man who killed her husband? Yes. She would if she didn't know that he was responsible. That was the key. Let her know enough to feel sympathy. Don't forget, she'd called him. She wanted him.

Wildman came out of the bathroom. He looked worried as he handed her the note.

'What is it?' Pandora stared at the Latin message.

'It's from your husband.'

'What? How do you know?' She was sick with confusion. 'Why would he send a message in Latin? He can't . . .' Pandora stopped. *Iacta Ilea Est*. Her heart stopped. The inscription on that model plane. 'The Die Is Cast'.

'I'll translate it. It means "If you don't come to me, I'll come to you."'

Pandora wanted to shout I know what it means. What I want to know is what's going on?

'I don't understand,' she said.

She did understand. 'If you don't come to me, I'll come to you. The die is cast.'

She couldn't get the phrase out of her mind. She had translated it for Alec. Now she remembered that Wildman had used that same expression when he came to the house, when the silence took over. He had whispered it to her.

'He's found out where I am. Where we are.'

'How could he?'

'He must have been listening when you called me.' Wildman left Laura out of it.

Pandora's mind was spinning. She knew Alec hadn't heard that conversation. There was something else.

'What do you think I should do?' he asked. Wildman considered it was an innocent, but effective question. She'd think he was as confused as she. He was asking for advice.

Pandora heard herself say 'I think maybe I should leave.'

'Leave? Why?'

'I don't want you to get involved with all this. It's not your affair.'

'I am involved. The note was sent to me.'

Pandora needed to sit, she needed to think. There was something else going down. There were missing pieces. Where had Alec gone when he disappeared? What really happened? Alec can't read Latin. So why would he write to Wildman in Latin? It had to be some kind of response to 'The die is cast'. That crazy model plane. The phonecall in the Japanese restaurant. He had passed it off. But what had that strange incident been about? She went blank.

'Why don't you leave?' she said. She had to be alone to think. Perfect, he thought. He'd leave for a while. Hammond was probably watching the place. With Laura. Let them make the next move. He'd just keep out of the way for a while. There was a problem with that. If Hammond came into the hotel it might put Pandora in some danger. That was bad. She'd had enough. On the other hand Hammond probably didn't want to harm her. It was him he wanted. It was still tricky.

'Why don't you leave?' Pandora said again.

'All right. I'll go down. I'll see if he's out there.'

'You think he is?'

'I'll find out.' He was pleased with that plausibility. 'Wait here. And for God's sake don't answer the door. Don't even answer the phone.' Wildman took Pandora in his arms. 'You look so beautiful. I'm not going to let anything happen to you.'

He kissed her. She felt a firmness in his lips. They were tense like muscles. It wasn't fear. He didn't seem scared. He seemed determined. She was scared.

'Don't answer the door.'

'No. I won't. Be careful.'

He went to the door. She watched him. They both privately thought the same thing – it was like a scene from a movie. The situation, the dialog, seemed to come from someone else's script. And the plot? That was different. He knew the plot. She didn't.

After he left, Pandora sat on the bed. She stared again at the Latin. A wild idea came into her head. Alec wasn't really crazy. He was just acting crazy. Maybe his violence had been real enough. But all that other stuff. The scene with Paulette? Could that have been staged? No. He was crazy.

She went into the bathroom. She sat on the toilet. In the plastic lined basket under the basin was a scrunched envelope. Pandora leant down to take it. She unfolded it. The envelope that had contained the message. It was addressed: 'Mr Hammond'. She didn't believe it. How could it be addressed to Alec? Not Mrs Hammond. Mr. This was impossible. Wildman was calling himself Hammond. My God. My God. Who's crazy?

3

Pandora came out of the hotel. She didn't look around. She went straight to her car which was parked around the corner, away from the ocean. She tried not to think of Alec somewhere out there on the street watching her. Her mind was ticking with interpretations of the message, disturbed confusions about Wildman's behavior. She now had a single intention in her head. To be with Paulette. Her daughter mustn't suffer any more.

It was Laura who saw her through the cruising traffic. Hammond was sitting next to her in the Mustang. He was imagining Wildman alone. Laura turned the ignition key.

'Please get out of my car,' she said as the engine started.

'What?' His thought train was disrupted.

'There's something I have to do. Someone I have to see.'

'Now?'

'Yes, right now.'

'How long will you be? I thought you were going to stick with me like glue.'

'I'll be back.'

Out of the corner of her eye she saw Pandora turn the corner. She knew where Pandora's BMW was parked. Hammond was put out by the suddenness of Laura's decision. But then he didn't care if she went. She'd been helpful but he was happy to be alone now. He prickled with excitement at the thought of his next encounter with Wildman. The car started to move as he climbed out.

'See you later,' Laura called.

She swung the wheel and spun the Mustang across the traffic to the sound of objecting car horns. Crazy woman. Hammond watched her go. He was suddenly alone on the street opposite the hotel. He looked up wondering which room they were in. He could see them together. Her on top of him. He suddenly wanted to get on with it. Wildman would have read the note by now. Perhaps she translated it for him. He would be panicked. I may be down, Hammond thought, but I'm not out. Here I come.

At the reception desk the night clerk, an older man, had just come on, taking over from the girl who had changed her clothing for a date. The girl hurried past Hammond with a smile as he approached the desk. The reception area was deserted. Eight thirty was a quiet time.

'Hi. My name is Hammond. I think Mr Wildman is –'

'– Yes Mr Hammond,' said the clerk. He was eager to please and he had done his homework. He knew the hotel guest list. '305. There you go.' He reached for the key and gave it to Hammond. 'Have a nice evening.' 305. Hammond and Harten. The clerk hadn't actually seen either of them. He knew the facts.

'Thank you.' Dazed, Hammond took the key. He looked at it. What the hell was going on? Don't hesitate. Check it out. He walked to the elevator and rode to the third floor.

This was crazy. Maybe he had the wrong key. How did the guy at the desk know his name was Hammond? Maybe there was someone else in the hotel called Hammond? But the guy had seemed to recognize him. Plus he hadn't reacted at all to the name Wildman.

Hammond walked along the third floor hallway to 305. He looked around. If there was another Hammond the guy was out. He inserted the key in the lock and quietly turned it.

The room was in darkness, but there was a shaft of light coming from the bathroom door which was ajar. Hammond froze. Without closing the door to the hallway he listened. Was someone there? He clenched his fist involuntarily.

'Dora,' he whispered.

There was no answer, no sound. He waited before closing the door. No, someone had just left the bathroom light on. He crossed the bedroom silently. He pushed open the bathroom door. A flash of scarlet caught his eye. Dora's red dress was draped over a chair. On the floor were her panties and bra. He picked them up. He was instantly aroused. It surprised him. Hadn't he gotten over that? Then he realized that he wasn't thinking of Dora. He was remembering Betty May. He hadn't thought of her for a long time. Strange. It had all begun with her.

He sat on the bed, tried to get his head straight. He could see the girl lying face down on the bed in the Arizona hotel. He could feel Betty May's firm flesh under his hands. As he pulled her panties down the tight buttocks moved up, the muscles tensing, towards him. He opened the crack, felt the heat. He could hear the cicadas outside in the parking area. He breathed the stale stuffiness of the motel room. He touched himself between the legs. He slapped the backs of the girl's thighs as she had asked him, cautiously at first, then harder. Her moving bottom slowly danced.

Had this memory been in his mind with Dora on the stairs? Was that what he wanted, to penetrate her as if she had been Betty May? Perhaps all that had happened was a desire for things he had never done? Wildman perhaps understood that and provided him with a scenario of violent sexuality. Why else had he checked into this hotel in the name of Hammond? There were two men merging in their relationship with two women living a secret desire to sodomise. Wildman had probably done that to Betty May. And to Dora. Yet he wasn't gay. Hammond wasn't gay either. Between them there must be something truly perverted. Was that what Wildman wanted, to bugger him? Hammond knew he was sick, had become sick. He knew that that sickness in him was Wildman. And if proof were needed Wildman now called himself Hammond.

Wildman was listening at the door to 305. He smiled. Got you! He almost said it out loud. You're in there, aren't you, trapped like a bug in a bottle. I'll let you sweat. I'll pick my time. Then I'll swat you flat. Wildman went downstairs. He felt like a beer.

Laura sat in her car on Alpine Drive across the road from the Wing's house. She couldn't figure why Pandora had gone there. Whose house was it? She had been sure that Pandora was going home to Rancho Park. She looked at the clock in the dash. It was nine thirty five. She would wait. She wondered whether Hammond had found Wildman. If he had, poor man, he'd be dead by now. Time stretched for Laura, like elastic. It wouldn't break but it would snap back.

Mrs Wing told Pandora that Paulette was out having dinner with David and a friend of the family, Mrs Long.

'I thought it would be nice for them,' Mrs Wing said.

'How long do you think they will be?' Pandora now wished she had called ahead.

'Not long. There's school tomorrow.'

Pandora didn't know what to do. She had interrupted a dinner party and she felt awkward.

'I'll go home,' she decided, 'and call her later. I'm so sorry for all this trouble. It's a very difficult time.'

'We're happy to help,' Mrs Wing said. 'Paulette is a charming girl. So grown-up for her age. But then, girls always are, aren't they?'

Pandora left and drove to her home. The place was dark. Alec's car was there in the garage. She asked herself why she had come back at all. The answer was because she had nowhere else to go. She wondered whether she wanted to return to Santa Monica at all. It was all so blurred. That Latin message. The silver dress. The black underwear. Meeting Beverly with Jimbo. And Wildman. Why had he checked in using Alec's name?

Pandora didn't get out of the car right away. She watched her house through the windshield. The place scared her now. It was like a movie horror house. A Gothic place full of terrors. Despite the car in the garage she felt sure Alec wasn't there. If Wildman had been right he was going crazy in Santa Monica.

Pandora finally got out of the car. The night air was chilling. The silver dress seemed cold to her skin like metal. She walked in the front door reaching into her bag for the key. She felt the weight of the gun. She was thankful to be armed.

The house was cold, like a tomb. She switched on the living room lights. The place became brighter but no warmer. She went to the kitchen and poured herself a vodka from the fridge. The cold alcohol warmed her throat, burned her stomach. In a few minutes she would call Paulette. As she sipped the drink she thought of Alec, how she used to be worried about his drinking. She remembered the anger it could produce in him, the hidden violence, and it made her shiver. The ice cubes clinked in her glass. The whole experience was almost supernatural. A prophecy fulfilled. It seemed to her that the seeds of this violence had been sown a long while ago in comfortable times.

Hammond realized Wildman wouldn't find a key at the desk when he returned. He would assume Pandora was in the room. So he would knock. Hammond would have to open the door. That was awkward. He planned to nail Wildman with a single blow. He had the brass column of the bedside lamp ready. But logistically it would be hard to open the door with one hand and strike the man with the other. Better fix that now. Hammond left the room with the door unlocked and hurried down to the desk. He prayed Wildman wouldn't be there. He was lucky. He put the key on the desk. The clerk was in the office. Then he quickly returned to the room and closed the door.

Hammond decided to position himself behind the door with the room in total darkness. He could see Wildman coming in, reaching for the light switch beside the door. He would catch him cold. He hoped Dora would not be with him. Yet that would be natural under the circumstances. He didn't want to kill Wildman in front of Dora. It might be good for her, the bitch, to see her lover die. But for practical reasons he didn't want her as a witness. She might do something stupid like go to the cops. This had nothing to do with the law. This was natural justice. Just two men, the way it must have been before anyone thought of having police.

What would happen if Dora came back first and alone? He would tie her up, gag her as he had been gagged, and put her in the bathtub. That might be good for her, considering the way she thought she could go on just as before, playing the good wife, after fucking her brains out. He assumed she had gone to see Paulette, wherever she was holed up, with the Balfours perhaps, or with that air-head friend of hers, Beverly.

As Hammond waited, sitting on the end of the bed, a great calm came over him. Should he fill the bathtub now? It would save time later. He was startled by a knock on the door.

'Room service.'

It was a man's voice. A waiter, perhaps. But he hadn't ordered anything. He decided not to answer. He didn't want anyone else to get a sight of him, certainly not in the room.

'Room service.' The voice again.

Shit. Would the waiter have a key? He mustn't come in and find him. Say something.

'Just leave it outside, would you.'

He waited for a reaction. When it came it was what Hammond most feared. The sound of a key inserted, turning in the lock. He positioned himself behind the door. He wasn't dumb. This could be a Wildman trick. Maybe it wasn't room service at all.

The door opened. And opened, and opened. The wide arc forced him back against the wall. Hammond felt a surge of panic as the door started to press against him. The brass weapon knocked gently against the advancing door. The wood pressed against his body, trapping him. He had to act. He pushed the door violently.

The door moved only an inch. Wildman had his foot against it. The door stopped. Hammond shoved it with all his strength. Wildman removed his foot. Hammond stumbled forward. Wildman took hold of the door and slammed it into him. He pounded Hammond over and over again. Hammond cried out in pain as the door struck the side of his face. He didn't let go of the lamp.

Wildman kicked the door shut and snapped on the light.

259

Hammond, blinded for a moment, lurched forward, bent. Wildman brought his knee up. There was a crack as it connected with Hammond's jaw. Hammond straightened. Wildman grabbed his left wrist, twisted it sharply and threw him across the room. Hammond gasped with pain. He still held the brass lamp column as he fell against the end of the bed. Wildman advanced on him.

Hammond swung at him with his weapon. Wildman tried to dodge it, but the metal struck his thigh, throwing him momentarily off-balance. Hammond saw his chance. He rammed the lamp upwards into Wildman's groin. Wildman felt a stab of pain. Hammond hoisted himself up, using the end of the bed. Wildman knew he had to get the weapon away from him. He backed away.

The two men were now facing each other, bruised and panting.

'I have to make a call,' Wildman said.

'What?'

Hammond watched Wildman go around the bed to the phone. He knew he was being deliberately provoked. Anger rose like vomit from his stomach. In a fury he jumped onto the bed, stamped across the cover, wobbling, and struck out at Wildman's sarcastic expression. Wildman had expected this. He dodged the swinging lamp which smacked into the wall above the bedside table. Wildman punched him in the neck. Hammong gasped and fell against the bedhead. He dropped the lamp. Wildman climbed on top of Hammond. Don't kill him here, a voice spoke. The two men wrestled like lovers in an extended spasm of passion. Hammond felt he was drowning again. Wildman was on top. He heard the bedsprings groan. He pressed Hammond's neck finding the pressure point. As he watched Hammond losing consciousness Wildman felt a hardening in his groin.

Laura waited five minutes before getting out of her car. She walked up the short drive and rang the bell. The sound startled Pandora. Who was that? She came out of the kitchen and went up to the door. She looked out through the spyhole. It was a woman. She didn't recognize her. Laura pressed the bell again. Cautiously, Pandora opened the door.

'Mrs Hammond?'

'Yes.'

'We've met before, or at least half-met.'

'We have?'

'At the Bel Air Hotel.'

Pandora stared at Laura. The distraught woman. The woman with the gun. But wasn't she dead? Hadn't she killed herself?

'Don't you think it's time we talked?'

'Come in.'

The two women sat in the living room. Laura had calculated what she had to say. It would determine whether or not she got Wildman back.

Pandora was now beyond confusion. She was distraught. She felt at a hideous disadvantage. She wanted to know so much. She had no idea where to begin.

'He told me you were dead. That you'd committed suicide.'

'That's not quite true, as you can see.'

'He didn't have to lie.'

'Men do that. I guess he wants to be rid of me. At least in his head.'

'What do you know about me? About my husband?'

Laura did not want to talk about the kidnap or the brainwashing.

'I know nothing about your life. Nor do I want to.'

'What do you want? Why are you here?'

'It's simple, Mrs Hammond. I want him back. That man is my life.'

'Look, the truth is I know almost nothing about him. All I know is that he's a photographer.'

'Is that what he told you? He's not a photographer. He's a stunt man.'

'A what?' Pandora remembered her conversation with Rosie. A stunt man? Didn't that girl on Alec's movie die in a stunt? 'Did he work on a movie with my husband?'

'I believe he did, yes.'

'What really happened?'

'I have no idea. I'm only interested in what's going to happen. That's why I'm here. I want you to give him up. I want you not to see him again. Ever.'

For the first time Pandora saw herself, not just from the outside, not simply as two people, Pan and Dora, but from someone else's point of view. The woman sitting opposite her in her own house had cast her as the other woman. To Hammond she was a whore, an adulteress. To Wildman she was an object of desire, someone to be rescued, or possessed. To this woman, whatever her name was, Pandora was the other woman. She had never been that before. She had never even imagined herself sharing a man. Now she was regarded as a girlfriend, a mistress.

She knew she ought to feel defensive. *If he prefers me to you that's his choice.* Instead, she felt aggressive. *I've been pushed around, scared, abused enough. I've had it up to here being manipulated. Object of desire, object of disgust, they came down to the same thing.* Now here was a woman telling her what she must do. A woman she didn't know existed.

'Look, I don't know who you are. Right now I've got enough problems without taking instructions from you. You come into my house and tell me that the guy I'm seeing is a liar and a philanderer. Maybe he did lie about his work. But then again, maybe he didn't. Maybe you're lying. How can I tell? Why should I believe you? Wouldn't you lie to get him back?'

'I'm not lying.' Laura spoke calmly. She was unnerved by Pandora's aggression. She hadn't expected it. *A woman would understand another woman,* she had thought. Now she saw this approach had been a mistake. Wildman had gotten to her. It was clear this woman had fallen for him. After all, she was only a Beverly Hills housewife. She would naturally be impressed by his advances, his compulsive sexuality. He wasn't just a trick to her. She might even imagine she'd found the real thing. So there was no point in trying to reason with her. Laura felt close to tears. She should never have come to see Hammond. Now she'd come to this house twice. She should have stayed out of it, sat on the sidelines, waited in her prison cell, waited for the sound of his footsteps again.

Laura got unsteadily to her feet.

'Forgive me,' she said.

Pandora watched Laura pick up her bag and leave the room. She heard her leave the house. She was pleased at her show of authority. It was more satisfying than her earlier vindictiveness. The only thing was, Pandora could see that this nameless woman had loved, did love, Wildman. Whereas she did not.

This time when she called the Wings', Paulette was there.

'Where are you, Mom?'

'I'm home right now darling.'

'Where's Dad?'

'He's not here. I don't know where he is.'

'What are you going to do?'

'I don't know, darling.'

'Mom, don't cry. Please don't cry. I know what to do.'

'What do you mean?'

'Don't worry. I've found out how to help.'

'Paulette, what are you talking about?'

'Nothing. Just don't worry. Things will turn out OK.'

'You're not going to try and come back here are you?' Pandora suddenly had a vision of Paulette coming home, while she wasn't there, talking to Alec, trying to reason with him.

'No. I'm staying here. Try not to worry about me, Mom.'

It was an awful, ridiculous thing, a mother not being able to see her daughter, be with her.

After she had hung up, Pandora wondered what Paulette had meant when she said, I know what to do. If only I did, she thought.

4

Pandora stayed alone in the house for two hours before she finally decided to return to the hotel. She had expected a call from Wildman who must be wondering where she was. She thought about calling the Shangri-La, but that would mean she would have to make up her mind right away whether to go to him or stay where she was.

She went up to the studio, turned on the lights, looked around. She had the oddest sensation she would never see Alec again. The room was still littered with his drawings of the box. Why had he done so many sketches? They all looked the same. It was only a box. Then she saw a small pile of handwritten pages. They were hers, her writings to Luke. So that was what happened. Alec had read them. That was what provoked him into attacking her, swearing obscenities at her. He had been quoting her own words.

Pandora felt weak. He must have thought that she had written them to Wildman. But that didn't make sense. If he thought that, Wildman himself would have them. Unless Alec assumed she had written but never sent them. If only she had left them where they had lived for years, in her father's desk. They meant nothing really, all that time ago, in adolescence, yet they had made her realize how her father despised her. Now she had made a gift of them to Alec who, like her father, had reacted with disgust. It seemed to Pandora that her fate had been lying around, hidden for decades, waiting to be excavated. Everything came back. She went upstairs and lay down on her bed. She felt like crying, crying out loud to release her misery and frustration.

She cried, but no sound came. She cried but heard nothing. She was deaf.

Laura saw Wildman walking across the street supporting the apparently drunken body of Hammond. Still numb from her visit to Pandora she had been sitting in her car near the hotel, for what seemed like hours, watching people pass, waiting, irresolute, for something to lead her. Lead her where? Not back to Wildman. She had failed. Pandora wasn't going to let him go. But the sight of him now with Hammond lifted her spirits. Whatever he had done to Hammond, he was alive, not lost to her. It wasn't over yet. She remembered the night at the house when she and Wildman had taken Hammond's soaking body to the car. Time had flashed back. They were where they had been before. There was a second chance. She got out of the car and started to follow them at a distance as the swaying couple went towards the pier where the funfair was blasting its violent music.

This was one of those nights when time ran backwards. Wildman dreamed again of the sea, of the sand dunes, the scattered rocks placed like markers for some ancient game for which the rules were long lost. When Pandora returned and climbed into bed beside him she joined him on the sunny shore. He moved towards her, found her, drew her to him. Her body felt as if it had been warmed by the sun. He knew that outside the hotel room was darkness and noise, but for him the here and now was noon and silence, the silence of the sea.

I am this man's mistress, Pandora said silently. This man is my lover. He wants me. I am not the other woman to him. On the drive from her home she had planned to ask questions, demand answers. About Alec, about the dead girl, about the woman who had visited her like a revenant. Now in the darkness of the room, in the warmth of this bed, that did not belong to her or him, she wanted nothing more than to be touched and held. Was that her weakness, to change emotional direction so quickly, from independence and aggression three hours ago to

265

longing and submission now? The deafness had come and gone again. She no longer looked on it as a sign to be interpreted. It was a condition to be accepted. The ebb and flow of silence was analagous to the movement of her feeling. It wasn't symbolic. It was simply a form of music. Like the sound of the sea it could be adapted to your moods. The calm sea could represent anything from peace to boredom, contentment to desolation. The storm of lashing waves could be fear or desire, a sound accompanying isolation or destruction. It was only liquid. When he entered her, when she absorbed him, she was mercury, running silver inside.

Laura found Hammond under the pier bound to a heavy pile with electric cable. The incoming tide was inches from his face. It took her several minutes to untie him. He watched her blearily. When she had to move him he groaned in pain.

'I'm not dead,' Hammond said. 'I'm not dead.' There was no sense of relief in his voice. It was a plain statement of fact.

Laura wondered why Wildman had left him like this. It was as if he was giving Hammond a last chance. Had he calculated that someone might free him before he drowned? Was it a game, the kind he used to play with her? Laura drove Hammond towards Malibu, to a motel just off the Pacific Coast Highway. He didn't protest. He was exhausted and in physical pain. Sitting dejected beside her in the Mustang he was aware of the irony. For a second time this woman had picked him up after a fight with Wildman. This time she had saved him. He probably owed her his life. He was getting used to being close to death.

Some instinct made Laura ask for a double room instead of two singles. She felt responsible for Hammond. She helped him undress. He was badly bruised. He washed in the bathroom, longed to brush his teeth, came to bed in his shorts. Laura was already in the bed. She had switched her light out. She had undressed. She couldn't bear the idea of sleeping in her clothes. She kept her panties on. Hammond climbed into the bed, turned away from her without a word and turned his light off.

During the night Laura woke to find Hammond clinging to

her, his face buried between her shoulder blades. She felt him shaking. He made no sound. He wasn't crying. Was he thinking of his wife? She turned herself around within the grasp of his arms. She could see the child in him. She felt the mother in herself. She shifted her position, placing his head between her breasts. His grip on her body weakened. He put his arms around her waist, one hand on her thigh.

What a strange couple we make, Laura thought. Two jilted people lying in each other's arms, needing comfort, reassurance, peace. This was a feeling that had no place with Wildman. Laura was unused to any sensation with a man without a sensual root. She yearned for Wildman between her legs. But here and now this man's warmth was surprisingly satisfying. It must be what regular married life was like.

Hammond imagined he could hear the ocean. His face resting in the soft flesh of a woman he hardly knew provoked memories that were dreamy rather than violent. This was another motel room far from Arizona. He felt no sensual desire. This woman was lying with him as he had so often lain with Dora, but she wasn't his wife. She was no one. He knew now what he had guessed before. He had lost his mind. He could see that he was a ridiculous man. He had lost any sense of progress in his life. There was no proper sequence of events, no routine, no pattern. It was all shapeless, a journey without direction. He pressed his lips to Laura's breast under her nipple. He didn't kiss her. It was only a touch. Hammond was loveless.

It was ten o'clock in the morning. Wildman settled the account at the Shangri-La, paying cash. He joined Pandora in her car. He would have to leave his own car in the hotel lot. Pandora had insisted on taking her BMW. She also insisted on driving. He didn't argue. It was enough that she was prepared to stay with him downtown at least for a day or two. He directed her along the highway towards the Santa Monica mountains. They would pick up the freeway over in the valley. It was a beautiful day. It would be a pleasant drive now Hammond was dead.

Pandora had woken with a strong desire to take charge of

things. She would go with this man, but it would be on her terms. The sensuality of the night had made her resolute in the day. She was optimistic. I want to be adored. I don't want to be screwed. I'll drive.

They were up in the hills when Wildman saw the Mustang in the door mirror. Damn you, Laura. Can't you leave it alone. Don't you know it's over. Finished. Get off my back. Pandora saw Wildman turning in his seat to look behind. What had he seen? She was physically aware of his agitation. She didn't see the Mustang at first. The road through the Santa Monica mountains curved and the following car was momentarily lost to sight. Wildman continued to look in the mirror.

'What is it?'

'We're being followed. Drive faster.'

'Who's following us?' Was it Alec?

Wildman wished he was driving. He would lose Laura in a few minutes. But there wasn't time to stop the car and change places. Shit. There was nothing to be done. He'd have to face it down sooner or later.

'You mean that Mustang?' Pandora could see the car clearly now. It wasn't Alec's. 'Do you know who it is?'

'Slow down.'

'Do you want me to stop?' Pandora knew now who it was. The woman.

As she slowed, the Mustang accelerated. It came straight at the BMW, gathering speed.

'God, what's she doing?' Pandora shouted.

Wildman jammed his foot over to the accelerator. He kicked Pandora's shoe off in the violence of his action. He had seen who was driving. It wasn't Laura. It was Hammond. The man was alive.

The BMW swerved to the right. Pandora kept control of the wheel. Despite the acceleration of her car the Mustang thundered into the rear. They were both jolted forwards. Pandora cried out.

'Now do what I say!' Wildman yelled. 'Don't be scared. Stay on this side of the road.'

268

In the Mustang Hammond accelerated again. He drove the fender of the car into the trunk of the BMW. His target was the license plate 'Pandora'. He wanted to crush it.

'You'll kill us!' Laura shouted at him.

'Not us. Them.'

'Stop it. Please stop it.' She took his arm. He shook it away.

'Just leave this to me.'

The Mustang now pulled alongside the BMW. Hammond swung the wheel. There was a smack of metal as the Mustang attacked the passenger door. Wildman prayed for a car coming from the other direction to take Hammond out. What the hell was Laura doing with him?

Despite Wildman's shouted instructions Pandora was terrified. When Hammond rammed her again she felt the violence of rape. Being thrown by the impact was a re-run of the scene on the stairs. That wasn't going to happen again. You're not going to do it to me. As calmly as she could she brought the BMW to a stop. The Mustang sped past.

'What are you doing?' Wildman was exasperated.

'I'm not going to die because of your fight.'

She reached over for her handbag and took out the gun. Now Wildman was nervous. Pandora got out of the car. Up ahead the Mustang had skidded to a halt. Hammond jumped out pushing Laura away as she tried to stop him.

Pandora held the gun in her hand and walked straight to Hammond. Wildman came after her. She's crazy, he thought. But he was impressed by her determination. Laura ran to Hammond, half-tripping.

'Come away. She'll kill you.' She could see murder in Pandora's eyes.

'You won't kill me,' Hammond looked straight into Pandora's eyes. 'Give me the gun.' He held out his hand.

Wildman came up and stood beside Pandora.

'Don't push your luck,' he said to Hammond.

'Give me the gun,' Hammond repeated. 'I need it for him.'

He came close to Pandora. She was chilled but she didn't waver. Hammond looked down at the gun. He saw her finger

269

tightening on the trigger. The gun was aimed at his heart. He knew Dora was a good shot. But that was at her gun club with targets. She couldn't do it like this. Hammond knew he wasn't going to die here on a road shot by his wife. He had survived too long, come too far, for it all to end here with a bullet.

'Pull the trigger, Dora.' That would stop her.

Pandora wavered. How could she kill him like this. It was absurd. She glanced at Wildman. As she moved her head Hammond grabbed the cold barrel of the gun. He wrenched it from her grasp. She cried out.

Wildman jumped forward. Laura screamed. Hammond struck Wildman's hand with the gun. There was a crack. Wildman gasped. Hammond hit him again. Across the left cheek. Wildman swayed. Hammond aimed his right foot, kicked at his legs with all his strength. Wildman fell to his knees. Hammond stepped forward, put the gun to Wildman's head. It was easy now. His finger nursed the trigger. The cries of the two women to stop seemed far away, out to sea. This was the moment of truth. Between men. The die was finally cast.

'Say goodbye,' he whispered.

Wildman looked up at him. For the first time in his life he felt he was about to die. He was going to lose Pandora.

Now I shall be free, thought Hammond. I shall be rid of him. Free. In the silence of this moment there was a distant echo of doubt. He glanced at Pandora. She was pleading with him. He couldn't hear her voice. He could see it in her eyes. Don't kill him. I'll do anything you want. Hammond suddenly realized he didn't want anything. Kill this animal, but then what? Go back to Dora. He didn't want her. He didn't want to go back to anything. He wanted only to be free. Would killing Wildman make him free, truly free? Being free was being alone. That's what he wanted. To be free alone. If Wildman died would he be free? Wildman was as good as dead now. If she wanted to live with a dead man, fine. She could go right ahead. It didn't mean shit to him.

And so Hammond stepped back from Wildman, took the gun away.

'Get back in her car.'

Wildman rose painfully to his feet. He showed no sign of relief. Laura closed her eyes.

'And take her with you.'

Wildman put his arm around Pandora. Together, followed by Hammond, gun in hand, they returned to the BMW.

'You drive,' Hammond told Wildman. 'Take her where you want.'

Pandora looked round at Hammond as she climbed into the passenger seat. Was he smiling? She almost said thank you. Hammond felt happy as he slammed the door. Wildman put his hands on the wheel.

'Start the car.' Hammond went around to Pandora. 'Give me your bag.'

'My bag?'

Hammond held out his free hand as Pandora fumbled to retrieve her handbag from the floor of the car. She gave it to him. Hammond opened it. He put the gun inside, zipped it up, and threw the bag into the back of the car onto the ledge behind the rear seats.

'Go,' he said. Vanish, he thought. Disappear.

Pandora was near to tears as Wildman drove away along the road. She looked back at him once. When the car was out of sight, Hammond turned to Laura.

'Aren't you pleased with me?' he said.

Part Six

1

On the freeway drive downtown Pandora felt that her body was made up of different parts not properly connected to each other. One thigh ached, the other was numb. Her left ankle throbbed with the movement of the car. She tried not to look at Wildman as he drove. When she did she saw two men sitting at the wheel, two flat profiles juddering, trying to merge themselves into a single three dimensional shape, an entity.

She tried to think of herself, how she felt, how she looked. Was her own reality any more solid? Two men had tried to kill each other because of her. But hers was no romantic tale. She had no feeling of power over their destinies. Two men seemed willing to die for one woman. So what? Where was the heroism of legend or the enduring archetype of myth? The truth was two sick souls had used her to project their own unfulfilled desires. She was an object, not the subject, of desire. She could see herself, from a distance, being driven, carried by a man towards the next place in her fate. This wasn't an open adventure, this was willful abuse. And she had allowed herself to be taken for this violent ride. Did she now have the courage to stop the car, get out, go her own way? But then why should she get out? For fuck's sake, it was her car.

Wildman was dissatisfied, oppressed by the fact that neither he nor Hammond had finished the thing. It was like a failed stunt. If it were a movie he would have wanted to re-shoot the scene. That he was still alive gave him no pleasure, no relief. He told himself that Hammond had lacked the courage to do what he had to. But that wasn't quite the truth. Hammond had decided not to kill him. He had made his choice. Hammond had left him with the woman he wanted. She was sitting now beside him. But he had also bequeathed him a sick sensation of defeat. A duel should not end this way. Why the hell hadn't he disposed of Hammond when he had the chance, in the hotel room or on the beach. Why had he let him live? Why had he let him win? Wildman was conscious of a terrible weakness in his character. It wasn't goodness or decency. It was fear, in effect cowardice. In the last resort he had been afraid to kill. All along, right from the start, that weakness had been there, a virus in his make-up. Now he had let Hammond make the final decision. Yes, it was final. He knew they would never fight again. When you came right down to it, he wasn't a man of action. He was a stunt man.

Once again, Hammond found himself hitching a ride after a fight in cars. Once again, he was waiting to be picked up, helped home, bruised and limping. This time though, he knew he had won. Last time it had been an illusion of triumph. This time it was fact. Maybe Wildman was hard to kill. All the same he was not worth killing. The man began to seem like a figment of his imagination. That devil inside him, who had used his name, had been left standing beside a road up here in the Santa Monica mountains. He might just as well have died in that antique car on the flats in San Bernadino. And Dora, who had stood next to him in clothes he'd never seen before, she had been left too. He felt as if he'd never known her, never wanted her. Thirteen years of marriage now seemed like a one-night stand. His home life no longer seemed like an anchor. It was a floating island he'd once visited and stayed on, a castaway.

As he waited beside the road he could see the sun shining on the distant ocean. There was no visible horizon beyond the mountains. It was just graded light. This ocean was not for drowning. It wasn't some vast swimming pool. It was simply part of the sky. An open house. A set without construction. It would provide light and warmth during the day. Like now. And when night came the stars might guide him if he could only understand their configurations. He had never studied astronomy but he knew a few of the names, Orion, the great bear, the small bear, planets you couldn't even see, named after Greek gods who had never even existed. An intellectual folly. The earth was under his feet, supporting them through the soles of his shoes. That was the full extent of his reality now.

Hammond turned at the sound of an engine. A truck carrying boxes of fruit pulled up beside him. He hadn't even raised his hand. The driver was a Mexican. He called to Hammond.

'Need a ride?'

'*Gracias.*'

Hammond climbed up into the passenger seat. He stepped back once, his legs weak, muscles exhausted, before he clambered up, hoisting himself like a rock climber into the passenger seat. He smiled at the Mexican. The truck moved on. This was reality. It was a ride that was not part of any plot. There were no more devices. The story was over.

Laura drove the clanking Mustang over the hills to the valley. She never cried but now she couldn't stop. Alone in her car she howled. Why not? She'd lost her love. Trite, but that's what it was. Her center was gone. He'd never come back. She'd never hear his footfall outside her cell again. Her happier prison days were over. She was freed, released into a world where she had no place, no role, no home. She would never again ride in that cage up to the loft. The drowsy dogs would never greet her again. The mirror on the wall would not reflect her again. She looked up into the driving mirror. She saw only the receding road. Nothing was following her.

Laura wondered what she could have done to change things. What had she missed? What trick could she have pulled off? What ritual dance could she have performed to bring the rain, to make things happen, or undo the things that had? She could have killed Pandora. Could have. Would have. Should have. She hadn't, wouldn't, couldn't. There was no murder in her heart. She was always a victim. Like Hammond. Why hadn't he killed Wildman? He swore he would. She had believed him too. What changed his mind? Was it Pandora? Did he have in his mind to get her back after all? Poor Hammond. Wildman had her now and he would never let her go. She would be the new Laura.

'Is this where you live?' It was a rhetorical question. Pandora leaned weakly against the cold metal wall of the elevator cage as it ground and squeaked upwards. It felt like going down. A shaft of light came in from somewhere, weakened through a wide and greasy window. Wildman's face lit up for a moment. The air smelled of rust.

Pandora had expected somehow to be taken to another hotel or an apartment that resembled a hotel. The cage clanked to a stop. He pulled the metal gates open. The two dogs ambled towards them.

'Romulus and Remus,' he introduced them to her. She looked around the large raw space. Huge though it was, she felt as if she were in prison. There seemed nowhere to go from here. This suspended space reminded her of downtown New York. There was no felt presence of the sun or the ocean, no sheltering sky. This was not California.

She sank into the leather couch. Without a word Wildman began to take his clothes off. He didn't look the same man in this setting. Only when he was naked did he resemble the person she knew. The person she didn't know.

'I want an explanation,' she said.

Wildman expected, feared, many questions about his relationship to Hammond.

'Tell me how you got that scar.'

'I'm going to take a bath. I'll tell you while you wash me.'

Pandora watched him while he prepared the tub on the far side of the loft. For the first time his nakedness was separate from his sexuality. She examined the surfaces of his body without desire, as if she were looking at an artwork. There was beauty in it, but distant and abstracted.

'I got this scar when I was three weeks old.'

'Three weeks?'

'Tiny babies, usually under six weeks, sometimes have a disease called pyloric stenosis. It's the sudden contraction of the stomach muscles leading to the digestive system. The baby can't digest food. The milk is swallowed, then suddenly vomited out. It's known as projectile vomiting. The stuff is literally thrown out. It can go several feet across a room. The baby needs an operation to cut the contracted muscle and stop the spasms occurring. That's how I got the scar. Not particularly romantic, although it was a matter of life and death.'

The domesticity of the scene, the man naked in the tub, the story of childhood illness, caused Pandora to think of Paulette. She desperately wanted to be with her.

'May I make a call?'

'To your daughter? The phone's over there.'

He always knew. 'I need to pee first.'

'Go ahead.'

Wildman's wet finger pointed to the toilet bowl a few feet away. Pandora felt a stab of embarrassment. The strange domestic intimacy again, enforced intimacy without sex, like being at home. Where was Alec now? He was certifiable. Was that what would happen? Would he be sent to a mental institution, some rural haven where he would be guarded by men in white coats? She could see driving with Paulette over there on visiting days. It would be like her own house in New Hampshire.

She hoisted up her skirt, pulled down her panties and sat on the toilet. The pee seemed interminable.

'What else do you want to know?' Wildman asked. 'The Kleenex is behind you.'

'I want to know about that girl.'

'What girl? Laura?' Wildman had been expecting this. He should never have lied that day at lunch when he told her Laura had killed herself.

'Laura? Was that her name? I mean the girl you and Alec knew in Arizona. The one who died.'

'Betty May,' Wildman said. How the hell had she found out about Betty May? Hammond must have told her. The asshole. 'Your husband was sleeping with her.'

279

'What was your relationship with her?' Pandora stood up, dabbed herself with some Kleenex, pulled up her panties, stood, straightened her dress. She looked straight at him. There was no escape. He had to tell the truth.

'She was my assistant. They wanted each other. I didn't try to stop it. It was none of my business. It made me think he didn't want you, didn't deserve you.'

'So you knew that all the time, when we first met. You knew about me then?'

'No, no. That was a coincidence. I was attracted to you. Then I discovered the connection. The coincidence made me even more certain that I wanted you.' He stood up and stepped out of the tub. 'Would you dry me?'

Pandora looked for a towel. She saw the bath robe. She walked to his dripping body and draped the robe around him. She started to rub his shoulders and arms through the material. His body felt soft, giving, despite the hard muscle. It was a contradiction.

Was he lying? Had they both fucked the same girl? Was that what was behind everything? Was she in the same boat as Betty May, as that other nameless woman, handed back and forth between two men? Would she meet the same fate, coincidental, accidental, destroyed in an accident for which they were both responsible. She was a fly trapped in a spider's web of desire, a web made up of fine strands of male sperm.

As she rubbed his chest gently and mechanically Pandora became aware that he was watching something over her shoulder, across the loft. She turned to see what he was looking at. In that instant she felt they were not alone, the woman had come in. But there was no one. Nothing but the drowsy dogs.

Wildman was staring at Betty May. The girl was smiling nervously at him from across the space. Slowly she lifted her heavy white sweater. Her breasts moved as the material passed across them. He looked away from the ghost of the girl and violently pressed his wet face between Pandora's breasts. He shook.

*

Laura turned the key in her apartment door. She was about to go in when a man's voice from along the hall stopped her dead.

'Pardon me, miss.' He walked up to her.

The man was about fifty, dressed casually with a gray crew-cut. Laura vaguely recognized him as a neighbor. She was in no mood for a discussion about the maintenance of the apartment building or a lost pet. She watched while the man removed a photograph from his shirt pocket.

'Do you recognize this girl?'

Laura stiffened. The guy wasn't a neighbor. He was a cop. She felt a stab of fear. She knew instantly who the girl was.

'I don't think so.'

'She lives . . .' He stopped. 'She lived in apartment 32A just upstairs.'

Laura hesitated, staring at the picture of the laughing face of Betty May. She was scared to look directly at the man.

'Maybe I have seen her.'

'I think you have seen her. At least, I think you've seen a man who used to see her.'

Laura shook. 'What happened to her?'

'The man you know is called Wildman. Charles Wildman. He knew her. Matter of fact, he killed her.'

Don't panic. For God's sake don't panic.

'You're looking worried.' There was menace now in the man's tone.

'Yes. I do know Mr Wildman.' She was too scared to lie.

'You know him well?'

'Casually, I guess.'

'I saw you with him once by the pool down there. It looked more than casual.'

'Who are you?'

'I want to know where Mr Wildman lives. That's all.'

'I can't tell you that.' Laura tried to sound firm.

The man leaned towards her. Laura could feel his deodorised breath on her face.

'Just the address.'

'Are you from the police?'

'My name's Lefevre.' He pronounced it Lefever. 'I'm Betty May's father.'

'I'd like to help, but . . .'

'. . . you will help.' He leant the flat of his palm against the door jamb near to her head.

Laura panicked. Give him an address. Any address. Get him away from me.

'He lives at 12570 Rancho Park Drive.'

'12570 Rancho Park Drive.' The man repeated it out loud. He wouldn't forget it.

'Thank you.' His voice was husky with emotion. He removed his arm from the door, and with the same hand took back the photograph from Laura's shaking grasp. 'Thank you for your help.'

He turned and walked away from Laura like an apparition. She went into the apartment, too weak even to close the door. She sank to the floor. She began to cry again. Out of self-pity, out of despair, she had committed a crime.

2

When Hammond returned home he was confronted by an image of himself. He closed the front door and stared at his own reflection in a mirror that had been placed at the foot of the stairs. The tall free-standing mirror from his bedroom had been brought down and placed directly facing the door. He was surprised but unworried. The question of how the mirror had gotten there, whether Dora or the maid had been responsible, hardly mattered to him. It was what he saw in it that counted. He faced a ruined man, bent, half-broken, thin faced with two days' growth of beard. It was the figure of a vagrant, an addict beyond rehabilitation. Hammond took off his dark glasses. After a few moments examining his portrait, he smiled. He saw in it a chance, a real and solid opportunity to change, to become another man, unshackled and free. He breathed deeply, feeling a small twinge of happiness. The image was only a mask. He went upstairs to pack.

The studio was in semi-darkness. Hammond saw that the venetian blinds had been lowered and tightly closed. There was music, quite faint, coming from his hi-fi. It was lyrical, a piano and orchestra, oriental in rhythm. It sounded like running water and gave him a feeling of immense calm. It reminded him of Debussy's orchestral suite *La Mer*.

He had entered a fresh real world. First, the mirror and now the watery music. What would, in an earlier existence, have seemed like a bad dream in which someone was trying to drive him crazy now added up to a lengthening glimpse of lighted hope. The quiet rectangular gloom of his studio was as wide as the ocean landscape without horizon that he had seen and felt for the first time among the Santa Monica mountains. The interior was an extension of the exterior. It was brilliant production design. The feeling of relief grew and enfolded him here in a setting he thought he knew so well. It was beautiful. Hammond felt transformed.

He looked to see what music was playing. The unfamiliar piece that so delighted him was, he saw from the CD cover beside the amplifier, a piece called *Riverrun* by Takemitsu, a Japanese composer he had heard of but never listened to. Well, he had found a new friend, an ally, a guide.

Of course he knew that he had not so much found it as been given it. For that he was grateful, but as when he discovered music for the first time on the car radio he didn't think to thank anyone for having sent it to him over the air. It was a natural gift, like a surprising view of a landscape or a dawn with broken clouds. It was pleasurably astounding.

He sat down on the sofa. He was on a boat at sea, comfortably and securely rocked to the rhythm of nature, in tune with the beating of his heart. He smiled at his new world. He became aware of other changes. The studio, habitually untidy, now possessed a new, calming order. The room seemed to have taken a different shape. There was a greater sense of formality and space. It was a film set ready for the scene to be shot the next day. Hammond felt pleasantly tired as he used to after hard, successful hours of preparation. I could have done this myself, he thought. Maybe I did.

He realized that his scattered drawings of that ridiculous box had gone. They had vanished, been swept away. By whom? He didn't care. It didn't matter. They had belonged to his unhappy past. That story was over and would eventually be forgotten. Hammond was no longer engaged by mystery.

Wildman's need for Pandora was overwhelming. Sucking her toes in turn he came close to orgasm. For the first time he examined her sex with no thought of entering her. The vulva was the most complex part of a woman's body, the most capable of change. In essence it was an unformed egg protected by hair. He told her that men used to believe that originally the vulva had teeth like a mouth. But they had been drawn out by a fearful god. There was a legend, he said, that it was a lucky charm. The horseshoe that was hung on stable doors for good luck was a representation of the vulva. When the first nymph stole fire she hid the flames inside. Men's fascination with the female vulva and the desire to enter it was a version of the quest for fire. The clitoris was not a small male penis at all but the finger of the beautiful princess that had been pricked by the spindle which sent her to sleep for a hundred years. Wildman told her that by kissing it he would awaken her from her sleeping existence before she met him.

To begin with, Pandora resisted his love-making. She wanted only to call Paulette. But as he whispered to her body, telling stories, she felt her consciousness melting. She listened to his words, his descriptions of her flesh, and entered his dreamlike adoration of her body. She began to expand. Her body changed shape under his hands and lips. It wasn't sex but pure feeling, abstract but compulsive, like music. All objective thought vanished, all confusion dispersed, there was no trace of fear, everything was subjectivity, the world was inside her.

This time Pandora was unconscious of her deafness. It was completely natural, this existence without sound. Silence was the unquestionable state of things. When she came she had no sensation of something being done to her. She didn't know whether he was inside her or not. Knowledge was music. She was the sound of it. Her climax was a long and soft explosion. Her fade out was slow, a weakening petal which fell unnoticed into the passage of sleep.

Pandora awoke from an indescribable watery dream. She was in the four-poster bed covered by an unfamiliar fur rug. She discovered herself. She was alone in the loft. She looked round seeing objects, all separate and sharply defined. She felt like a child returned to a nursery full of significant objects. But the objects she saw were unknown to her. Their significance was obscure. There was the large box, closed, containing what?

Where had it come from? What was it for? Her memory stirred. She had never been in this place before, yet the image of the box was irritatingly familiar. How? It connected somewhere with her home. Did she have a box there? In the garage? In Paulette's nursery bedroom? No. No, it was Alec. As she remembered she sat up in the bed. The cool air chilled her warm, damp skin. Alec had been drawing boxes. There had been sketches of boxes all over the studio floor. Hundreds of boxes. Designs for some movie project. She had taken it as a sign of his madness. But this box was right here. A disturbing presence. Where was Wildman?

Pandora's fears returned with an improbable connection. Alec had drawn this box. So had he seen it? No, wait. There had been a screenplay. It was called *The Box*. He'd been making sketches for that. She remembered reading a couple of pages. It had been a strange story. Someone in a box. A woman. Pandora felt a wave of unease.

Call Paulette. That's what she had to do. She climbed out of the bed. It was cold. She went to the bath and took Wildman's bathrobe. Pulling it around her she felt the dampness of the cotton. How long had it been since she had dried him after he got out of the tub? She had no idea. She looked at her left wrist. She wasn't wearing her watch. She wasn't wearing anything. Then she remembered he had taken it from her wrist before they made love. Had she put it with her clothes? The silver dress. The black underwear. There was no sign of any of her things. Where were they? She saw a white phone on a table beside the leather couch. Call Paulette.

Pandora caught sight of herself in the wide mirror as she picked up the phone. She looked at herself, saw a half-stranger, someone she didn't completely recognize. As she lifted the receiver she realized she didn't know the Wings' number. It was in her book. Where was her book?

Pandora hunted for her bag. There was no sign of it. The two dogs followed her as she searched. The bag had gone, along with her clothes. She began to panic. Just call enquiries. She knew the Wings' address. She returned to the phone. When she picked it up, there was no sound. She shook it. The line was dead. Her body twitched. She could feel sweat forming under her arms. She was a prisoner.

Before she could think what to do, alone in this huge interior, she heard a small creaking sound. So she could hear. She wasn't deaf. She turned fearfully. The door of the box was opening slowly. Pandora was transfixed.

Out of the darkness of the interior Wildman appeared. He was naked. He stood up and walked towards her. Involuntarily, she backed away. Her voice cracked.

'I want to call my daughter. The phone's dead.'

'I'm sure she's fine,' Wildman said. 'You don't need to call her.'

'What are you talking about? Where are my things?'

'You don't need them.'

'What are you trying to do?' She quivered with fear. I must get out of this nightmare. For God's sake let me wake up. But Pandora knew she was awake.

'You have everything here you need. With me.'

Pandora began to run, her feet on the cold wood floor. She ran, ran as fast as she could to where she remembered the elevator had been. Wildman walked after her. The dogs came too.

At dinner the night before Mrs Long had explained to Paulette and David the meaning of re-arranging objects in a house where evil spirits dwelt.

'There are spirits everywhere, evil and good. To fight the evil spirits you must create a balance in your surroundings. Natural things like wind and water and light can be arranged so that the evil spirit cannot find a place to live and flourish. The world is a garden. It has to be controlled by us, otherwise the weeds take over and strangle the flowers. We have to create a balance between man and nature.'

'We don't really have a garden.' Paulette didn't fully understand. David explained Mrs Long's analogy.

'Think of your house, the inside of your house as a garden.

If your dad is possessed by an evil spirit, it's because the balance of things inside your house is wrong.'

'So we could help him by moving the furniture? Is that what you're saying?'

'Not only the furniture, but we might make an atmosphere of calm.'

'You know that my dad's a production designer on movies. He builds sets and decorates them.'

'What a wonderful job,' said Mrs Long. 'It means he would be sensitive to *fung shui*. He would respond to a different balance.'

When Paulette and David got home Mrs Wing told Paulette that Pandora had called to see her. Talking to her mother later on the phone, Paulette knew what she had to do to help. She still had her key to the house. She would go with David and Mrs Long the next morning before school and do the *fung shui*. Pandora told her that her dad had gone away again. When he came back there would be a new balance of objects waiting for him.

Paulette didn't totaly believe in it all, but David was insistent that it would help. And David, her love, knew. She believed him. She felt elated when she went to bed. The earlier disgust about Hammond now became pity. That was good. It made her feel good. It showed that *fung shui* was already working. It had changed her. Don't worry, Mom, she told herself, I'll protect you.

Before she put out the light, Paulette set the portable tape recorder to play one of her favorite albums, an oldie by Don Maclean. She idolised Don Maclean and *American Pie*.

Paulette was almost asleep when David climbed into the bed and lay next to her. After a few moments, he put his hand on her thigh. He could feel the welcoming warmth of her through the cotton nightdress. Paulette didn't look at him. She took his hand and placed it between her legs. He pressed gently, feeling the softness and the bone. Later, when she held his penis in her hand and felt it move, Paulette was close to tears. They held each other, gaining courage from the music of Don Maclean's song *Vincent.* The sad romance of a misunderstood artist, a

288

genius who went unrecognized, who killed himself in loneliness under the starry, starry sky of his painting, overwhelmed them both. The breathless rush of love gave Paulette a feeling of invincibility. If only her poor sick father and unhappy mother had this.

Hammond slept in his studio. He was awakened by the front door bell. He came to immediately. He was oddly pleased by being woken. A fresh new day. He pulled on his robe and went down to open the door. He felt great. He glanced at himself in the mirror before opening the door. He liked the man he saw. He had no thoughts about who was out there. It didn't matter now. He didn't look through the spy hole. Let it be a surprise. Any visitor would be welcome, the first in his new life.

'Mr Wildman? My name's Lefevre.'

Hammond looked puzzled. The man stepped inside the door. Someone looking for Wildman? Funny thing. He was about to speak when he felt a sudden pressure in his chest. Lefevre's combat knife entered his heart with a single thrust. The last image that came into Hammond's mind before he died was a book about UFO's on a shelf in a store in Santa Monica.

By the time Lefevre had finished he couldn't see his own reflection in the tall mirror, it was so lacquered with Hammond's blood.

3

Don't run. Don't try to run. You won't get out of here running, Pandora told herself. He won't let you go. Find another way. There has to be a way out. Relax and think. Don't worry about Paulette. She's fine, safe with the Wings. Concentrate on yourself. Let your mind go blank. Just relax, Pandora. Re-lax.

Pandora lay back on the bed, her head and shoulders comfortably propped by several pillows. Wildman sat in a chair beside her, listening to her voice.

She told him the story of the woman at the masked ball in the forest outside Paris. She told him how the stranger had approached the woman, and how they had run away together to a hotel. She told him how, after a night of love, the stranger had turned out to have been just a man looking for an adventure, how the woman had been misled, and how she had been transported by love.

Wildman adored the story with its memories of Paris. He brought her food and drink and asked to hear more tales. Pandora wished she had read Paulette's book all the way through. Now she was forced to invent stories herself. She knew she was no writer. She fell back on describing events that had happened to her. But she made them sound like made-up fairy-tales. She recounted the story of her affair with Luke and how her father found out about it. But she described herself as the Princess and Luke as the poor woodcutter who was really a prince in disguise. Her father naturally became the King, jealous of his daughter. Her house in New Hampshire was transformed into a magic castle with a hundred bedrooms. And she herself, the story teller, became Scheherezade, entertaining the tyrant to keep him at bay.

To her surprise Pandora began to enjoy her role. She became adept at her trickery. When she was tired of talking she found she could sleep without fear.

Wildman wanted to watch her sleeping. She was transformed into a character from one of her stories. She belonged to him and at the same time she was a fiction. While she slept he re-wrote his screenplay. What was happening now in the loft was more imaginative than the scenes in his movie. His story of a man who captures people to transform them through sensory deprivation became less of a suspense thriller, more of a fairy-tale romance, something like *Beauty and the Beast*. His leading male character, the hero-villain, was gradually metamorphosed into a young prince who is enchanted by the mysterious woman he has made captive.

There were times when Pandora was awake while Wildman slept. These were moments of temptation. She almost reverted to her first plans for escape. But when she walked across the loft towards the elevator, the dogs began to growl and Wildman awoke. No, she thought, the only way out is to wait until he leaves. He can't stay in here for ever. Can he? They would eventually run out of food. Eventually? When was that?

Pandora established one golden rule. Do not make love with him. Don't let him seduce you. She half-expected an assault. But it didn't come. There were times when, in bed together, she longed for his touch. He would reach for her sometimes, but she would turn away. She wondered why he didn't persist.

Wildman understood. She was playing with him. In her place he would do the same. He could wait. He knew her nature. That was what he loved. Pandora's flesh was her character: her desire was her personality. That was why she was with him. She might struggle but she would never escape. There would come a time when she wouldn't want to. He adored her and kissed her feet.

One morning Wildman decided to give her a present. She opened her eyes. In front of her on the bed was the model plane.

'I sent it to you,' he said.

She lifted the light object in her hands. She examined the fuselage. *Ilea iacta est*. She caught herself smiling. She wasn't afraid. Why doesn't this make me scared, she wondered. A few days ago I would have been terrified. A few days ago I was a victim. I know I'm still a prisoner. But I'm not scared any longer.

Pandora's fearful confusions had given way to an almost pleasant sensation of puzzlement. Like a child recovering in bed from an illness she felt relieved, knowing that the fever had passed. The deafness which had plagued her for so long had mysteriously left her. She realized she hadn't suffered from the silence since she had come here, to his castle. How strange that was.

It had been four days since Paulette had heard from Pandora. She had become increasingly frightened. She thought Hammond had killed her mother. She couldn't allow herself to confess these fears to Mrs Wing. David guessed them. He was good at guessing her. He said she must go to the police. Tell them everything, he said. Paulette knew it was the right thing to do, but she was ashamed of her father. She didn't want strangers to know. The *fung shui* hadn't worked. She was angry about that. Repressing her tears she became violent. When David tried to reason with her one night she hit him and ordered him out of her room. She never wanted to see him again. She was going to run away. Her violence scared her.

Paulette consoled herself by listening to the Don Maclean tape. Every night she listened and sang along softly. She couldn't sleep. David stayed away. She had scared him. One night she opened the plastic bag in which she had kept all Hammond's sketches of the box. She spread them out on the floor of the bedroom. What did they really mean? She felt sick. Her head was spinning. The music was suddenly no comfort.

Paulette had an idea what to do. It came to her. Get rid of the evil spirit. Destroy it once and for all. She gathered up the sketches and carried them downstairs to the kitchen. While the house was asleep she turned on the gas stove. She fed the papers one by one to the blue flames. As each paper burned yellow she

292

dropped it into the empty wok on the counter beside the stove. Smoke filled the kitchen. Paulette choked as the flames leaped in front of her. She didn't care. That was the death of the evil spirit. Suddenly, there was a loud high-pitched ringing sound. It frightened her. It must be the spirit's death agony. She had set off the smoke alarm. By the time Mrs Wing appeared in the kitchen Paulette was sobbing wildly. She'd done it.

David thought she shouldn't go to school the next day. Mrs Wing wanted to call the doctor. But Paulette had calmed down and insisted on going. She refused help or sympathy. The fire had given her courage. The smoke was proof of the purge.

In the school yard two police officers were waiting for her. They'd found out about the fire. She was terrified. They took her aside into the teachers' relaxation room and told her quietly that a terrible thing had happened. Her dad was dead.

'How did she die?'

'She? Not she. He. Your father's dead.'

My father? Paulette couldn't grasp it. Her father was the violent one, the evil spirit. It was her mother who was dead. Her mother. Her father had killed her mom.

The officers and her class teacher sat with Paulette for a while. The teacher knew that for some time there had been trouble at home. Paulette started to cry when they asked her where her mother was. She knew the truth now, but she couldn't tell them. She mustn't ever tell them. She would protect her mom to the death. They would never, never find out what had really happened. That her mom had killed her dad. That was a secret between her mom and her.

Pandora asked to go into the box. She had become fascinated by it. She wanted to know its significance. Wildman explained what it was, how it worked, what it was for. To begin with she disbelieved the theory. It was simply crazy, the whole idea. Some wild obsession of his. But now her feelings for him had altered. This man had not become her tormentor. He hadn't forced her to do anything. If she didn't want sex with him, she didn't have to. He seemed just to enjoy her company. He made

293

no demands. On the contrary, he would do what she wanted. She asked for strawberries. He got dressed and went to get them. He was gone for more than an hour. Yet she hadn't tried to escape. Wasn't that the opportunity she had been waiting for? Why hadn't she run away? Strange. She only thought of it after he had returned. While he was away she missed him. She wanted him back with her. Instead of running she waited.

I must go into the box, she told herself. He would like that, I know. It's open. It's waiting. After all, my name is Pandora.

Wildman left the loft after he had had a call from his agent, George Elliott. George wanted a meeting immediately.

'I'm not interested in working right now.'

'This isn't work.' He sounded grim.

'Can't you tell me on the phone?' Wildman did not want to leave Pandora alone. She could still want to run away. Although she had changed, and now wanted to be with him without reservation, his fear remained. He couldn't risk losing her now after all that had happened.

George was so insistent on seeing him right away that Wildman was nervous of some kind of trap. Was Hammond there, waiting?

'It's personal, Charles. And important.'

Wildman sat down in his agent's office. He felt danger. George closed the door, cutting them off from his secretary. He took a sheet of paper from his desk. It was a fax. It was from a lawyer in Paris.

'Dear Mr Wildman, it is with great regret that I have to inform you that your sister Florence and her daughter were killed ten days ago in a car crash on the Côte d'Azur. I have had difficulty tracing you. I finally received the fax number of your agent through the union of technicians in Los Angeles. The funeral was last Saturday . . .'

There was more but Wildman couldn't read it.

'Would you like a drink?' George asked.

'No. I have to get back.'

'I didn't want to tell you on the phone. I'm so sorry.'

'It had to happen,' Wildman said, without emphasis.

'Why? Was your sister a bad driver?'

Wildman drove slowly back downtown, keeping well within the limit. It had to happen. And in a car crash. It was that alternative pattern of events, the script behind the script. His desire for Pandora had cost Florence her life. This was no coincidence. This was the revenge of the gods. They couldn't let him get away with Pandora. He had opened the box. For what he had taken from it there was a price to be paid. And this was it. The gods didn't give a fuck about Hammond. They didn't want the sacrifice of men. They wanted women. First, Betty May. Now Florence. The heroes took what they wanted. But they had always to lose something. That was the classical way. And you had to live with it. It had nothing to do with coincidence or luck, good or bad. It was destiny.

He could see Florence now, her face blurred by the flames and smoke of a burning car high on the Corniche road on the French Riviera. It was noon and the flaming wheeled coffin momentarily obliterated a view of the shining ocean. There was music playing on the car radio to accompany Florence's immolation. No one would reach her or her daughter before the gods had taken their sacrifice. Far below the hillside road was a sea port, probably St Tropez, the town didn't matter, it could have been Alexandria in Egypt or Minos on the island of Crete. The blue Mediterranean was the swimming pool of the gods. They enjoyed themselves there. Fine, fine as long as he could keep his Pandora.

Paulette was in bed listening to Don Maclean. She had dizzy spells a lot of the time now. Mrs Wing came in to her to tell her that there was a lady who wanted to see her, talk to her.

'What lady?'

'A friend of your mom's.'

Mrs Wing showed Laura into the room. Laura smiled. Paulette didn't. Mrs Wing left them together.

295

'It's terrible about your dad. I'm so very, very sorry.'

Laura had heard of Hammond's murder on the car radio. She had to pull over. For days afterwards she expected a call from Lefevre. It didn't come. She hadn't seen him around her apartment building. She had spent sleepless nights expecting a visit from him, knife in hand. She knew she ought to call the police. She knew it. She was shielding a killer. But then the cops would want to know how she knew that, how Lefevre had gone to the wrong address. In a way she was Hammond's murderer. If she confessed it would all lead back to Wildman. She wanted to protect him more than she wanted to save herself. She had to live with her guilt. Silence was golden.

'I know where your mom is,' she told Paulette.

'You do? How?' Paulette was excited.

'That doesn't matter. I can take you to her.'

'You can?' Paulette's heart leapt. 'When?' She couldn't wait.

'Tomorrow or the next day.'

'Why not now?'

'I said tomorrow or the nextday. I have to plan it.'

'You're not going to the police?' Paulette was scared of the police. They were the enemy. They would discover the truth and arrest her mom, they would send her to prison.

The police had not told Paulette the circumstances of Hammond's murder. They figured it would be the wrong thing to do. Paulette was too young. They could have told her they didn't suspect her mother of the murder, despite the fact that Pandora couldn't be found, but they saw no reason to upset the little girl any more than was necessary. It was always the children who suffered most. One of the investigating officers had the idea that it was a crime of passion, that Pandora knew Hammond had a lover somewhere who had committed the murder. It would explain her disappearance now. According to this theory, the two lovers were together in hiding. But on this, and other theories, the police kept silent.

'I'll call you tomorrow,' Laura told Paulette.

'I wish it could be today.'

Paulette allowed Laura to kiss her on the cheek before leaving.

She had a vague suspicion of this strange woman she'd never seen or heard of before but who claimed to be a friend of her mom. But it was better than the police. Much better. There was hope.

Pandora knew the police must be looking for her by now. But how would they find her? No one knew where she was. She was untraceable. Even she didn't know where she was. And she felt oddly at home. It wasn't a home like her Rancho Park house, not home like Old Hampshire, but a fresh new place she'd moved into and found she liked. It surprised her. Pandora was no longer afraid. She had entered a house of pure feeling, or rather, the house had grown around her. It wasn't the objects in the loft that gave her a feeling of belonging, though they had now become a familiar witness to her experience. The presiding box was no more frightening now than the loft itself which contained it. A box within a box. The model plane, by which he had enigmatically made his presence felt to her naked in the pool at night. The leather couch on which he had spread her to relieve her pain through ecstasy. The bathtub, that emblem of sinlessness, was the crucible for an experiment that washed away her guilt. These were no longer objects. They were presences.

She no longer believed she was in prison, though she had not been outside at all. Was it already a week? It didn't matter. How long had Alec been away after he disappeared? She couldn't remember. No, this home was a place constructed of flesh. The loft was awareness. That was not a word Pandora used, awareness. Too old-fashioned and phonily spiritual. But that's what this place was. A state of awareness. It was defined by a man's body and her response to its touch and feel, to its very presence. That was how she had come to know herself.

She had asked to be tied to the bed. She wanted to be touched without being able to return the caress, to find out what it was like. She would be a character in a story. She would become a different woman and actually know something she had only read about.

When he sat on top of her he weighed no more than a cushion.

He let his balls rest on her eyes. It was a kiss between testicle and eye. She opened and closed her lids brushing him with her lashes. She saw his penis rise and lengthen.

Later when he removed himself from her vagina, he brought his penis to her face for her to look at. Its glistening length had changed color. Before, it had been like amber wood carved from a tree. Now it was purple silk, an exotic plant form, moving, breathing through its tiny mouth.

Mouth to mouth, she could taste him and herself in a single scented flower. She massaged him with her tongue. She felt her sex begin to contract and throb. She desperately wanted her hands free. The ropes allowed for a helpless expression of her fingers, but they could only feel each other. He ignored their entreaties. Instead, he pressed his clenched fists gently into her exposed arm pits.

Pandora could feel her underarm glands. They were swelling. Was that the same sensation he felt in his testicles? She could feel her helpless breasts, relaxed and flattened, tighten inside. She swallowed. Her neck throbbed rhythmically. Her ovaries were moving deep inside. She imagined them swelling, hardening. She was close to a different orgasm, an explosion of all her glands. She shook from head to foot. Without speaking, she begged him, begged him to come into her.

Wildman heard her silence. He had never been wanted like this. He quivered with a profound, churning fear. Her power over him while she was tied up, spread out, apparently helpless and at his mercy, was almost complete. He had made her his mistress. She could ask him anything. He would obey. He feared his own orgasm. It would bring this passage of desire to an end. Longing was so much stronger a sensation than release.

In the days and nights Pandora had been here with him he had begun to understand something new about himself. Having thought for his entire life that making love to a woman was what he perpetually desired most, he now saw that he needed something more. He could see his life upside down, reversed in a mirror. From this woman he discovered his deepest need. To be loved, made love to, always. It wasn't his desire that mattered. It was hers. He could see Florence, her face cautiously smiling, her tentative hands on him, looking for him. Her death couldn't alter that. She would understand. The truly forbidden thing, the seemingly unattainable state was her need. Not his. The goal was to be loved, to be desired, to be possessed.

If he came now with Pandora it would be his last orgasm. It would be the end. If she could touch him, hold him, he would be lost. But she couldn't. She couldn't make him come. She couldn't move. He was saved.

'Come inside me,' Pandora didn't know whether she actually spoke or not. For God's sake, release me. With tears glowing in her eyes she watched him. He moved away. Don't go. His warmth receded. He climbed off the bed. She raised her head and looked down her body, past her breasts, to the hair on her pubic bone. She ached with longing. He was leaving her. Why? For God's sake, what had she done?

Wildman knew he must resist. For the first time, resist. If you come now you'll die. This orgasm will be your last. The feeling was overpowering. If you touch her, you'll lose her. He stood naked looking down at her. She willed him to come back to her. Lie on her. She twisted against the ropes that bound her wrists and ankles. She moved as violently as she could, every limb was in motion, every muscle tensed. She would snap the ropes that held her. She had the power. She knew it.

Wildman watched Pandora's writhing, struggling body. Cut her loose. She wants you to cut her loose. The knife was there. It would be easy. Don't. Don't. He could feel her pain as if it were his own. He marveled at the extraordinary force of her body. The strength of a wild animal. He watched her, fascinated. His penis lifted towards her thrashing flesh. Her thighs lifted themselves, shining with sweat. Her mouth was moving. She was speaking, shouting, singing, but without sound.

His fear returned. He could feel himself getting close. Turn away. Turn away now. Don't look. Her vulva, that most adored flesh, was moving. The lips quivered. The pale yellow hair, slick with passion, parted. Her lips were trying to open. Don't watch. He felt dizzy. His balls rose, struggling to return to his child's abdomen. The lips parted slightly. Impossible. He was helpless. Weak and tense, he felt his sphincter gasp and take in air. His body shook. Liquid flowed visibly from her lips. Pandora screamed. He gripped his penis with both hands as he started to come. It was unstoppable. He felt the sperm pulsing upwards. She seemed to levitate. Her lower body arched upwards, became rigid. The semen spurted and shot and flowed out of him. He began to cry. In her blurred ecstasy she could see his tears. She felt his sperm warm on her legs. She shuddered and fell back softly. She was going free. Wildman fell to his knees still quivering. He lowered his tear-stained face to her vulva. Lips pressed into lips. He sighed, goodbye. He knew he had lost her. He would soon be dead.

Wildman dried Pandora's hair with the electric hair dryer Laura once used. He kissed her neck, the skin heated by the electric air. He arranged her hair. It was black now. She had asked him to do it. She remembered his suggestion in Eugenie.

'If you don't like it, it will grow out.'

'I shall like it because I want it. I like the dress now.'

He led her to the mirror. She examined herself in her black underwear. He had washed and dried that too.

'I do like it,' she said.

He took her in his arms. 'You can go out if you like. I mean, you can go and see your daughter. You must miss her. And she must miss her mom.'

Pandora was shocked. He was letting her go. To see Paulette. 'Alone?'

'She's not my daughter.' He smiled. 'Whenever you want. You're free. Just go.'

Wildman knew after she had been tied to the bed that he couldn't, mustn't keep her. She must want him because she wanted him. Her freedom is his. She would know that now. He could let her go and she would come back. He only wished he'd never tried to keep her by force.

Pandora still didn't understand what he had said. What did it imply? She didn't think he would ever have let her go. She

300

had thought of asking him if she could bring her daughter here, not to meet with him, he wouldn't have to be here, but to ask Paulette to this strange new home, just so they could kiss and talk for a while.

Pandora wished she had never even thought of those deceptions, those plans to escape. When she had realized that she was not Scheherezade, she didn't need that woman's tricks. She needed only to fall back on being Pandora. He wanted to hold in his arms the woman who had opened the box. She wanted to be held by someone who saw that in her and would not mind. This man understood Pan and Dora. It was hard for her to realize she didn't have to lie to him. If she wanted something, all she needed was to ask. He would give it to her. It would thrill him. She could see that. She could have anything she wanted. And what she wanted most, with him, was Paulette. She thought to herself, this is the way you fall in love.

Laura parked the Mustang across the street from the entrance to the loft. She switched off the windshield wipers. On the drive downtown from Beverly Hills there was a sudden freak rainstorm. The morning had been threateningly warm and humid. Laura, who seldom sweated except in the exertions of her dance practice, dripped under her leotard. She hurried round the car in the rain and opened the passenger door for Paulette.

Paulette hadn't told Mrs Wing that Laura was picking her up from home. David and his mother were out. Paulette left a note saying she'd return in a little while, that she was with her mother. Don't worry, she wrote. Paulette was always telling people not to worry while she herself was in torment. She hadn't asked Laura where they were going. She looked up at the building. She'd never been anywhere like this before.

'What is it? A factory?'

'No, it's a kind of apartment.'

'You mean people live here? It doesn't have proper windows. It's filthy.'

Laura inserted her key in the lock. She prayed they would be there. She hadn't dared call ahead of time. Now, because of the pelting rain, she hadn't see the BMW parked on the lot across the wide street. She wanted to confront them with Paulette. Faced with a direct choice Laura knew Pandora would take her daughter over Wildman. Any mother would.

Paulette was her weapon.

INT. LOFT. DAY

Rain beats relentlessly against the great window. The running water ripples the surfaces of the interior. The white box is bathed in tears.

Naked in a chair, Wildman watches Pandora getting dressed. She puts on the silver dress, glances at herself in the mirror. There are two of her. She prepares to go out. Something calls her back to him. She comes up to Wildman, bends over and kisses him. She whispers 'Thank you'.

There is the clanking sound of the elevator. The noise mixes with the drumming rain.

Pandora: (*nervous*) Who is it? Alec? The police?

Wildman smiles to himself. He shifts in his chair but makes no attempt to cover himself. Pandora relaxes somewhat.

Wildman: None of the above.

Pandora: You know who it is.

The dogs wander over to the elevator, wait, wagging their tails sleepily.

Pandora: They don't bark. Why don't they bark?

Wildman: They know who it is.

Pandora is not reassured. She opens her bag and takes out her gun.

Wildman: You won't need that. Put it down.

Pandora is getting scared. The elevator cage clanks to a stop. The doors open. Footsteps. The dogs come back into the main loft area leading Laura and Paulette. Paulette is shocked. She sees her mom with black hair. She sees the man, naked in the chair. She screams at Wildman.

Paulette: You killed my dad! You killed my dad!

Wildman doesn't move. He is icy calm. Pandora goes to quiet Paulette.

Pandora: Dad's not dead, darling.

Wildman: (*to Pandora*) You don't have to go after all. Everybody's here.

Suddenly, Paulette grabs the gun from her mother's hand.

Laura watches in horror as Paulette aims the gun and fires at Wildman. He smiles as if to say 'Go ahead'. There are four shots. Four bullets strike his flesh.

Pandora rushes forward screaming. She throws herself on Wildman's twitching body. Blood spurts from his wounds. He puts out his shaking hand to her and kisses her fingers, covered in blood. Pandora stops crying, becomes calm.

Laura screams. She runs forward. Paulette still grips the gun. She is rigid. She doesn't fire again. Pandora kisses Wildman. Blood oozes between their lips. Wildman slides back into the chair. He dies with his eyes open.

Smoke from the fired weapon drifts across the loft. It is sucked into the open box, like cigarette smoke into a mouth.

Part Seven

Pandora, who had for so long avoided the police, had now to face them to have Hammond's body released from the morgue for burial. She was questioned at length about Hammond's friends and enemies. She had expected to see the man who came to her house when Alec disappeared. But the officers referred only to his filed report. These cops were less aggressive even though they found the mystery of his murder seemed as impenetrable as his disappearance. The police privately believed that Hammond must have had some kind of secret life, probably gay. One of the officers had recently been involved with two brutal homosexual murders. Pandora did nothing to challenge his homophobia. Let them think what they want. All that mattered was Wildman had not killed Alec. He had been all the time with her. Loving her.

Pandora's one thought today was to protect her daughter. They must never know. Wildman's death had traumatised Paulette. The police obligingly took her state of shock to be the effect of her dad's murder. At the same time the police psychiatrist who interviewed Pandora was satisfied that her disorientated response was completely consistent with the revelation of Hammond's murder. He advised counseling for both of them.

Paulette said nothing for two days. She appeared not to hear people who spoke to her. Bells and banging doors had no effect on her. Pandora wondered whether she had contracted her disease of silence. In a way it was fortunate. Pandora was afraid that Paulette might talk about Wildman, about whom the police knew nothing. If she did, Pandora was ready to say that it was she who had shot him. It was, after all, her gun.

Pandora carefully read the *Los Angeles Times* each day looking for some report of his death, the discovery of the body, anything. She couldn't get the image of his body out of her mind, alive and dead. And there was the woman, the other woman whose name she still did not know, what would she do? If she talked to the police, everything would have to be faced. Should she try and contact her? At the loft? No, she would never go back there, never call there, except perhaps in her dreams, her nightmares.

Pandora was engulfed in silence. Physically, her hearing was now perfect. With his death, the disease would never recur. She knew that. The silence which surrounded her now was the silence of secrecy, of the events and feelings that would remain unvoiced for the rest of her life. She would live with that silence and get used to it.

At Hammond's funeral, which in its misery resembled the funeral of her father, Pandora thought hardly at all about Alec. She had been numbed by the police account of his murder. The question of who had done it was something she would leave to the police. Her husband had long been a stranger to her. She watched his coffin disappear on its short journey to the embracing flames and thought only of Wildman. It was he who lay in the box. Memories of his body, alive and dead, crowded out everything else. That overwhelming sensuality would never leave her. Whether she had loved him or not she knew she would never again experience anything close to it. If one day she formed another relationship with a man it would be never more than tepid.

After the funeral Pandora went to pick Paulette up from the Wings'. It would have been crazy to have brought her to the chapel. Paulette was sitting silently with David in the living room. She hadn't spoken now for five days. David was near to tears when they left for the airport. He kissed Paulette goodbye. She didn't respond. She didn't seem to recognize him.

★

Pandora awoke from a dream. She had been making love to Wildman on a beach somewhere in the Mediterranean. It was three in the morning. She looked over to Paulette's bed. They had been sleeping together in the same room since coming to New Hampshire. The bed was empty. Pandora was suddenly panicked. She grabbed a robe and began to search for her.

She went from room to room in the house, calling her name. In the conservatory Pandora was alerted by a draught of cold air. The glass doors were open. She ran outside calling for Paulette. She saw her in the moonlight standing on the lawn in the white nightgown her daughter had insisted on wearing. Paulette was looking up at the clear black sky. The stars glistened and winked like crystals. She fancied she could hear them crackling millions of miles away.

Paulette was humming to herself as she looked up at the heavens. Pandora said nothing. She put her arms tightly around her daughter. She felt a new fleshiness there. Womanhood. Paulette began quietly to sing. Pandora couldn't make out the words. She heard only the name Vincent.

In fact, Wildman's death had been reported in the *Times*, but Pandora had missed the item.

> 'FATAL COUPLE FOUND – Police today discovered the naked bodies of a man and a woman in a downtown loft. The man had been shot four times. The woman sustained a single lethal wound in the heart. The discovery has led the inquiry to presume that the woman slew the man and subsequently shot herself with the same weapon. Two dogs were in the loft at the time of the deaths. The names of the fatal couple have so far been withheld. Police have not ruled out the possibility that both were killed by a third party.'